SPACE PLANNING
BASICS

SPACE PLANNING BASICS

Third Edition

Mark Karlen

Space Planning Illustrations by Kate Ruggeri and Mark Karlen

Building Shell Drawings CAD-generated by Peter Hahn

Stair Design Illustrations by Kathryn Hunchar and Mia Kang

WILEY

JOHN WILEY & SONS, INC.

Published by John Wiley & Sons, Inc., Hoboken, New Jersey

Published simultaneously in Canada

For general information on our other products and services or for technical support, please
contact our Customer Care Department within the United States at (800) 762-2974, outside
the United States at (317) 572-3993 or fax (317) 572-4002.

Wiley also publishes its books in a variety of electronic formats. Some content that appears in
print may not be available in electronic books. For more information about Wiley products,
visit our web site at www.wiley.com.

Library of Congress Cataloging-in-Publication Data:

Karlen, Mark.

   Space planning basics / Mark Karlen; space planning illustrations by Kate Ruggeri and Mark
Karlen; building shell drawings CAD-generated by Peter Hahn; stair design illustrations by
Kathryn Hunchar and Mia Kang. — 3rd ed.
      p. cm.
Includes bibiographical references and index.
   ISBN 978-0-470-23178-4 (pbk.)
   1. Interior architecture. 2. Space (Architecture) I. title.
   NA2765.K37 2009
   729—dc22

                                  2009004202

Printed in the United States of America

10 9 8 7 6 5 4 3 2

CONTENTS

Preface

I remain pleased that *Space Planning Basics* continues to be used by students and their faculty at many colleges and universities across the country. The previous edition focused on the increasing impact of digital technology on design procedures, from web research and the design process to importing standard design elements and presentation techniques. In the past five years since that publication, those relatively new methods have become entrenched as standard practice. The Third Edition features revised and expanded Skill Development Exercises, clearer illustrations, and updated information on building codes.

A primary purpose in creating this 3rd Edition is the addition of a stair design component. Over many years as a design studio teacher and critic, I have been regularly reminded of the significant difficulty that many students have in learning to design and draw stairs correctly. From a design perspective, stairs are among the more complex elements within buildings, particularly when there are multiple levels to be accommodated and/or complex building configurations to be considered. There are very few resources to turn to: the graphics standards publications offer a very limited number of pages, and that's about it. As is the case with space planning, most designers learn stair design in a mentorship mode with the help from a teacher in a classroom setting, or an experienced professional in a professional office. It is intended that the Stair Design Resource in this book will serve as a handy reference source.

The initial thoughts about an instructional resource for stair design were generated by sitting in on a critique of the work of second year design students.

Stefan Klein (one of the most gifted teachers I've ever known) made repeated critical comments on his students' stair designs, a central element of the design project being critiqued. With each project, Stefan was necessarily critical about the stair design and the drawing conventions that were used. As I listened to Stefan, I heard my own voice making the same critical comments to countless students in the past. Listening to Stefan that day was the impetus for writing this stair design resource.

In addition to my appreciation for Stefan Klein providing a focus for this effort, I want to thank several people for their help in making this Third Edition possible. John Wiley and Sons, the publisher, provided the results of anonymous critical reviews of the Second Edition, from several faculty who have used it in their classrooms; as a result, several revisions have been made to improve and clarify the material........................Thanks, whoever you are. Thanks to a young design professional, Liyan Wan, who has been of unusual help in reviewing and suggesting revisions to the space planning Skill Development Exercises. Over a period of more than a year, a young professional in Philadelphia, Kathryn Hunchar, and I have worked together to create the stair design illustrations. To help refine those illustrations and ready them for publication, Mia Kang, a professional designer in New York (and a former graduate student of mine), was of great help. Finally, special thanks to Paul Drougas, my editor at Wiley, who has been a consistent supporter throughout the entire process.

Again, my hope is that the resulting book is of significant value to students in mastering space planning and stair design skills.

Introduction: How to Read and Use This Book

This book is an instructional tool designed to develop interior space planning skills for typical building uses in spaces up to 4,000 square feet in size. Although this book may be used by an individual learner, it is geared for use in a conventional studio classroom setting. Its contents are threefold:

1. Explanatory text
2. Descriptive graphic examples
3. Recommended practice exercises

Space planning is an inherently complex process. For this reason, a series of planning exercises, starting with very small spaces and building to larger spaces with more complex program requirements, are provided as the primary technique in the development of space planning skills. In addition, basic information about space planning, the use of planning rules of thumb, guidelines for appropriate drawing techniques, and recommended reading and reference sources are included.

As an introduction to space planning, this book is primarily directed to intermediate-level (sophomore and junior levels in a baccalaureate or first-professional-degree program) interior design students. To be more specific, it is assumed that its users possess adequate drafting skills (defined here as basic experience with drafting tools and architectural scales) and ease in understanding and preparing orthographic projections (plans and elevations). In addition, users are expected to be competent in planning conventional furniture arrangements within fixed rooms, not including large-scale arrangements of office systems furniture, which is a basic space planning process in itself. Ideally, some background in design program development has been previously gained, but that is not necessary for a successful learning experience. Background in the planning of undivided or "raw" space is not required. Although specific direction to prepare for the National Council for Interior Design Qualification (NCIDQ) examination is not an intended purpose here, the basic space planning skills learned are applicable to the practicum portions of that exam.

Space planning is not a simple process involving a single category of information; rather, it is a complex dovetailing of several processes involving many categories of information related to the organization and construction of buildings. Such processes range from program analysis and use of building code principles to environmental control techniques and the development of desired spatial qualities. Even with space planning problems of relatively small size (a few thousand square feet) and relatively simple programmatic requirements, it is impossible to completely avoid these complexities of process and information. For this reason, such issues will be dealt with in enough depth to provide a realistic context for design problems, while maintaining focus on the central issues of space planning. Over a long period, the experienced space planner will gain in-depth knowledge of all these complexities, but it would be counterproductive to attempt to deal with them here except in the simplest manner.

The great majority of professional space planning work lies within existing structures, rather than in the interior planning of new buildings still on the drawing board. For this reason, the greatest emphasis in this book is on spaces within existing structures. Interior space planning for buildings still on the drawing board is an endeavor that requires some experience in the design of structures and building shells and therefore demands additional knowledge and skill on the part of the space planner. Those additional areas of professional involvement lie beyond the intent of this text and will be discussed in a general manner in Chapter 8.

Finally, this textbook is meant not only to be read, but also to be worked with as a hands-on guide in the development of a creative skill. Space planning skills grow from consistently repeated practice and experience; consequently, learners are encouraged to apply sufficient hours of concentrated effort at the drawing board to gain professional-quality technique. The quality of space planning solutions, particularly at the beginning of one's experience, is difficult to assess. Unlike some other forms of problem solving, space planning problems usually have many "right" answers. Rarely are there "perfect" answers. Space planning solutions involve satisfying program criteria on a priority basis where the issues at the top of the list must be solved, but where some of the issues near the bottom might only be partially solved, if at all. In its simplest terms, space planning almost always involves compromises, when one looks for good and workable solutions rather than "correct" or "perfect" solutions. Identifying and satisfying high-priority or major planning criteria is part of the learning experience presented here, but the best tools to assess quality in space planning solutions are personal exchange and critique with others. Classroom discussions, both formal and informal, are of great value. Seeking out the opinion of fellow students, as well as offering criticism of others' work, will help immeasurably to develop strong critical skills. Taking advantage of classroom pinups and critiques, particularly with the expert view of the classroom teacher available (and possibly that of a guest critic), is essential in this growth process. In time, as consistent evaluation of one's own work and the work of others continues, skills in criticism improve, and one becomes a better judge of one's own work. Despite this, at every level of professional growth, value exists in seeing another approach and in hearing objective criticism.

The step-by-step process of space planning described in this text is deliberately geared to the learning of a complex skill. It should be understood that many worthwhile and productive planning processes are used by professionals in the field; one process is not superior to the others. This is true because of the creative element involved in space planning. As one's skills grow beyond the learner's level. it is assumed that each designer will develop variations in the planning process geared to his or her individual thinking patterns, and will ultimately create a complete and personalized design methodology.

Note should be made of the issue of terminology. This text contains many words and phrases that must be considered as professional jargon; they are unavoidable. They are also not universal in their use. Words and phrases such as "criteria matrix," "prototypical plan sketches," "relationship diagram," "bubble diagram," "block plan," "barrier-free," "suite," "rough floor plan," "speculative office building," and so on are used by some professionals and not by others. The use of the same word or phrase by different individuals may convey varying connotations. Do not allow this lack of universality in terminology to become a stumbling block in the learning process presented here.

As your space planning skills grow and achieve professional quality, you will probably find that these new elements in your repertoire also sensitize and sharpen other, related design skills and bring you several steps closer to the status of the "compleat" professional.

Recommended Reading

The bibliography at the end of this book is kept brief. It is worth taking a few minutes to read the introductory paragraphs to that list of books. The recommended reading that relates to this introduction has been selected for its introductory qualities. The following numbers refer to books listed in the bibliography.

6*, 8*, 12*, 27*, 30

Books marked with an asterisk are also included in the recommended reading for other chapters.

SPACE PLANNING
BASICS

Chapter 1   PLANNING METHODOLOGY

The space planning process begins when a person, or a group of people, decides to put a building, or a portion of a building, to a new and practical use, running the gamut from small residential or work spaces to vast, complex business and institutional facilities. Except in the simplest space, such as a small apartment or office, making efficient and functionally satisfying use of space is a complex task that is far beyond the capabilities of most building users; this is when and why the space planning specialist, interior designer, or architect, is called in to solve the problem.

Space planners are presented with their task in a great variety of ways. Most users or clients are inexperienced in working with planning professionals and present their space planning problems without significantly prepared data. It is not uncommon for a business owner or manager to come to an interior designer and say, in effect, "Our staff has grown by 60 percent over the past few years, and we are still growing at a very fast rate. Our space is terribly overcrowded; what should we do?" In cases of this

kind, the designer must begin with the basic tasks of charting organizational structure; identifying personnel, their tasks, and necessary equipment; analyzing the operational process; and gaining an understanding of the human and cultural qualities of the organization. In effect, the planning professional must take full responsibility for organizing, analyzing, and interpreting the problem at hand.

At the other extreme, with clients who have had considerable experience in planning their spaces and who may have an in-house facilities manager or staff, the designer or architect may be presented with a bound volume of extensive data on the number and types of personnel (including their equipment and square footage needs), spatial adjacency studies, and the desired human and esthetic qualities of the completed project—in effect, a complete space planning program. In such cases, the planning professional is relieved of the responsibility of data gathering, organization, and analysis. Obviously, the design problem or program that is presented must be fully absorbed and understood by the designer, and some tasks of program interpretation may need to be performed. These issues will be discussed later in this chapter.

There is a full range of client or program situations between the two extremes presented above. Most clients have given some thoughtful consideration and analysis to their spatial needs before engaging professional services but do not have the in-house expertise to make a complete analysis of their problem and present it in terms easily translated into a planning solution. It is this middle ground into which most professionals step when presented with a space planning problem.

Regardless of a client's experience with planning professionals, the issues of design sensitivity and insight play a major role in their discussions. Some space planning programs that are prepared by in-house facilities management personnel deal only with hard data and are of little use in understanding the subtleties of organizational dynamics or the detailed requirements of lighting or acoustics. What at first glance may appear to be a complete and professional program may still require a great deal of organization, analysis, and interpretation on the part of the designer. Conversely, some clients who are completely inexperienced in space planning matters will bring invaluable design sensitivity and insight to the project, despite their lack of categorized data.

It is very difficult to simulate real client or program situations in the classroom. Typically, students are presented with a written program that defines all the detailed requirements of a project, along with floor plans (and possibly additional drawings) of a real or imagined space. A space planning solution is drawn from this data. Though good and useful for the student's learning process, these exercises lack the dynamics of personal interchange with a client, ignoring as well such real problems as internal conflicts in the client's organization, corporate mergers or takeovers, changes in management personnel, budget constraints, and dealings with building code administrators—all of which exist in actual practice situations. Bringing real or role-playing clients to classroom assignments can be helpful, just as using actual spaces that students can walk into and survey has value in making the space planning problem realistic. Despite these simulations of reality, students should be aware that dealing with a broad variety of personalities, unusual time frames (from projects with tight deadlines to those that extend over years), and stringent budget requirements will add unexpected and challenging elements to the space planning process when they move from the classroom to the professional setting.

DEFINING TERMS AND INTENT

The title of this chapter, "Planning Methodology," is a phrase used throughout this text to describe the phase of the space planning process that begins when the planning problem is presented to the planner (with or without a program) and ends when physical planning commences, usually with bubble diagrams or block plans. In some professional circles, this is called the pre-design process—meaning all the necessary steps of data gathering, research, analysis, and interpretation before actual planning. For many in the design fields, "planning methodology" and "programming" are synonymous, although some would argue that the charting and diagramming described here as part of planning methodology fall outside the bounds of programming and are part of the design process.

A great deal has been written about the general area of planning methodology. Books and articles are available about the interview process, questionnaires, observation techniques, idea generation, spatial analysis and theory, programming, design methods, problem solving, graphic thinking, and so on. As noted in the Introduction, a unified terminology universally used or accepted by professionals in the field does not exist. Despite this lack, comprehensive reading in this subject area will reveal a body of knowledge that provides a broad variety of useful approaches to the pre-design process.

Very little has been written about space planning techniques, particularly from an instructional viewpoint. Space planning skills have generally been learned in a mentorship mode, at the drawing board or workstation, in the studio classroom and/or the professional design firm. The primary intent of this book is to provide a written foundation for the space planning process. Although a planning methodology is described and recommended here, it is dealt with in a concise manner so as to give full attention to the more elusive planning- and design-related parts of the process. This should not be construed as minimizing the value of the pre-design process; to the contrary, good space planning cannot be accomplished without the professionally thorough pre-design analysis generally defined here. A simple and workable method will be succinctly presented so as to move on quickly to the physical planning phase. Students are strongly encouraged to read about and acquire skills in a broad range of pre-design techniques, both verbal and graphic, in order to gain many analytical tools to apply to the problem-solving challenges they will ultimately face as professionals. The recommended reading at the end of this chapter provides direction for expanding that knowledge and those skills.

Another brief note on terminology: Several steps in the space planning process described and recommended throughout the text are identified by words or phrases unique to the text, such as "criteria matrix" and "relationship diagram." In each case, these words or phrases will be defined thoroughly, and potential conflicts with other terminology common to the field will be identified.

THE SYNTHESIS GAP

Among professionals working in the field, a generally accepted process or sequence of tasks occurs from the point at which the planner begins to work on a project to the point at which project analysis is complete and the physical planning process begins. Despite many variations in technique or terminology that planners may apply, the basic process of creating a design program consists of the following steps, presented here in an extremely abbreviated form:

1. Interview

a. Executive level (organizational overview)

b. Managerial level (departmental function)

c. Operational level (process and equipment detail)

2. Observe (existing or similar facilities)

a. Assisted observation

b. Unobtrusive observation

c. Inventory of existing furniture and equipment (when it is to be reused)

3. Establish architectural parameters

a. Acquire complete base plan data (including mechanical and electrical services)

b. Compile contextual data (architectural, historical, social)

c. Research code constraints

4. Organize collected data (the first-phase program)

a. Place data in sequential format most useful for planning

b. Summarize confirmed quantitative factors (square footage, FF+E count, equipment sizes, etc.)

c. Record first thoughts on conceptual planning approach

5. Research the unknowns

a. Gather detailed information on process and equipment

b. Gather case study information on similar facilities

c. Integrate researched data with first-phase program

6. Analyze the data

a. Discover planning affinities (working interrelationships, public/private zoning, special acoustic needs, etc.)

b. Discover scheduling affinities (maximize use of space)

c. Identify planning or architectural relationships (site, structural, mechanical, and electrical conditions)

7. Interpret and diagram the data (the complete program)

a. Define the functional problems in planning terms

b. Establish a basic conceptual approach (in terms of human/social and image/esthetic objectives)

c. Prepare relationship or adjacency diagrams (for client and designer visualization)

8. Summarize the data (the finished document)

a. Finalize project concepts—STATE THE PROBLEM

b. Outline and tally basic budget issues

c. Prepare a package for client approval and to serve as the designer's manual for space planning

The analytical process described above will never produce a space planning solution. Regardless of how thorough the process may be, creating a physical solution requires that analysis be put aside and a process of synthesis begun. That synthesis requires a creative understanding of all elements of the analysis, to place the programmatic elements in a physical juxtaposition that will satisfy the users' needs. The word "creative," in this context, must be seen in its broadest sense, in which functional, esthetic, and technical issues must be addressed and resolved. The heart of the problem-solving task in space planning occurs in making the transition from the analytical pre-design phase of the project to the creative design solution phase.

The entire design process is one of synthesis, in which many disparate factors are integrated into a useful whole, but the initial mental or creative leap from the analytical phase to recording or drawing on paper the first physical solution is the most difficult single step in the process. If the pre-design process is very thorough, it may bring the planner several steps closer to a physical solution or may make the creative leap a shorter, easier one. For the purposes of this text, the void between the completed design program and the planning solution will be referred to as the "synthesis gap," and it might best be visualized graphically:

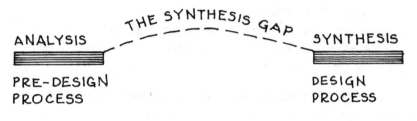

If the pre-design process has been skimpy or inadequate, the synthesis gap will be wider and more difficult to manage:

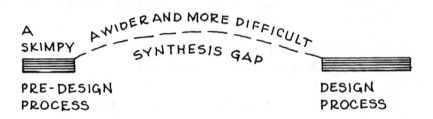

If the pre-design process has been thorough and insightful, the synthesis gap will be narrower and easier to manage:

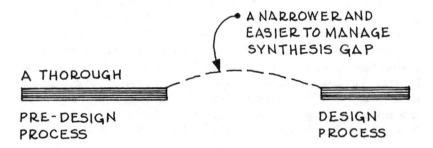

From a practical, professional setting viewpoint, the planner needs an efficient and reliable process to turn to each time a space planning project is encountered. Gathering a few basic facts and then staring at a blank floor plan waiting for inspiration to strike is an utterly impractical approach. A well-established design methodology is needed to meet the typical time pressures of the profession and to solve space planning problems in a manner that fully satisfies the needs of the client and user.

When space planning problems become both large in scale and complex in function, solutions become elusive or less obvious and the problem-solving process can feel intimidating. A basic principle, fundamental to all design methodologies and helpful to remember when projects loom too large and difficult, is this: Break down problems to their smallest and most manageable elements. Rather than be confronted by a maze of complex and seemingly unrelated factors, take the problem apart and reassemble it. View the elements as smaller, more controllable components, and then reorganize them in a sequence or in groupings that relate to the space planning problem. This is all part of the process to narrow the synthesis gap.

THE DESIGN PROGRAM

In space planning terms, design programs are written documents that qualify and quantify the client's or users' needs for a given project. In addition, most programs are accompanied by adjacency or relationship diagrams that often express physical planning relationships more articulately than verbal descriptions do. While the basic skills required to prepare a program are not unusual or complex, do not expect to be able to prepare a professional-quality program in the first attempts. After repeated experience, the skills required for interviewing, observation, research, analysis, and documentation become well honed, and one is then prepared to accomplish the real goal of programming—setting the stage for the planning and design process.

Interviews
When planning projects are small and groups are tightly managed, it may be necessary to interview only one person: a proprietor, manager, or director. As projects increase in size and/or complexity, the number of people who must be interviewed increases correspondingly. Size and complexity are quite different issues. Even though the project may be small in size, it would be unusual to plan a typical residential renovation without interviewing both wife and husband, or both partners of a small law firm when planning new office facilities for the firm. When size or complexity demands interviewing

several people, selecting the most appropriate people for those interviews is a skill unto itself. That selection is often dictated by the client and not left up to the designer's discretion.

It is essential that the interviewer be prepared with an organized and consistent set of questions—winging it just doesn't work. Generally, it is advisable to give the set of questions to the interviewees in advance of the interview, to better prepare them to respond in an organized manner and (when employees are involved) to lessen their chance of approaching the interview session with apprehension or anxiety. Rather than use a recording device, most experienced planners take interview notes, because recorders can be an intimidating intrusion on the easy rapport desired between programmer and interviewee. Except to gather dimensional and other quantitative data, questionnaires are not in widespread use; personal exchange is necessary to get beyond the superficial issues and to uncover the subtleties of space planning requirements. A great deal of informational and instructional literature exists concerning the acquiring and developing of interview skills valuable in approaching the interviewing task from a knowledgeable and professional perspective.

Observation

Observing existing facilities to see and understand operational and equipment-related processes is often an integral part of the interview process. Typically, a manager, senior partner, or department head will take the interviewer on a tour of the entire facility, or the portion of the facility for which he or she is responsible. In many cases, this kind of guided walk-through is adequate to the situation. But particularly when complex interpersonal relationships are involved, a walk-through may not be sufficient. The fact that people act differently from the norm when they know they are being observed is well known. Some special situations warrant the use of unobtrusive observation, in which the observer is not seen, or at least not noticed —the proverbial fly on the wall. While the instructive literature concerning this observational technique is limited, enough exists to direct the learner in acquiring appropriate skills.

It is not unusual to plan a project in which a facility or operation for observation does not exist. In this case, it is advisable to visit and observe facilities having similar functions or operations. Even if the facility being planned does not involve unusual processes, as might be the case in a conventional business or legal firm, unless one is especially knowledgeable about the day-to-

day functions, observing similar facilities is time well spent. This observation falls into the category of case studies and will be discussed further in "Research the Unknowns," later in this chapter.

Many space planning projects require the complete or partial reuse of existing furniture and equipment. Inventorying and dimensioning great quantities of existing furniture and equipment is usually a tedious but necessary procedure.

Establish Architectural Parameters

Ideally, the basic architectural constraints and parameters of a given project should be established during the programming phase so that the relationships between client needs and the qualities of physical space can be considered from the outset. Highly detailed information about the physical setting is not necessary at this early phase of project involvement; too much detail might even get in the way at this point. The basics here are:

1. A base floor plan(s), at a scale large enough to be useful, and accompanied by enough data about mechanical and electrical services so that plumbing constraints, HVAC delivery systems, and primary electrical access points are known

2. Contextual data concerning the basics of architectural, historical, and social factors

3. Building and zoning code requirements in enough detail to avoid basic code violations in general space allocations

Most of the detailed architectural data are not needed until the physical planning and design phases of the project have begun. In some cases, the contextual factors, particularly those related to the human and social environment, will play a major role in determining the conceptual approach to a project. In these instances, significant data gathering and research of the critical contextual factors should become part of the programming process.

Organize Collected Data (First-Phase Program)

After the interviewing and observation tasks have been completed and the basic physical setting information has been acquired, it is time to organize the data accumulated to date. Although it is unlikely that all the necessary project information is known at this point, great value exists in organizing a first-phase program, in which the collected data are put into a useful sequential format, and quantitative factors, such as square footage and furniture and fixture tabulations, can be easily seen and extracted. This organizational process requires a basic analysis of the client's organizational structure and the project's planning needs. Most importantly, it should identify what is still lacking. What critical information not obtained in the interview process will require additional interview time or research? What conflicts in the given data require investigation? What subtleties in interrelationships have been hinted at but not really defined? What technical equipment and processes need to be researched and more fully understood in order to plan intelligently? These and other questions will arise, requiring investigation and research. Techniques to organize the collected data will be discussed in "Analyze the Data," later in this chapter.

Research the Unknowns

From planning nuance to hard dimensional information, the kinds of gaps in program data described previously should be sought out at this point in the process. As with architectural parameters, too much detail is unnecessary and can even be a hindrance; a lot of dimensional and process data are more appropriate to research later, during the design process. The programmer must draw the line between what is needed to analyze the project and what will be needed later to design the project. Some case study research is often valuable at this stage. Again, complete case study data are unnecessary, but some basic factors on spatial organization, corporate or institutional space standards, circulation percentages, and the like for facilities of similar size and function can provide a realistic comparison and guidelines for the project at hand. For example, enough common factors exist among law offices, medical clinics, or day-care centers to make such information useful. Additional case study research is also useful during the planning and design phases of the project, but its value during the pre-design phase should not be overlooked.

Analyze the Data

With all the informational material now at hand, a comprehensive analysis of the project's planning factors must be made. When a project is large enough to require it, the analysis process might begin with making or adjusting an existing traditional organizational chart, identifying lines of authority, and grouping functions. Beyond this traditional technique, many other analyses should be made:

1. Spatial adjacencies need to be articulated.
2. Working relationships, both inter- and intradepartmental, require identification, including traffic flow of personnel, visitors, and materials.
3. Public and private functions and zones should be identified.
4. Special acoustic requirements should be defined.
5. Needs for natural light, air, and view (more simply, windows) should be evaluated for each function and area.
6. Groupings of facilities requiring plumbing connections should be identified.

These and any other factors that will bear on the space planning process should be understood fully and seen in proper perspective to the whole of the problem.

One planning factor that warrants separate analysis but which is too often overlooked, because it involves time rather than space, is scheduling the use of facilities. An analysis of how space is scheduled for use, coupled with knowledge of moveable partition construction techniques (sliding, folding, coiling, etc.), can result in significantly more efficient and economical use of space.

The format in which the data can be placed varies tremendously. In addition to the collected data, one may also wish to record planning and design thoughts and ideas. Data and ideas can be itemized in a conventional prose paragraph style or in bulleted phrases. Categories of data and ideas can be developed and recorded in related groupings. Charts or matrixes can be developed to further organize the data and ideas. This issue of format is discussed in some depth later in this chapter under the heading "Criteria Matrix."

Interpret and Diagram the Data (Complete Program)

As they relate to programming, a fine line often exists between analysis and interpretation. Despite the similarities in their meaning, value is derived in making a distinction between the terms. "Analysis" here refers to creating an understanding of the problem that is directly deduced from the gathered data, while "interpretation" refers to insights about the problem that have been gained through the unique perspective of the trained designer. Designers often have the opportunity to get to know their clients' needs in great detail and are subsequently able to make penetrating and ingenious interpretations of the programmatic information. Those interpretations are often among the most creative contributions a designer has to offer within the problem-solving process. The nature of the insights gained can range from a relatively small and internal process to a major shift in the client's organizational structure.

Although significant new perspectives cannot be guaranteed, they are not uncommon, since the designer comes to the problem from a fresh, outsider's point of view, unfettered by the history of the client's circumstances, and is asked to see the organization as a whole. From this unique vantage point, the designer can make invaluable evaluations and recommendations, since no one else is in a position to gain that special perspective.

Another form of interpretation that occurs during the programming process is in the translation of the verbal program content into diagrams. The use of this diagramming technique is well established and is a part of many design programs. A wide range of graphic styles is used, and a great deal of verbal terms identify these styles, from "adjacency diagrams" and "bubble diagrams" to "space adjacency studies" and "program analysis studies." Despite the graphic quality of these diagrams, they are still clearly part of the pre-design process, since they are a graphic abstraction of the written program and not an attempt to realistically create a design solution. Particularly with larger-scale projects, diagrams are often drawn of both the entire organizational structure and various segments or departments within the organization. Often a series of diagrams will accompany the written program to provide a comprehensive graphic translation of the verbal document. As every designer knows, the graphic view can say precisely what words may still leave unclear. Later in this chapter, a graphic technique, a relationship diagram, will be described and recommended as an integral part of the pre-design process.

Summarize the Data (Finished Document)
The programming effort must be summarized and documented before moving on to the design phase of the project. In some cases, the program material is recorded in an informal manner and is used only by the designer as an internal design tool; it is not seen or used by others. In most cases, however, particularly in a formal designer-client relationship, the program is finished in a bound document and presented for client approval before the beginning of the design phase of the project. Regardless of format or designer-client relationship, it is necessary to bring the programming process to an appropriate close.

If the programming process has been thorough, the programmer has become completely immersed in or surrounded by the problem and is now able to make an overview statement about the problem as a whole. Whether this is referred to as a "concept statement" or "statement of the problem," significant value exists in crystallizing one's thoughts in a comprehensive verbal perspective of the problem that will precede the detailed program data. This statement should deal with the spirit of the problem, not its

details, and represent the broad human, social, aesthetic, and philosophic aspects of the programmer's thoughts concerning the project.

In its final form, the program should be a well-integrated package containing:

1. An overview statement
2. A detailed, function-by-function written program describing all project needs and concerns
3. Diagrams that translate the planning relationships into visual terms
4. Numerical summaries of spatial and furniture and equipment needs as a first indication of project budget factors

When the entire programming process is complete, a great deal has been accomplished. Most importantly, the designer has a complete and documented understanding of the problem. It should be noted that it is not uncommon for the programmer and the designer to be different people; in those cases it is particularly important for the program's language to be clear and free of personalized idiosyncratic words and phrases. The program document is the ideal tool to communicate both broad conceptual issues and the detailed planning concerns of the project to the client. In many cases, client response to the program document may require revisions to the program before the design phase begins. Once the design process has begun, the program serves as the primary guide for space planning and design considerations. Despite this, the program cannot be slavishly followed; many new and worthwhile ideas related to planning and design are likely to emerge during the design process, and it would be foolish to ignore them just because they are not contained in the original program document. As planning and design solutions take form, the program becomes the designer's best evaluation tool for measuring the success of the solution. In other words, has the design solution met the carefully programmed needs or requirements of the program?

CRITERIA MATRIX

Whether the designer has personally compiled the program or has it presented by the client in a completed form, it is typically a multi-page document in a format that is far from ideal for space planning purposes. This is usually true in the classroom also, where students are given a lengthy verbal description of a space planning problem that is difficult to immediately translate into space planning terms. The designer needs a concise and abbreviated format, with program elements organized in a practical sequence, to find information without flipping constantly through many pages of data, and where spaces, rooms, or functions are categorized and grouped in relation to the project's adjacency requirements.

The matrix format is a widely used technique for visually organizing information of a variety of factors that is sometimes referred to as a chart or table. The criteria matrix, described in the following paragraphs, is a useful technique to condense and organize the conventional written design program. It is applicable to both small and large projects and is adaptable to both tight and open time frames or deadlines. When time permits, the matrix can include all the project's design criteria; when time is tight, the format can be condensed to identify only the most critical planning considerations.

BLANK CRITERIA MATRIX   ILLUS. 1–1

In this context, the word "criteria" refers to the program requirements, and the word "matrix" is best defined as a "rectangular arrangement of elements into rows and columns" (*Webster's New Collegiate Dictionary*). The criteria matrix attempts to verbally and visually organize design program requirements in as concise a form as possible, achieving an overview of the problem in an "at-a-glance" format. In its most basic form, it is a rectangular grid of notation spaces with names of rooms or spaces (or functions) listed in the column to the left, and columns for verbal and/or numerical indications of program requirements in the succeeding columns to the right. A hand-drawn, basic blank matrix for Design Program 2S (see Appendix, page 179) is shown in Illustration 1–1, indicating notation columns for the most critical space planning factors: (1) square footage needs, (2) adjacency requirements, (3) public access, (4) daylight and/or view, (5) privacy needs, (6) plumbing access, (7) special equipment, and (8) special considerations. Turn to page 179 now and read Design Program 2S ("S" stands for "sample") in order to fully understand the structure of the criteria matrix and the many references to Design Program 2S that follow. A format as abbreviated as this can be of great value in making the planning process more efficient, while avoiding the potential for overlooking critical factors.

When time and the designer's interest permit, the criteria matrix can be expanded to include a broader range of factors, including furnishings, HVAC requirements, lighting design, color, materials and finishes, and future planning needs. When appropriate, the privacy factor can be split into two columns, one for "visual privacy" and the other for "acoustic privacy." When project size requires it, rooms or spaces (or functions) can be grouped or clustered in departments or divisions. Further on in this chapter is a demonstration of how the criteria matrix can be used with larger and more complex planning and design problems.

The degree of complexity or completeness of the criteria matrix can be adjusted to meet the needs of the size and scope of the project, as well as the amount of time available. Even when time constraints are unusually tight, the matrix approach can be used as a rapid organizer of basic planning data. The matrix can be hand-drawn or computer-generated with one of many available chart-producing software programs; this is a decision in which time availability and the size and complexity of the design problem are contributing factors. To be more specific, if the designer will come to reasonably quick decisions, a completed criteria matrix for Design Program 2S could be accomplished within a half hour, particularly if the designer develops a legend of letters and/or symbols, as shown in Illustration 1–2. Note that the square footage column has been left blank.

CRITERIA MATRIX: DESIGN PROGRAM 2S   ILLUS. 1–2

CRITERIA MATRIX FOR: UNIVERSITY CAREER COUNSELING CENTER	SQ FOOTAGE NEEDS	ADJACENCIES	PUBLIC ACCESS	DAYLIGHT AND/OR VIEW	PRIVACY	PLUMBING	SPECIAL EQUIPMENT	SPECIAL CONSIDERATIONS
① RECEPTION		② ⑤	H	Y	N	N	N	TRAFFIC HUB ADJ. TO MAIN ENTRANCE
② INTERVIEW STA. (4)		① ④	M	I	L	N	N	FEEL LIKE A TEAM OF FOUR
③ DIRECTOR		④	M	Y	H	N	N	HIGHEST IMAGE ACCESS TO REAR DR FOR PRIVATE EXIT
④ STAFF		③	M	Y	M	N	N	
⑤ SEMINAR RM		① ⑥ ⑦	H	I	H	N	Y	A/V USE IMPORTANT CLOSE TO ENTRANCE
⑥ RESTROOM (2)		↑ CENTRAL ↓	M	N	H	Y	N	
⑦ WORK AREA		② ④ CENTRAL	L	N	M	Y	Y	
⑧ COFFEE STATION		CENTRAL	H	Y	N	Y	Y	CONVENIENT FOR EVERYONE
⑨ GUEST APARTMENT		REMOTE	L	Y	H	Y	N	RESIDENTIAL CHARACTER

LEGEND
H = HIGH
M = MEDIUM
L = LOW
Y = YES
N = NO/NONE
I = IMPORTANT BUT NOT REQUIRED

NOTE: IN "ADJACENCIES" COLUMN ⊗ – INDICATES ADJACENCY IMPORTANCE
⊗ – INDICATES MAJOR ADJACENCY IMPORTANCE

The one aspect of the matrix that involves more than fundamental intellectual analysis is the development of square footage figures. The process for assigning figures to that column is a skill unto itself. Before attempting any of the suggested criteria matrix exercises, it is necessary to understand the critical importance of square footage figures and how they can be quickly approximated.

PROTOTYPICAL PLAN SKETCHES

As one gets further into the space planning process, it will become more obvious why it is important to have reasonably accurate square footage approximations for each room or space before the physical planning process begins. Without explaining any of the details here, suffice it to say that almost all space planning projects have strict budget limitations; consequently, square footage figures have a direct relationship to interior construction and furnishings costs. At this point, let us simply note that if the space-by-space square footage requirements total more than the square footage contained in the building shell, the spaces will not fit within the exterior or demising walls. Conversely, if the space-by-space total is significantly less than the square footage contained in the building shell, the building will be underutilized and is likely also to have awkward and oversized circulation spaces.

For certain kinds of spaces, the square footage column may be filled in with relative ease and speed. For example, if one has considerable experience in office planning, it may be possible to quickly respond to the program description of an executive office, counseling room, or conference room with an estimate of square footage needs. The same may be true of almost any kind of typical space, such as a reception room, kitchen, or public restroom. Generally speaking, accomplished designers can make quick (without sketches or calculations) approximations of square footage needs by using their personal store of past project experiences of a great variety of rooms and functions. But spaces with unique requirements will have to be dealt with differently, as past experience will not help in making quick approximations. And for less experienced designers, particularly at the student level, approximations for many typical rooms or spaces may be difficult.

When past experience will not help, the use of prototypical plan sketches will usually provide the needed information. The word "prototypical" is synonymous with "generalized" or "abstracted," and "sketch" is defined as a quick drawing done for informational purposes only. For example, a design program may call for a director's office with a 36" × 72" desk, a matching credenza, a desk chair, two guest pull-up chairs, lounge seating for four people, and 35 linear feet of bookshelves. Unless one's professional experience provides a quick and certain square footage figure for this room, it is best to take a few minutes to quickly sketch one or more floor plans of such a room to establish approximate size needs, as shown on the left side of Illustration 1–3. Keep in mind that these quickly drawn sketch plans are not intended to be directly incorporated in the floor plan, but are meant primarily to serve as generators of square footage requirements.

If drawn by hand, almost any kind of paper and drawing tool are acceptable for this purpose (probably a roll of sketch tracing paper and a medium-weight pencil are best), and drawing quality is not an issue. Some designers find that working over a ⅛" or ¼" grid paper background (or directly on grid paper) is helpful to keep the plan sketches quick and reasonably proportional. But don't be too careful in making these sketches, since their use is limited; it is even unnecessary to work in a particular scale, as long as one keeps track of the dimensional factors. If the sketch is computer-drawn, as shown on the right side of Illustration 1–3, the same principles related to drawing style, quality, and accuracy apply. The inherent accuracy of computer drawings can be a negative quality in this particular process, leading to unnecessary and deceptively finished-looking sketches.

It should be obvious that a basic knowledge of typical furniture sizes, arrangements, and dimensional relationships between individual pieces of furniture is essential here; otherwise, one cannot work with appropriate speed. Many interior designers tend to work in only one aspect of the field (residential, hospitality, offices, health care, etc.); if a designer finds him- or herself working outside of his or her accustomed area of expertise, familiarization with a new set of furniture standards may be necessary. Certainly for students, whose knowledge base is less complete, regular referral to standard reference sources and furniture catalogs will be required. Specific exercises given in Chapter 6 are designed to bolster those skills.

To demonstrate the use of the prototypical plan sketch technique, Illustrations 1–4A and 1–4B, each developed by a different designer, provide several examples. These sketches are for rooms and spaces described in Design Program 2S and have been reduced from their original size so that more examples could be shown.

An additional advantage, beyond the value of approximating square footage needs, that derives from producing prototypical plan sketches during the pre-design phase of a project. is the development of an intuitive sense of the specific needs of each space, providing a feel for better room proportions (square, or a long and narrow rectangle), window locations, door access points, and internal furniture and equipment relationships within each space.

PROTOTYPICAL PLAN SKETCHES: DIRECTOR'S OFFICE

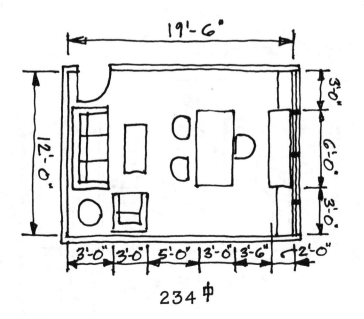

185 ⌀

234 ⌀

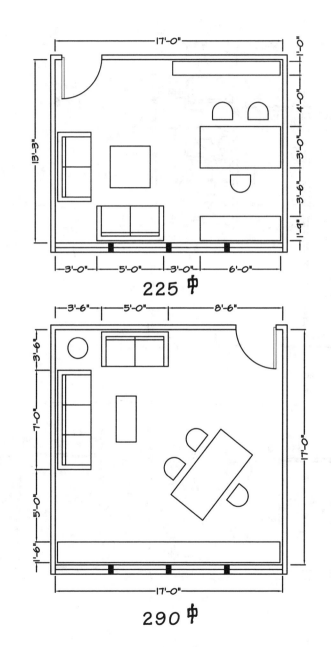

225 ⌀

290 ⌀

PROTOTYPICAL PLAN SKETCHES: DESIGN PROGRAM 2S

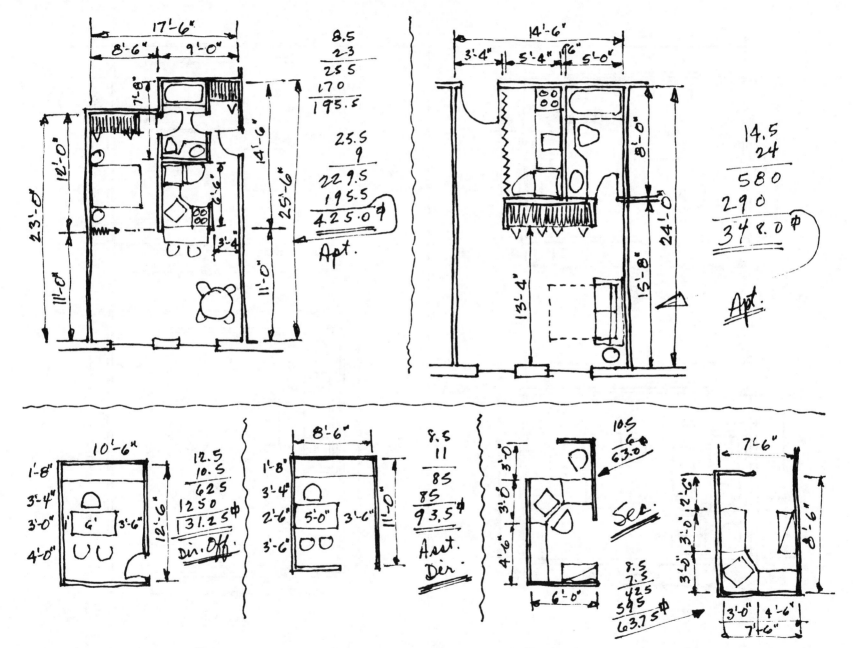

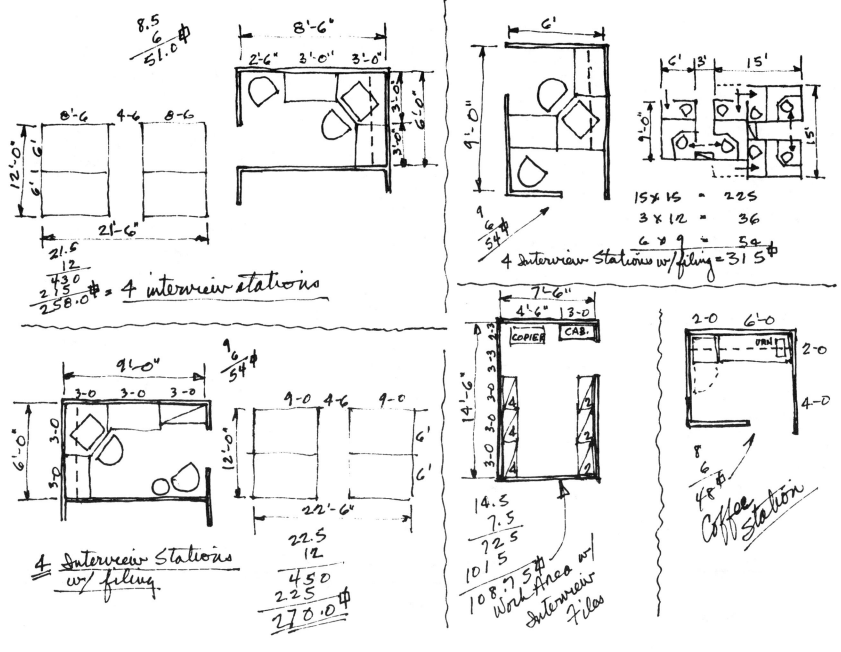

PROTOTYPICAL PLAN SKETCHES: DESIGN PROGRAM 2S

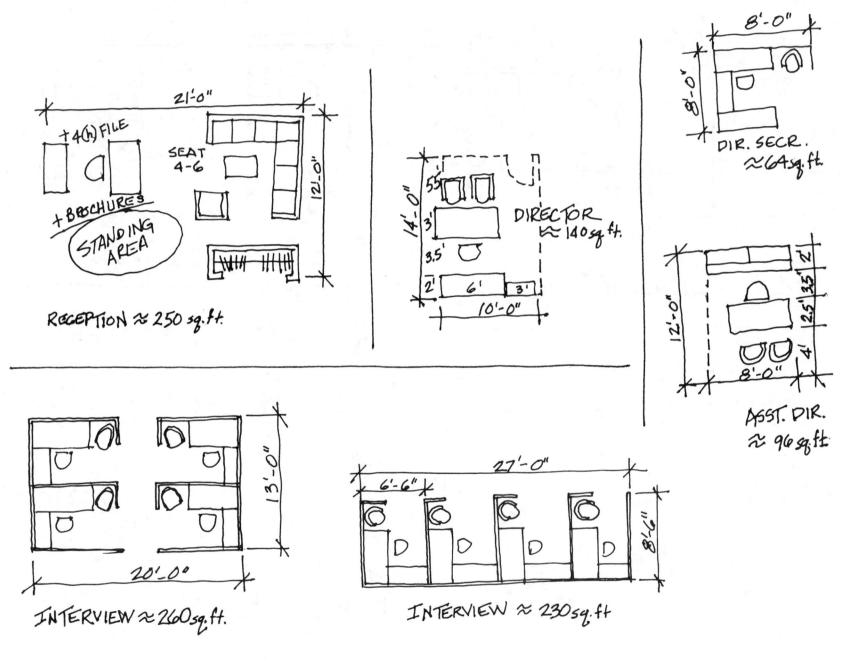

RECEPTION ≈ 250 sq. ft.

DIRECTOR ≈ 140 sq. ft.

DIR. SECR. ≈ 64 sq. ft.

ASST. DIR. ≈ 96 sq. ft.

INTERVIEW ≈ 260 sq. ft.

INTERVIEW ≈ 230 sq. ft.

ILLUS. 1–4B

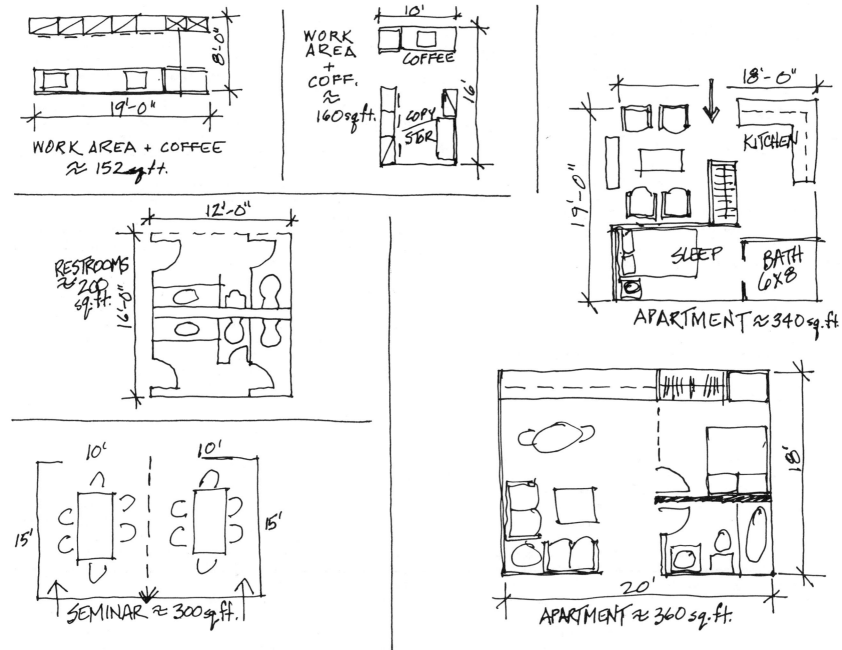

WORK AREA + COFFEE ≈ 152 sq.ft.

WORK AREA + COFF. ≈ 160 sq.ft.

COFFEE

COPY STOR

RESTROOMS ≈ 200 sq.ft.

KITCHEN

SLEEP

BATH 6×8

APARTMENT ≈ 340 sq.ft.

SEMINAR ≈ 300 sq.ft.

APARTMENT ≈ 360 sq.ft.

To work quickly and efficiently with this pre-design technique takes considerable practice. Under conventional professional conditions, prototypical plan sketches are accomplished with dispatch, since they are generally left as an unfinished product developed for informational purposes only. On some occasions sketches may be refined and then serve as corporate or institutional standards for a particular organization, but studies of that kind are usually full-blown projects of their own.

EXERCISE 1-1

Using Design Program 2S (page 175), as well as one or more of the design programs in the Appendix, develop several groups of prototypical plan sketches in order to build skill and efficiency in this process. Try using both hand-drawing and computer-drawing techniques. Save the results of these exercises for use in further exercises that will be presented and recommended later in this chapter, as well as in Chapters 2, 6, and 7.

COMPLETING THE CRITERIA MATRIX

With the prototypical plan sketches completed, it is now time to go back to the criteria matrix and fill in the square footage column for those spaces for which one was unable to estimate size based on previous planning and design experience. But even with this accomplished, an element is still missing in the square footage figures—the space needed for circulation (halls, corridors, vestibules, etc.) and partition thickness.

For most non-residential interior facilities, a factor of 25 to 33 percent of the square footage total for all required spaces will be a reasonably accurate estimate of the space needed for circulation and partitions. An absolutely reliable factor for this element does not exist; it will vary from project to project, depending on the configuration and construction of the building shell and the nature of the functions to be performed in the space. In general terms, when building or space configurations are complex, structural spans are short (with interiors having closely spaced columns or bearing walls), or when functional planning requirements demand a lot of separate spaces (such as offices, examining rooms, or lab booths), it is likely that the circulation or partition factor will be higher than normal. Only extensive experience in space planning will permit a designer to make an educated guess at what the factor might be for any specific user or building situation. The definition of "space" for interior planning purposes can take many forms, particularly in the real estate industry. Forms such as gross, usable, and several others must be defined when working in these contexts. For the pirposes of this book, a simple square foot number measured inside exterior and demising walls is used, with the circulation factor as part of the total. A 25 percent factor is practical for most space planning problems because it permits one to err on the side of safety; it is recommended for use with the space planning exercises accompanying this text.

Until this point in the pre-design process, it has not been specifically necessary to know the size of the available space, but with the criteria matrix now complete, it is time to use an architectural scale and measure and calculate the useable interior square footage available within the building shell. After the available square footage has been determined, then calculate 75 percent of the available square footage; that result should be approximately equal to the total square footage of all the spaces listed in the criteria matrix. Another approach to this calculation that will bring the same result is to divide the total square footage of all the spaces in the criteria matrix by three and add the result to the square footage total (or $1.33 \times$ total square footage); this result should approximately equal the useable square footage available within the building shell. An allowance or tolerance of approximately 5 percent in either direction is usually workable; however, it is likely that an adjustment in the square footage column figures (up or down) will be required to attain a fairly close match between space needed and space available. One's first attempts at "juggling" the square footage numbers may seem difficult and tedious; as with all aspects of the space planning process, experience will permit this awkward trial-and-error numbers game to be accomplished easily and quickly. This is an essential part of the process, since a significant mismatch between the estimated amount of space required and the actual amount of space available will make the physical planning process very difficult. Using the square footage numbers arrived at in the prototypical plan sketches shown in Illustrations 1–4A and 1–4B, the square footage column in the criteria matrix for Design Program 2S has been completed in Illustration 1–5. With a one-third circulation factor added, the square footage total (2,443 square feet) compares favorably with the square footage available in Building Shell 2S (2,500 square feet). The use of program/shell combination 2S for illustrative demonstrations will continue throughout the text.

An additive variation to the criteria matrix that some designers find useful can be made part of the matrix with little extra time. Probably the most widely used matrix technique among space planners is the adjacency matrix. Although limited to defining the adjacency aspects of the program data, its graphic qualities can be very useful. With a simple addition to the left of the criteria matrix, this graphic approach to visualize the adjacency factors of the design program can become a valuable supplement to the other factors already accounted for in the matrix. Illustration 1–6 demonstrates the ease with which this can be accomplished, using a very basic set of legend symbols to articulate the relative levels of adjacency importance.

CRITERIA MATRIX: DESIGN PROGRAM 2S (WITH SQ. FOOTAGE NEEDS)   ILLUS. 1–5

DESIGN PROGRAM 2S

CRITERIA MATRIX FOR: UNIVERSITY CAREER COUNSELING CENTER	SQ FOOTAGE NEEDS	ADJACENCIES	PUBLIC ACCESS	DAYLIGHT AND/OR VIEW	PRIVACY	PLUMBING	SPECIAL EQUIPMENT	SPECIAL CONSIDERATIONS
① RECEPTION	250	② ⑤	H	Y	N	N	N	TRAFFIC HUB ADJ. TO MAIN ENTRANCE
② INTERVIEW STA. (4)	220	① ④	M	I	L	N	N	FEEL LIKE A TEAM OF FOUR
③ DIRECTOR	140	④	M	Y	H	N	N	HIGHEST IMAGE ACCESS TO REAR DR FOR PRIVATE EXIT
④ STAFF	180	③	M	Y	M	N	N	
⑤ SEMINAR RM	300	① ⑥ ⑦	H	I	H	N	Y	A/V USE IMPORTANT CLOSE TO ENTRANCE
⑥ RESTROOM (2)	200	CENTRAL	M	N	H	Y	N	
⑦ WORK AREA	120	② ④ CENTRAL	L	N	M	Y	Y	
⑧ COFFEE STATION	50	CENTRAL	H	Y	N	Y	Y	CONVENIENT FOR EVERYONE
⑨ GUEST APARTMENT	350	REMOTE	L	Y	H	Y	N	RESIDENTIAL CHARACTER

LEGEND
H = HIGH
M = MEDIUM
L = LOW
Y = YES
N = NO/NONE
I = IMPORTANT BUT NOT REQUIRED

TOTAL NEEDED =1810 S.F.   TOTAL AVAILABLE = 2500 S.F
2500 S.F – 625 S.F.=1875 S.F.   LESS 25% FOR CIRCULATION = 625 S.F.

NOTE: IN "ADJACENCIES" COLUMN ⓧ - INDICATES ADJACENCY IMPORTANCE
                               ⓧ - INDICATES MAJOR ADJACENCY IMPORTANCE

COMPLETED CRITERIA MATRIX WITH ADDED ADJACENCY MATRIX   ILLUS. 1–6

DESIGN PROGRAM 25

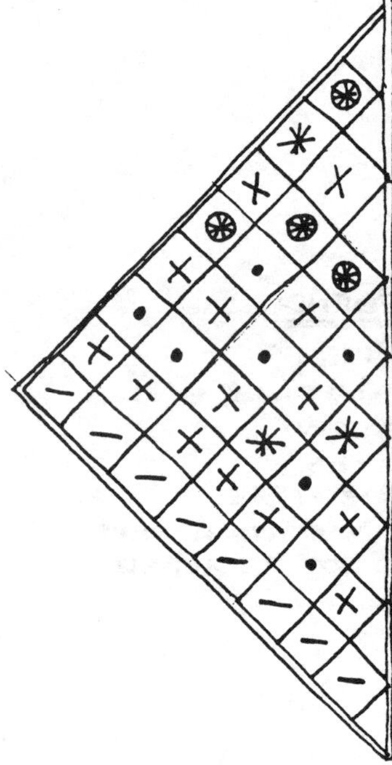

CRITERIA MATRIX FOR: UNIVERSITY CAREER COUNSELING CENTER	SQ FOOTAGE NEEDS	ADJACENCIES	PUBLIC ACCESS	DAYLIGHT AND/OR VIEW	PRIVACY	PLUMBING	SPECIAL EQUIPMENT	SPECIAL CONSIDERATIONS
① RECEPTION	250	② ⑤	H	Y	N	N	N	TRAFFIC HUB ADJ. TO MAIN ENTRANCE
② INTERVIEW STA.(4)	220	① ④	M	I	L	N	N	FEEL LIKE A TEAM OF FOUR
③ DIRECTOR	140	④	M	Y	H	N	N	HIGHEST IMAGE ACCESS TO REAR DR FOR PRIVATE EXIT
④ STAFF	180	③	M	Y	M	N	N	
⑤ SEMINAR RM	300	① ⑥ ⑦	H	I	H	N	Y	A/V USE IMPORTANT CLOSE TO ENTRANCE
⑥ RESTROOM (2)	200	CENTRAL	M	N	H	Y	N	
⑦ WORK AREA	120	② ④ CENTRAL	L	N	M	Y	Y	
⑧ COFFEE STATION	50	CENTRAL	H	Y	N	Y	Y	CONVENIENT FOR EVERYONE
⑨ GUEST APARTMENT	350	REMOTE	L	Y	H	Y	N	RESIDENTIAL CHARACTER

LEGEND

H = HIGH
M = MEDIUM
L = LOW
Y = YES
N = NO/NONE
I = IMPORTANT BUT NOT REQUIRED

⊛ – IMMEDIATELY ADJACENT
✳ – IMPORTANT ADJACENCY
X – REASONABLY CONVENIENT
• – UNIMPORTANT
– – REMOTE

TOTAL NEEDED = 1810 S.F.
2500 S.F. - 625 S.F. = 1875 S.F.

TOTAL AVAILABLE = 2500 S.F.
LESS 25% FOR CIRCULATION = 625 S.F.

NOTE: IN "ADJACENCIES" COLUMN

Ⓝ – INDICATES ADJACENCY IMPORTANCE
Ⓝ – INDICATES MAJOR ADJACENCY IMPORTANCE

To summarize the value of the criteria matrix as a space planning tool, four important steps in the process have been accomplished:

1. The basic program elements have been considered, evaluated, and organized for planning purposes.

2. This analysis has been put into quick reference format.

3. If referenced regularly in the planning process, the matrix ensures thoroughness and attention to detail.

4. The matrix becomes an excellent evaluation tool at the completion of the space planning process to check the finished solution's ability to fulfill the design program requirements.

To demonstrate how the criteria matrix can be effectively employed as a pre-design tool for larger and more complex planning and design problems, including those that require departmental categorization, the first two sheets (of a total of five) for a (new construction) 20,000-square-foot one-story suburban office building are shown in illustrations 1–7A and 1–7B. Make note of the expanded number of factors, such as acoustics, lighting, color, and materials, that can be appropriately considered in the pre-design process. The "size" column, unlike the abbreviated matrix format, typically indicates a square foot range figure rather than a single square foot number; this provides the opportunity for developing a "low" and "high" square foot range for the project, including a corresponding "low" and "high" range for the circulation factor. While this "low/high range" approach adds another level of complexity, it provides an additional tool for manipulating and balancing square foot needs, particularly when the available square feet are on the skimpy side in terms of optimally solving the space planning problem at hand. It should be noted that the full five-sheet matrix is the result of more than 100 hours of professional time extended over a period of several weeks.

EXERCISE 1-2

Using the design programs provided in the Appendix, develop a criteria matrix for at least one or two of the 1,500-square-foot and 2,500-square-foot problems, including the square footage column and any prototypical plan sketches required. These matrixes should be done in an unhurried manner so that the exercise provides a meaningful learning experience. Save the results of these exercises for use in further exercises that will be presented and recommended later in this chapter, as well as in Chapters 2, 6, and 7.

RELATIONSHIP DIAGRAMS

The relationship diagram is an excellent transition between the essentially verbal analysis of program development and the completely graphic techniques used in physically planning a space. As described earlier in this chapter, the relationship diagram is still part of the pre-design process, because it represents a graphic abstraction or interpretation of the program information, rather than a planning solution. If handled efficiently, the essential values of the relationship diagram process can be gained over a relatively short period; the expenditure of time is certainly warranted for a procedure that may reveal the essence of the interrelationships and adjacencies between and among the rooms and spaces called for in the program. As is true of all the other steps in the pre-design process, developing relationship diagrams helps the planner become immersed in the project's requirements and relationships.

Here's how to proceed. With the criteria matrix just completed and the required rooms and spaces fresh in one's mind, draw a circle for each required space so that its position on the paper represents a correct or appropriate relationship to the other spaces. Rooms or functions that should be close to one another should be drawn close together, while spaces that do not require closeness (or may even suffer from being placed in close proximity) should be drawn at a distance from one another. Use connecting lines between the circles to indicate travel or circulation patterns between spaces; those connections should be coded by using heavy or multiple lines for important or heavily traveled connections, and lighter connecting lines between spaces where circulation adjacency is less important or less traveled. The diagram should not be related to the building shell shape or configuration or to any architectural scale. It is a good idea to have the circles approximately proportional in size; ideally, a circle representing a 300-square-foot conference room should be about three times the area of the circle representing a 100-square-foot office. At least two or three diagrammatic arrangements should be attempted to explore a variety of viable sets of relationships. All this should be done relatively quickly and intuitively. As with the prototypical plan sketches, drawing quality is not an issue here, since the diagrams are a design tool, not for presentation. A short roll of inexpensive tracing paper and a soft pencil or felt-tipped marker are fine for this purpose. Rather than bothering to erase in order to revise, it is usually more efficient to make changes by placing another layer of tracing paper over the original and redrawing it. To demonstrate one basic graphic approach to relationship diagrams, Illustration 1–8 provides a few examples of visually interpreting the requirements of Design Program 2S, for which a criteria matrix was prepared and shown in Illustration 1–5.

ELECTRONIC DISTRIBUTORS, INC. BUILDING & DESIGN PROGRAM

Department	Space	Description of Function	Size	Proxemics	Equipment/Furnishing	Thermal
EXTERIOR	STREET ENTRANCE	Vehicular entrance to site from Hornig Rd.	2–14' lanes w/splayed sides for easy turns.	On Hornig Rd., easy access to both office and warehouse.	Signage—easy to read for approaching vehicles.	
	PARKING	For employees and visitors.	Now—128 employees, 10 visitors Later—214 employees, 20 visitors.	Convenient to Hornig Rd. entry, office, reception area, and pedestrian warehouse entrance.	Directional signage.	
	BUILDING EXTERIOR	Creates corporate image to employees, visitors, and passersby.		Visual outreach to Roosevelt Blvd. and Woodhaven Rd. is of secondary importance.		
	PEDESTRIAN ENTRANCE	Primary—for office employees and visitors. Secondary—for warehouse employees.		Primary—adjacent to main reception room. Secondary—direct access to warehouse employee locker room.	Exterior seating, such as benches, sitting walls, etc., for small parklike setting.	
	LOADING AREAS	Daily and frequent loading and unloading. Admin. plus oper. could share same exterior area, if specific dock and door areas are separated.	Admin. needs 4 truck bays of varying sizes. Oper. needs 3 truck bays of varying sizes.	Immediately adjacent to staging areas and shipping tables within both admin. and oper. warehouses.	Admin.—both med. spaces to have dock levelers. Oper.—med. to have wedge on ramp.	Deep overhang protection for loading docks, plus radiant heaters.
	RECREATION	Break, lunch and other non-work time exterior rest plus leisure activities.	Accom. one-third of total staff in passive activities (conversation, chess/checkers, sunning, etc.)	Immediately adjacent to large group functions (lunch, mtg, training) could be next to main pedestrian entrance. Could be a major view space from office areas.	Seating (benches, walls), tables (dining, games) table umbrellas (semi-protection, decorative), moderate exercise.	
RECEPTION	**The main entrance point for all office employees and all visitors. The hub of all internal office circulation.**					
	VESTIBULE	Wind and temperature break between interior and exterior.	50 sf. to 100 sf.	Transition area between exterior pedestrian entrance and the receptionist desk.		Air surge for slightly exaggerated temperature change.
	RECEPTION STATION	Greeting point for visitors. Check-in/check-out point for staff. Basic security checkpoint.	250 sf. to 350 sf.	Immediately adjacent to and direct visual contact w/ vestibule, doors. Adjacent to waiting area. Hub of internal office circulation. Easy-to-understand paths to entire building.	Two workstations, both visible, or one screened. Parcel ledge to separate visitors from receptionist.	TC-1; avoid entrance door drafts.
	WAITING	Visitor waiting.	6–8 guests; approximately 200 sf. to 300 sf.	Adjacent to reception station gallery and circulation paths to major office departments.	Upholstered lounge seating (not too low or too comfortable)—use system for easy change or additions.	TC-1
	POWDER ROOM	Toilet facility for guests.	25 sf. to 35 sf.	Immediately adjacent to waiting area. Visual supervision by receptionist.	Toilet. Sink in vanity.	TC-1; high ventilation.
	GALLERY	A small space for exhibiting fine artwork in a traditional gallery setting.	300 sf. to 400 sf.	Immediately adjacent to waiting area. Access from vestibule without walking through waiting area. Visual access from reception for basic security against theft/vandalism.	Picture hanging system for walls. Pedestal system for sculpture. Freestanding exhibit system for additional 2-D display.	TC-1

Date: _____
Revised: _____

Acoustics	Lighting	Color	Materials	Environmental Qualities	Future Factors
	Low-level lighting 2 +/- above grade.			Welcoming/use plants to identify.	None.
	Mid-level lighting 8'–10' above ground.			Avoid "sea of cars" appearance—use earth berms and plants to humanize.	Future parking could be on upper deck.
	Not required.	Colorful and warm.	Use a variety of materials—natural and man-made.	Present an image of professionalism and human-ism—avoid monumentality.	Future add-ins to maintain original image.
	Well lighted with low and medium level fix-tures—incorp. walls, planting, sculpture, foun-tains, and/or wall murals.	Concentrated use of color—potentially in both building materials and fine artworks (sculpures, glazed tiles, walls, etc.)	Most personal contact with building exte-rior—special attention to scale and texture of building material.	Major focal point—use sculpture and/or foun-tains—an extension of reception rm.	Original image could be expanded.
	General driveway area, lighting and general lighting of dock areas.	Light, reflective surfaces.	Wall material able to take regular major abuse. Dock floor material tough and smooth.	Paved area must drain off easily. Snow removal must be efficient; consider use of electrically heat-ed paved areas.	Loading areas will grow pro-portionally with their respec-tive warehouse areas.
	Decorative lighting of foliage.	Opportunity for lots of color in furnishings, plant material, paving adjacent wall sur-faces, window awning, etc.	Fast-drying, easily maintained.	Create a parklike setting. Utilize water and foun-tains; lunch, business meetings, and training ses-sions could move out to this area.	Must accommodate one-third of ultimate workforce.
	Ambient. An integral part of planned lighting for main reception spaces.	Subordinate to main reception spaces.	Very durable. Glass indoors for safety; floor to absorb water and snow.	An integral part of the planned reception area.	None.
A-1	Special lighting required for sculptural quali-ties of the reception area. Not overly dramat-ic. Task lighting for desk.	Colorful. An integral element in the plan-ning of the main entrance space of the building.	Very durable. Appropriate luxury. Consistent for entire reception area.	Spacious; express firm's success. Use of permanent fine artworks. Large environment with high ceiling.	Third workstation required; screened.
A-1	Ambient. Daylighting and view desired. Articulate sculptural quality of space.				More people in future.
	Ambient.	C-2	Durable and water-resistant.		
A-1	Ambient, plus track system for exhibit light. Control natural light.	Neutral colors to avoid conflict with exhib-ited works.	Tackable wall surfaces desirable.	A special space, inviting, to bring pleasure and enlightenment to employees and visitors.	Could expand if successful.

ELECTRONIC DISTRIBUTORS, INC. BUILDING & DESIGN PROGRAM

Department	Space	Description of Function	Size	Proxemics	Equipment/Furnishing
CORP. MANAGEMENT		An executive suite that is conveniently located, but a little removed from other office functions and departments. As a group, it should be immediately adjacent to the other corporate functions (Accounting, Computer, Marketing, and Personnel).			
	STEVE	Executive office with conversation area.	300 sf. to 350 sf.	In a central operating position within the management team. Adjacent to a secretary shared with Murray. Adjacent to a small conference room for exclusive corporate management use.	Desk, credenza, desk chair, 2 guest chairs, lounge seating for 6 (personal choice for furniture selections).
	6 CORPORATE OFFICES	Executive offices for very active and busy people.	200 sf. to 225 sf.	No prioritization of placement, all 6 executives work together. Each should have easy contact with their immediate staff.	Desk, credenza, desk chair, 2 guest chairs, and (A) conversation seating for 3 or 4 or (B) conference table for 4.
	SUPPORT STAFF	Administrative assistance and secretarial duties directly related to the corporate management group.	2 large stations now at 100 sf., 3 medium stations later at 75 sf.	One station between Steve and Murray. One station adjacent to Joe. Three future stations adjacent to Adam and Roger.	System furniture (including wall panels when required) and operational seating. Immediately use files adjacent when and if required.
	CONFERENCE ROOMS	To serve corporate management conference needs of 5 or more people.	Small—8 to 10 people, 225 sf. Large— 20 people, 575 sf.	Small is best placed between Steve and Mary. Large should be convenient for all executive offices and outside visitors.	Pedestal-leg conference table, uphol. swivel chairs w/pedestal base, projection wall and marker surfaces, beverage counter, misc. storage.
	FILE AND WORK ROOM	Files for corporate management only. Also coats, small copier, general workspace.	100 sf. to 120 sf.	Primarily accessible by support staff.	Portable steel cabinets, small copier.
	POWDER ROOM	Corporate management group visitors only.	25 sf. to 35 sf.	Convenient for corporate management group visitors.	Toilet. Sink in vanity.
ACCOUNTING		A corporate function, generally adjacent to Corporate Management and specifically adjacent to Joe's office. Also generally adjacent to the Computer Department.			
	MANAGER	General supervision of the department.	150 sf.	Adjacent to controller's office. Positioned to supervise the department.	Desk, credenza, desk chair, 2 guest chairs, shelves, 10 file drawers, EDP workspace storage.
	STAFF ACCOUNTING	Concentrative and detailed work.	100 sf. to 110 sf. (status I)	Adjacent to accounting manager.	F-4
	CREDIT DEPARTMENT	Concentrative and detailed work. A lot of telephone activity.	Manager = 90 sf. Staff = 75 sf.	Adjacent to assistant controller.	F-4
	BOOKKEEPING	Bookkeeping and general office functions. Accounts payable and receivable, secretary, clerical staff.	6 stations and 75 sf	Physically central to the department.	F-4
	PAYROLL	Confidential and concentrative work.	100 sf. to 110 sf. (status I)	Easily available to accounting managers, but in a fairly remote or private location.	F-4
	FILES	For exclusive departmental use.	200 drawers, 40 with 5 drawers each; 300 sf. to 350 sf.	Physically central to the accounting department, closest to bookkeepers.	5 drawer, vertical type, lockable.
	LIBRARY WORK ROOM	Central reference and equipment room.	120 sf.	Physically central to the department.	Shelving for reference books and manuals. Storage for EDP files. Work space for common equipment, i.e., Fax machines, 2 P.C.s and small copier.
	HUDDLE SPACE	Casual, impromptu conference space for up to 4 or 5 people.	65 sf. to 90 sf.	Physically central to the department, but positioned for minimum acoustic distraction to others, without requiring physical enclosure.	42" dia. Or 36" X 60" table, 4 pull-up chairs.

ILLUS. 1–7B

Thermal	Acoustics	Lighting	Color	Materials	Environmental Qualities	Future Factors
TC-1	A-2	Task/ambient, plus accent.	Personal choice.	Personal choice.	Exemplify the corporate image of professionalism and humanism. Clearly a customized interior. Personal art selections. Personal coat closet.	None.
TC-1	A-2	Task/ambient, plus accent.	Personal choice or corporate selection could be made.		Environment to express dynamism, not pomp. Some opportunity for personalization. Personal coat closet.	2 to 3 more offices.
TC-1	A-1	Task/ambient.	C-1 plus decorative accents of corporate management group.	M-1	Efficient, open dynamic, professional. This area important to interior corporate image.	None.
TC-1 plus high-level air change.	A-2—at least a 50 db. STL enclosure.	Task lighting for table. Separate switch wall washers for track and marker surfaces. Dimmer for projection.	Medium-level contrast, medium and light tones (avoid deep tones, except on floor).	M-1. Highly customized for important image space.	Important to convey corporate image of professionalism and humanism. These spaces should also be distinctive and sophisticated; clearly customized.	None.
		Task/minimal ambient.	Consistent with adjoining spaces.			More filing needed?
TC-1. High ventilation.		Ambient.	C-2	Durable and water-resistant.		
TC-1	A-2	Task/ambient.	C-1	M-1. Ceiling can be non-acoustic.	Appropriate for both concentrative work and informal conferencing. Personal coat closet.	None.
TC-1	A-1	Task/ambient.	C-1	M-1	EQ-1	NOW = 1 LATER = 2 to 4
TC-1	A-1	Task/ambient.	C-1	M-1	EQ-1. A little remote because of telephone activity acoustics.	Grow to 3 to 4.
TC-1	A-1	Task/ambient.	C-1	M-1	Mix of concentrative work with a lot of personal interaction within the bookkeeping group, and some interaction with others.	Grow to 8 to 10.
TC-1	A-1	Ambient, plus track system for exhibit light. Control natural light.	C-1	M-1	EQ-1 with an added degree of visual privacy.	None.
		Task lighting for file search, plus minimal ambient lighting.	Consistent with adjoining spaces.		Purely functional.	Not identified.
TC-1. Additional airflow if required by electrical equipment.	A-1	Task/ambient.	C-1	M-1	EQ-1	Identify future needs.
TC-1	A-1	General.	C-2, plus strong accent color in furnishings or on ltd. wall surface or panel.	M-1, plus added absorbing material on walls.	Conducive to stimulating verbal exchange. (Good place for graphic art work.)	Not identified.

RELATIONSHIP DIAGRAMS: DESIGN PROGRAM 2S

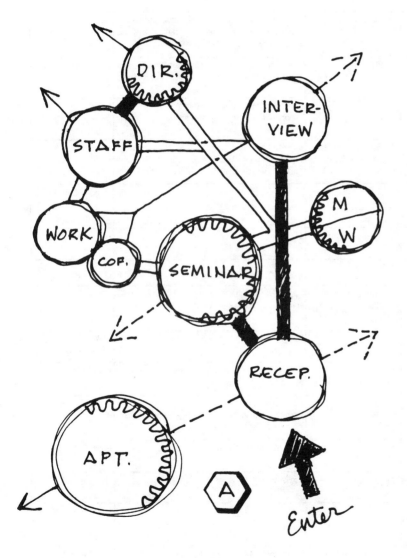

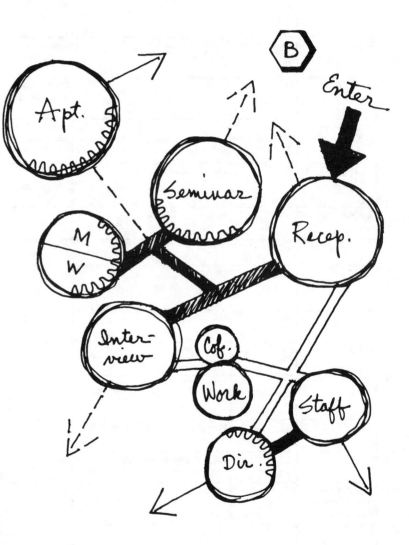

LEGEND

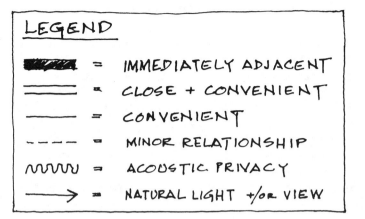

- ▬▬▬ = IMMEDIATELY ADJACENT
- ═══ = CLOSE + CONVENIENT
- ─── = CONVENIENT
- ----- = MINOR RELATIONSHIP
- ∿∿∿ = ACOUSTIC PRIVACY
- ⟶ = NATURAL LIGHT +/or VIEW

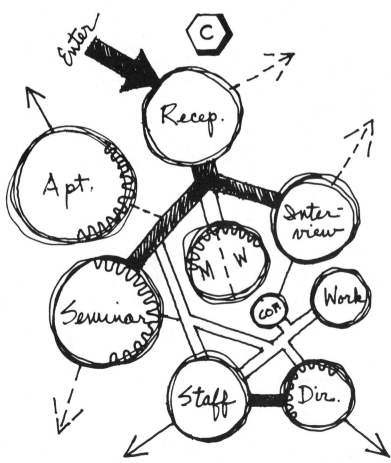

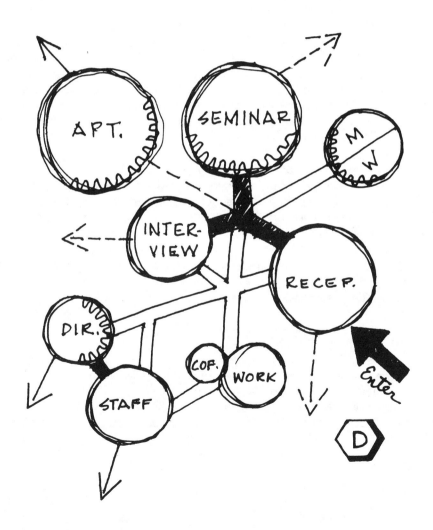

As one begins to develop skill in drawing relationship diagrams, graphic and/or verbal notations should be added to indicate important planning needs such as windows, segregation of public and private areas, acoustic barriers, and so on, as shown in Illustration 1–8. Color can be used as a coding tool to identify similar functions or planning relationships, such as privacy or adjacency. Over time, designers develop a personalized visual notation system that they are able to draw upon as an efficient and expressive pre-design tool.

There are appropriate alternatives to the hand-drawn diagramming process described above and shown in Illustration 1–8. There are several computer graphic software programs with which circles (or other shapes) can be manipulated on the computer screen, and lines of varying types and visual weights can be drawn to connect them. Text notations, legends, and color coding are also easily incorporated with computer graphic techniques. Still another alternative is the use of heavy paper (such as cover stock) cut into circular or rectangular labeled templates for each of the rooms or spaces and then moved about on a white or other neutral paper background, with lines drawn to represent the level of adjacency. In this technique, it is important to remember to record each viable diagram before shifting the templates around to create a new diagram.

As mentioned earlier, relationship diagrams, after some modest graphic refinement, are made a part of the finished design program document. Although their primary purpose is to help the planner gain a first visualization of program requirements, if skillfully drawn (and if the non-professional's limited visualization capabilities are kept in mind) they can often help clients and users to better understand the content of the design program. In this context, it is important to ensure that the diagrams do not resemble a floor plan, so that the non-professional will not confuse them with actual floor plans to be developed later.

EXERCISE 1-3

Using the criteria matrixes developed in the previous exercise, draw at least a few relationship diagrams for each of them. Make an attempt to begin to create a personalized diagramming and symbol language. Again, save the results for use in continuing exercises in Chapters 2, 6, and 7.

A FINAL NOTE ON PLANNING METHODOLOGY

This concludes the discussion of programming and the pre-design process. It is time to move on to the physical planning process and the development of a floor plan, with all its broader spatial and design implications. As mentioned earlier in this chapter, it is important to note that programming and its graphic products are rarely completely developed at this point. As one begins to develop bubble diagrams and rough floor plans for the project, it is natural for new concepts, functional relationships, multiple uses of space, and so on to emerge—ideas that had not surfaced in the pre-design phase. If the new ideas are an improvement on those embodied in the program, it would be irresponsible to ignore them and not revise the original program. In the professional setting, it is common to have new planning factors introduced after the initial programming phase has been completed—factors completely outside the designer's control. For example, programmatic changes could be created when new management decides to change organizational structure, or a lease agreement is rescinded by the client's landlord. These situations leave the designer no choice but to go back to the program and make revisions. Said in its simplest terms, design programs are rarely static documents after their original development and completion. Rather, it is common practice to revise the program as design ideas develop and outside factors evolve and change. The space planner must face the problem-solving task from a position of flexibility equal to the demands of the process.

Recommended Reading

9*, 16*, 18*, 20*, 21*, 22, 23*, 24*, 26*, 28, 29

Books marked with an asterisk are also included in the recommended reading for other chapters.

Chapter 2   THE FIRST PLANNING STEPS
Bubble Diagrams and Block Plans

To this point, efforts to solve a space-planning problem have been carried out through methods of data gathering, analysis of user needs, and first attempts to establish a general concept or approach to the project. Although some physical planning has taken place, in drawing prototypical plan sketches of specific functions or rooms and abstract relationship diagrams of the organization as a whole, the overall plan has not yet been approached from a realistic planning viewpoint.

The initial leap from these pre-design steps to the more creative development of a floor plan that solves the practical and esthetic problems of the users is the most difficult and critical element in the space planning process. Programming is essentially a process of analysis; planning (and design) is essentially a process of synthesis. Transition from the analytical mode of programming to the creative mode of planning will never be easy—a gap will always exist. Ideally, one makes the gap as small and manageable as possible. This "synthesis gap" will be narrow to the degree that one's programming results are complete and thorough.

The narrowness of the gap is the reward of good programming. But the gap will always be there, and a creative synthesis spanning it is required to bring together all the divergent elements of the space planning problem.

BUBBLE DIAGRAMMING

With the programming phase completed, one could simply begin by sketching or drafting a floor plan. However, with a problem involving more than a few spaces or functions, the likelihood of developing a good plan the first time around is slim. It's not very likely that a good plan would emerge after the first few attempts, and each of these attempts would be relatively time-consuming, since floor plans involve partitions, door swings, the placement of plumbing fixtures and equipment, and so on. Furthermore, when a good plan has emerged, it is difficult to know whether a significantly better plan (or plans) can be developed. Surely a better or more efficient approach to solving the problem exists than this trial-and-error development of full-blown floor plans. To eliminate this time-consuming approach, the technique used most by experienced space planners is the bubble diagram. Simply stated, it is a trial-and-error method to quickly explore all the planning options, both good and bad, of a given space planning problem. Although its purpose and results are primarily two-dimensional, some basic three-dimensional issues can also be dealt with in the process of arriving at a floor plan solution.

The tools required are simple. Obviously, a base floor plan of the building is needed. In addition, the planner needs lots of tracing paper, an architectural scale, and soft or flowing media with which to draw. Most typically, rolls of inexpensive yellow tracing paper (sometimes called "trace," "yellow trace," or "bumwad") are used, although any reasonably transparent tracing paper, yellow or white, can be used. Almost any drawing medium can be used, but markers or soft wax colored pencils are among the best, since they flow on the paper easily and make a bold mark without effort.

Despite the fact that the great majority of architectural drawing is computer-generated, a freehand approach has advantages for this initial phase of space planning. The immediate creative connection between hand and thought process, without the intervention of the computer's digital rules and processes, more easily permits the designer's intuitive processes to take over and react spontaneously to spur-of-the moment thoughts.

If one has a computer-connected stylus and digital drawing pad, computer-generated bubble diagrams can be accomplished in the same manner as those hand-drawn on paper. The drawing tools are then of little consequence. The block plan, an often-used alternative to the bubble diagram, is much more compatible with typical computer-drawn techniques and is discussed in detail further on in this chapter.

Regardless of the drawing tool employed, the general approach and attitude should be free and intuitive, roughly to scale, and (at least at the outset) essentially non-judgmental. In this context, "non-judgmental" can be defined as "uncritical" or "without evaluation." The purpose is simple: to efficiently explore and record all the basic planning options of the problem.

Just as the design program must be read and analyzed before one starts the planning process, the floor plan of the existing space must be "read" and analyzed before the physical planning process begins. It is important to study the existing space to understand its configuration, geometry, and structural framework or elements; the location, type, and quantity of windows; unique architectural elements (such as a fireplace or monumental stair); HVAC system; plumbing supply and waste lines; and so on. To some degree, a full

understanding of the relative importance of each factor will slowly develop as the bubble diagramming process continues. Despite this, it is useful to take some time (exactly how much depends on the size of the space and the time pressures of the circumstance) before the bubble diagramming process begins in order to (with architectural scale in hand) study, analyze, and understand the nature of the space within which you are working.

First, tape the floor plan of the building shell to the drawing board. If the reflected ceiling plan contains graphic information that might have a bearing on the planning solution (such as low ductwork, significant changes in ceiling height, skylights, etc.), it is a good idea to place this under the floor plan so that those influencing factors can also be seen. (If the floor plan is not on translucent paper, you can lightly sketch the influencing information on the floor plan.) As shown in Illustration 2–1, roll out the tracing paper over the floor plan, hold the roll in your non-drawing hand (each diagram is drawn too quickly to bother with taping down the tracing paper), and begin to draw.

With the completed criteria matrix in front of you, try all the planning options that come to mind. From one viewpoint, the correct process would be to methodically try each room or function in each location where it could fit (except for fruitless possibilities such as trying to place plumbing fixtures too far, codewise, from a plumbing chase). However, much of the intuitive potential of bubble diagramming would be lost with so rigid a process. Conversely, if one were to be exclusively intuitive, without any planned order or approach to the process, it would be difficult to know if all the possibilities had been

ILLUS. 2–1

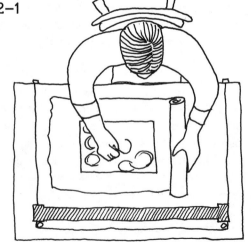

explored. Some middle ground between being laboriously systematic and erratically spontaneous should be found; it simply takes some experience with the process to find a personally comfortable track between these extremes.

An existing main entrance door or primary elevators may automatically locate an entrance area or reception room. Often, one large or major space requires accommodation and will fit well in only two or three locations in the existing space; each of these locations can become the generator for more bubble diagrams. Plumbing accessibility is usually a significant planning limitation; placing rooms with plumbing fixtures (kitchens, baths, public restrooms, etc.) within the maximum distances to existing plumbing chases permitted by the prevailing plumbing code presents another basic starting point from which a series of diagrams may be generated. Some rooms or functions demand immediate access to light and air (windows), while others are often better placed in the deep interior regions of the available space. All these factors can become the initiator for a whole series of diagrams.

Acoustic considerations, such as the segregation of quiet and noisy functions, may be a significant planning factor. Leaving space for circulation (corridors, stairs, aisles, etc.) is a must in the development of workable bubble diagrams. If these travel paths are not incorporated within the bubble diagrams, the results will be of little value when it is time to translate the diagrams into floor plans. Circulation issues are often important enough to require a series of diagrams of their own, in which travel paths and patterns are studied independently, as seen later in Illustration 6-3. It is common for space planning problems to present unique factors that demand the location of an important function in one area only—for example, the specific location of major computer equipment due to the unreasonable cost of relocating the electrical wiring throughout an entire building. Chapters 3, 4, and 5 will elaborate on the important influences on the space planning process.

Each bubble diagram should take only a few minutes to draw. Do not belabor any individual diagram; rather, move on to the next variation on a fresh section of tracing paper (certainly an eraser should not be anywhere in sight). Try all the variations that come to mind, even if they don't appear to be particularly promising; they could generate other ideas that otherwise might not have come forth. The non-judgmental approach is utilized here—don't be too tough or self-critical in evaluating the bubble diagram results while they are still in process. One good and basic approach to generate many possibilities is to take each of the generating conditions, such as entrance points, plumbing chases, a very large space, need for light and air, and so on, and, utilizing the limited number of planning positions permitted by that condition, draw as

many diagrams as are reasonable on that basis. As an example, suppose that architectural constraints and plumbing stack locations will permit only two solutions to public restroom locations; then generate as many reasonable diagrams as you can (and possibly a few unreasonable ones), starting with each of those two placement solutions. This process can be repeated with each of the determining existing conditions. It is impossible to draw too many bubble diagrams; exhaust all the possibilities to ensure that all planning options have been explored. Even for a relatively small space, such as the one shown in Building Shell 2S (used throughout for demonstration purposes), it would not be unusual to generate 20 to 30 bubble diagrams.

While the bubble diagrams are in process, it's a good idea to record thoughts about many special factors. This becomes a personalized notation system in which one develops a group of graphic symbols to quickly express planning needs and ideas. As explained earlier, some indication of traffic flow and circulation spaces is important. Interior door and window locations, new plumbing chases (if possible), acoustic barriers, barrier-free accessibility, and so on should all become part of the notation system. Even esthetic and spatial issues, such as notations about ceiling heights, interior vistas, and visual rhythm or sequencing, are worthy of recording at this stage. Some planners like to use several colors while diagramming, to visually color-code important factors such as public versus private spaces; acoustic and visual privacy; need for light, air, and view to the exterior; and so on.

This process is not limited in its use to one type of interior space, such as office spaces, health care facilities, or restaurants; it is relatively universal in its applications and should be thought of as a first-step space planning technique for all types and sizes of interior spaces. Although the described process may sound like a by-the-numbers approach, bubble diagramming is a complex, creative process and cannot be confined to a mechanical procedure. Negotiating one's way over the synthesis gap is a creative leap. Each planner invariably develops a personalized method to deal with the number of variables at hand and to record his or her ideas. No one "correct" way to develop or draw bubble diagrams exists, nor is there an accepted professional standard for the final product of the process. The graphic result is usually a personal notation system that the planner uses to go on to the next planning step (the development of a rough floor plan), and the diagrams are usually not seen or used by others.

To give you some ideas about what your bubble diagram results might look like, the next three double pages (Illustrations 2–2A, 2–2B, and 2–2C) contain the graphic results of three experienced designers solving Design Program

BUBBLE DIAGRAMS: DESIGN PROGRAM 2S

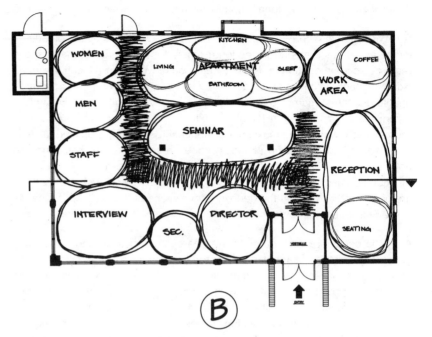

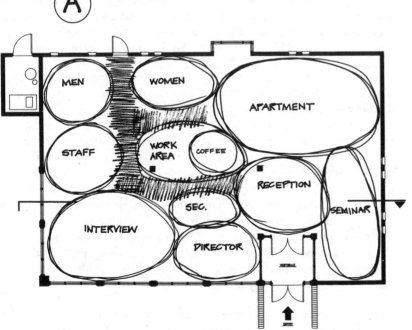

ILLUS. 2–2A

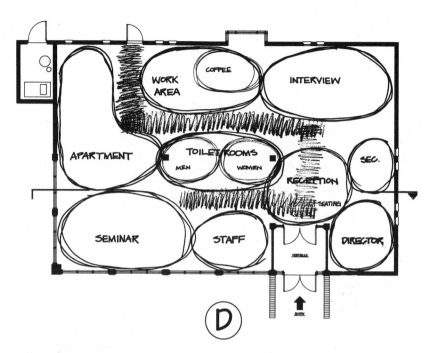

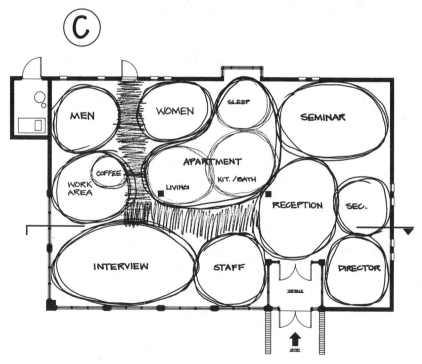

BUBBLE DIAGRAMS: DESIGN PROGRAM 2S

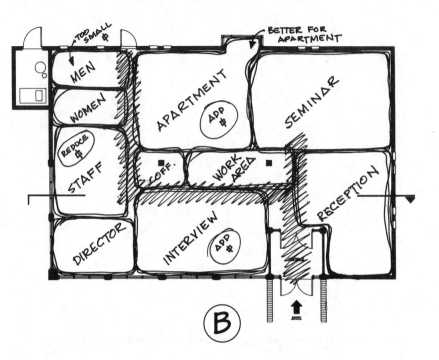

B

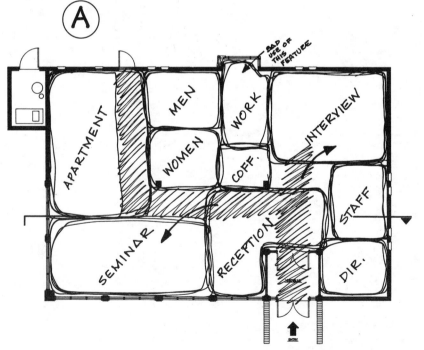

A

ILLUS. 2–2B

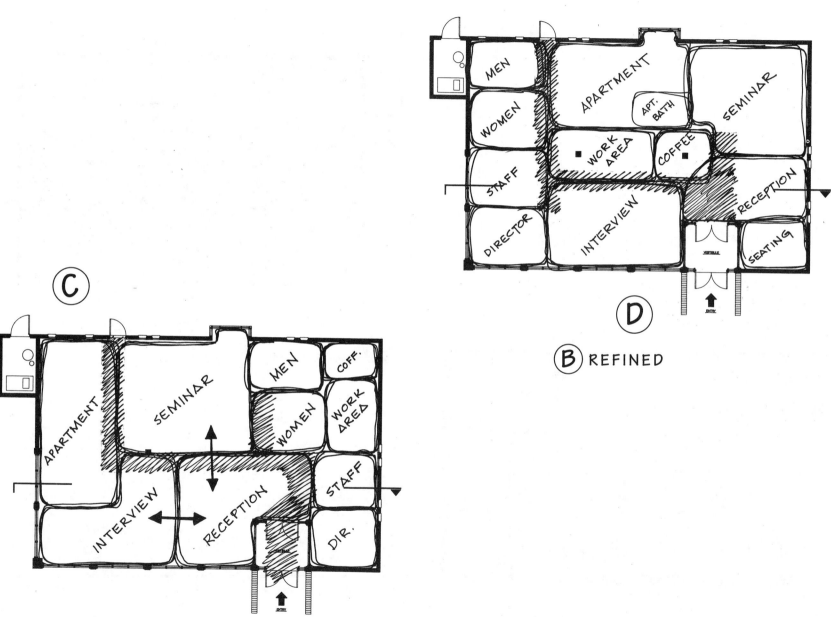

MEN

WOMEN

STAFF

DIRECTOR

APARTMENT

APT. BATH

WORK AREA

COFFEE

INTERVIEW

SEMINAR

RECEPTION

VESTIBULE

SEATING

ENTRY

D

B REFINED

C

APARTMENT

SEMINAR

MEN

COFF.

WOMEN

WORK AREA

INTERVIEW

RECEPTION

STAFF

DIR.

VESTIBULE

ENTRY

BUBBLE DIAGRAMS: DESIGN PROGRAM 2S

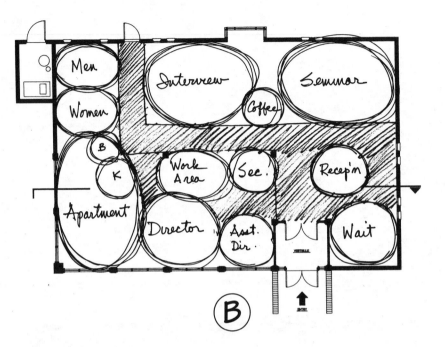

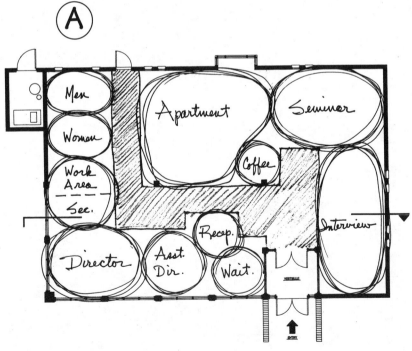

ILLUS. 2-2C

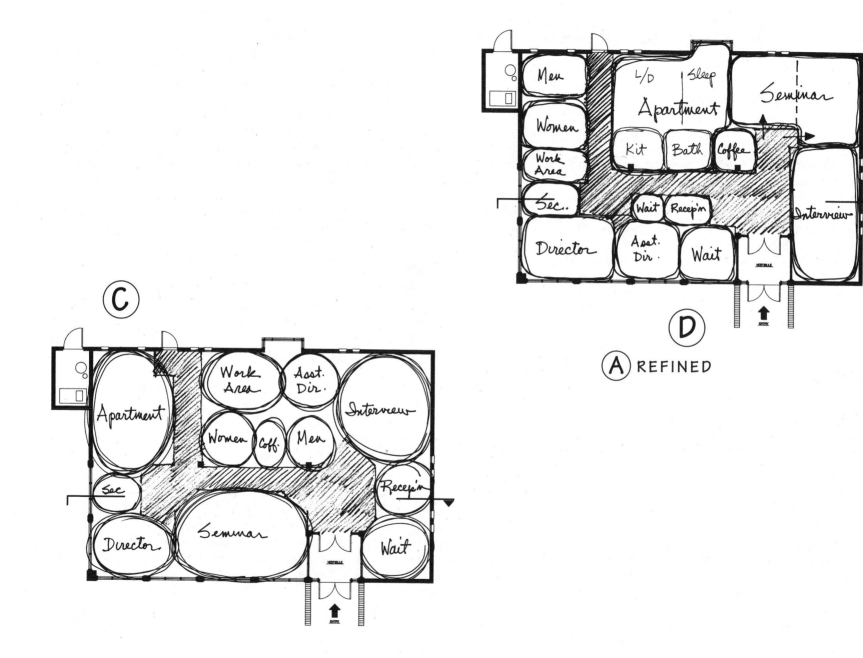

C

D

A REFINED

2S in Building Shell 2S. (These program and shell designations are explained in the following paragraph.) It is obvious that both method to solution and graphic style vary among the designers, yet each has produced a workable result and is ready to move on to the development of a floor plan.

SPACE PLANNING EXERCISES

Three series of space planning exercise problems are provided in the Appendix, starting on page 122. Each series contains three design programs and three building shell floor plans, providing the potential for nine planning exercises in each series. The first series involves spaces of about 1,500 square feet; the second, spaces of about 2,500 square feet; the third, spaces of about 4,000 square feet. Although prepared exercises of this kind will not be helpful in the development of programming skills or in coming to terms with the detailed requirements of real spaces, they are helpful in quickly getting down to the specifics of the space planning process. Ideally, classroom projects will provide additional planning problems where program development and the detailed idiosyncrasies of existing spaces are included in the process. Note that the letter designations used to identify the programs and shell are not related; Program 3B can be used in planning Shells 3A and 3C, as well as with Shell 3B.

EXERCISE 2–1

At this point in your learning process, it would be very valuable to try your hand at bubble diagram solutions for at least two or three of the program shell combinations provided in the Appendix, starting with one or two in the 1,500-square-foot series, followed by one or two in the 2,500-square-foot series. It would be time-efficient to use the criteria matrixes and the relationship diagrams developed in Exercises 1–2 and 1–3 (in Chapter 1) as the basis for the bubble diagrams developed here.

After the diagramming possibilities of a particular planning problem have been exhausted, the results should be reviewed and the two or three best diagrams selected from the many diagrams that have been drawn. In this context, the best diagrams are those having the greatest potential for further development into a good and workable floor plan. One by one, place each of these selected diagrams over the floor plan, place a fresh section of tracing paper over the diagram, and revise the diagram by modifying the shapes and sizes of the bubbles, more clearly identifying circulation spaces and paths, more accurately locating plumbing chases, doors, or access locations, acoustic barriers, esthetic or spatial features, and so on. One could have a second overlay diagram, in which the bubbles evolve into round-cornered rectangles (assuming rectangular rooms and spaces). This revising process moves away from the quick and spontaneous approach of the original diagrams and toward a deliberate, selective problem-solving mode. Despite its amorphous graphic quality, this is the first design step in the space planning process. Regardless of the specific drawing and refining technique, by the time the bubble diagram process is complete, a very rough or abstract floor plan should emerge. Partitions, door swings, fixtures, and other such elements are not yet identifiable, but a roughly-to-scale allocation of floor space has been established, along with several basic design and construction determinations. The results of this refining process are shown in the extreme right-hand examples in Illustrations 2–2B and 2–2C.

EXERCISE 2–2

Perform this refining process with the bubble diagrams developed in the previous exercise. It cannot be overstated that the successful development of each phase of professional-quality space planning skills is directly related to the amount of time and effort put into it. Save these bubble diagram exercises to use in the development of rough floor plans recommended in Chapters 6 and 7.

BLOCK PLANNING

Another well-established technique for this initial step into physical planning is conventionally referred to as "block planning." Its use is particularly widespread in large-scale retail and store planning. The process of development and the results are similar to those in bubble diagramming. Its primary advantage over bubble diagramming is that the result is more like a floor plan, and some planners feel more comfortable working with its more geometric quality. Its primary disadvantage in relation to bubble diagramming is that it lacks some of the free-flowing spontaneity and intuitiveness inherent in the bubble diagramming process; it also has a tendency to ignore curvilinear and other non-rectangular solutions. While block planning is readily accomplished with hand-drawing and computer-drawing techniques, CAD methods are particularly applicable. Since one can repeatedly copy a new base plan image on the screen, each copy then becomes the origin for a new block plan—a plan that can be both saved and printed. With a simple line technique (or, better yet, a double-line technique to represent partition thickness), allocate room locations and identify them with a room title (or an abbreviated title, such as "Rec." for "reception" or "Apt." for "apartment"). If using hand-drawing, it is best to avoid the use of a parallel edge and triangle, because they will tend to make the process slow and rigid. Instead, place a piece of grid paper under the base plan as a drawing and scale guide and work freehand. As with bubble diagrams, try many block plans, working intuitively and non-judgmentally, exhausting all the planning possibilities, and remembering that this is a primarily trial-and-error process. To get a general idea of what block planning diagrams might look like, the computer-generated drawings of Illustration 2–3 show one designer's use of this approach in the solution of Design Program 2S in Building Shell 2S, including a refined block plan at the

---

EXERCISE 2-3

Using the block planning approach, solve one or more of the 1,500-square-foot and 2,500-square-foot program/shell combinations in the Appendix. Try your hand with both computer-drawing and hand-drawing techniques. As before, select two or three of the best diagrams and refine them in the same manner by which selected bubble diagrams were refined. Again, save these exercises for continued use in the exercises recommended in Chapters 6 and 7.

A variation on the block planning technique some designers find advantageous is the use of paper templates for rooms and spaces, because the templates can be moved quickly and changes in planning relationships are seen immediately. The process begins with cutting and labeling a square or rectangular piece of substantial paper (such as cover stock) for each room or space, making sure it contains approximately the correct square footage. The templates are then moved about over the floor plan, leaving appropriate circulation paths or spaces, until some sort of workable solution is achieved. Each reasonably workable solution must be recorded by a hard copy of some kind (a quick sketch, or a Polaroid or digital photo). Since the particular proportions of the cut templates may be very limiting in terms of achieving workable solutions, it is advisable to make two or three templates of varying proportions for each room, being careful to use only one template

for a given room in each of the overall solutions. The approach of manipulating room-sized templates has a computer technique variation in which colored or hatched, labeled templates are created on the screen and manipulated over a copy of the base plan, with block plan solutions saved and printed. As with all these first-phase planning techniques, the process must be concluded with the refinement of the few most workable solutions into rough or abstracted floor plans.

It should be obvious that no single or "best" method exists for this first phase of the space planning process. Because it is at the heart of that process, it is inherently creative and without confining definitions. Because it is creative, most designers ultimately develop a highly personalized method that is specifically tied to their thinking process. Until a planner's experience builds to this level, the approaches shown here, if given enough time and practice, should provide adequate tools to solve most space planning problems.

Critiquing one's own work in this first planning phase is difficult. Graphic qualities are not the issue here; although graphic articulateness is of value, it is the planning qualities that are critical to a good solution to the problem. In a classroom, with the direction of a teacher and with the ability to see and discuss the work of other students, the evaluation of first-phase planning solutions is easier. It is outside the classroom where one must learn to evaluate the qualities of space planning solutions. Those evaluations must begin with making use of the program document's information.

With the use of the project's criteria matrix, review the refined bubble diagrams or block plans for all the basic planning requirements. Among the questions to ask are: How well are adjacency requirements met? Will traffic flow easily? Are square footage requirements adhered to? Are windows well located in terms of daily functions? What about the needs for visual and acoustic privacy? Are basic esthetic and spatial desires attainable with the plan arrangement? Will basic equipment and furniture be easily accommodated? In very general terms, place yourself in the users' position and ask, "How do I go (or get) there?" or "What do I see?" Don't become attached to these first-phase plans; remember that they are a work in progress. Use the results of the programming process as an objective evaluation tool in critiquing the first planning results. Has a basic function been forgotten? Are some interfunctional relationships not working well? Are code requirements a problem? In general terms, place yourself in the users' positions and ask "How do I go (or get) there?" or "What do I see?" Don't become attached

BLOCK PLANS: DESIGN PROGRAM 2S

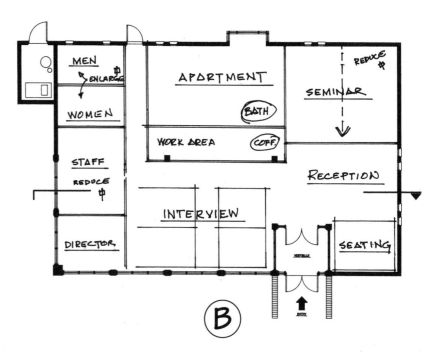

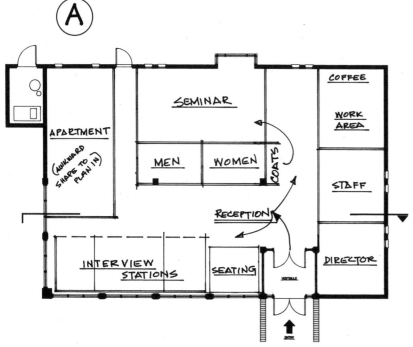

ILLUS. 2-3

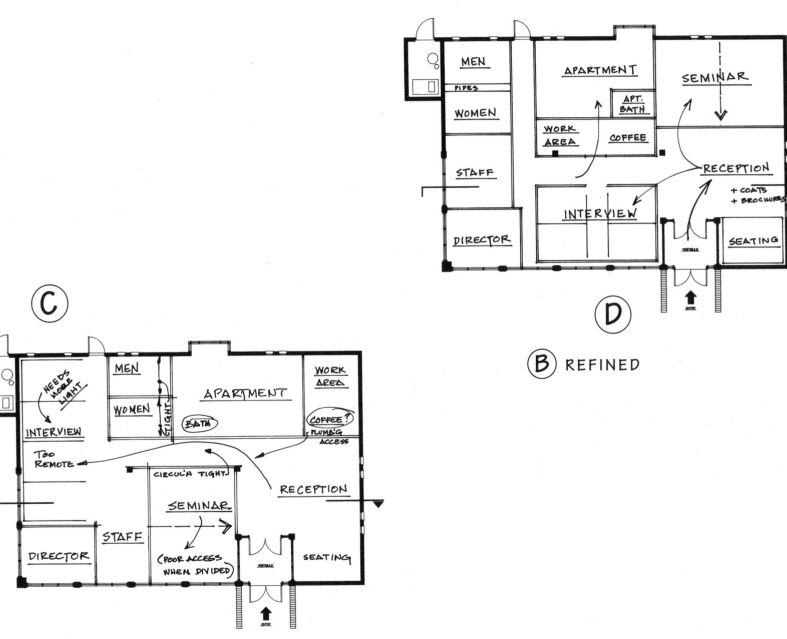

D

B REFINED

to these first-phase plans; remember that they are a work in progress. Now is the time to make revisions, not later, when plan changes become more difficult. It is entirely possible that the physical planning process will create some new insights about the design program, and it may be the program, rather than the spatial layout, that demands revision. Make the revisions needed at this early stage, before other planning and design elements become incorporated and every small change has complex consequences.

As the planning process progresses, the design program will again serve as an excellent evaluation tool. Throughout the space planning process, the designer must learn the techniques of self-criticism in order to work well independently. Do not be too self-critical; remember that in space planning, perfection is a rare commodity. Strive for the blend of compromises that produces workable results.

Recommended Reading

4*, 6*, 9*, 13*, 15*, 18*, 20*, 23*, 24*, 26*, 31*

Books marked with an asterisk are also included in the recommended reading for other chapters.

Chapter 3   SMALL AND DIMENSIONALLY DEMANDING SPACES

Before attempting to solve conventional space planning problems, it is important to have a mastery of planning typical small and dimensionally demanding spaces. To be more specific, competence should be achieved in planning typical residential spaces (kitchens, bathrooms, powder rooms, and laundries) and typical non-residential spaces (public restrooms and small serving kitchens). To a lesser degree, consideration should be given to such non-typical spaces as computer equipment rooms, darkrooms, and scientific laboratories. The common denominator for all these spaces is that they are equipment-intensive and expensive to construct; hence, they are usually planned with an eye to maximum economy and efficiency in their consumption of space.

The planning of these small spaces is not unusually difficult, but if one is inexperienced in planning them, they can become a serious stumbling block to efficiently and effectively solving general space planning problems. Miscalculations concerning square footage requirements, misunderstanding of the detailed aspects of placing points of access, and lack of knowledge concerning codes and standards related to plumbing and piping requirements are typical issues related to these specialized small spaces that impede the inexperienced space planner. Depending on one's current knowledge and skill in these areas, this chapter can be used as a refresher or as a primer before taking on the more complex qualities of general space planning.

EXERCISE 3-1

There are a lot of good, easily accessible resource materials concerning the planning of typical residential spaces of this kind (see "Recommended Reading" at the end of this chapter). One of the best methods to establish these planning skills is to trace (or, better, hand-copy) *many* examples of residential kitchens, powder rooms, and bathrooms. In the process, the designer will become familiar with a variety of fixture and cabinet sizes, fixture and appliance planning relationships, and necessary details such as points of access, use of accessories, avoiding door swing conflicts, and so on. After tracing or copying many plan arrangements on paper or with CADD, draw more without the aid of this kind of replication. The issues of scale and precision are important here. Because of their detailed nature, there is an advantage in working with CADD on these small spaces. CADD is inherently precise; the ability to zoom in permits one to visualize the detail more easily, and block libraries of bathroom fixtures (either generic or from manufacturers) provide a time-efficient tool. Kitchens and bathrooms are typically documented at ⅛" and ¼" = 1'-0"; if working on paper, try these spaces at larger scales (⅜", ½", and ¾" = 1'-0") in order to gain control of the critical dimensional issues, despite the fact that plumbing fixture templates are generally not available at these larger scales. Once some basic familiarity with typical arrangements has been established, a great deal can be learned from going beyond these basics by planning some non-typical kitchens and bathrooms, incorporating less common functions and equipment such as bidets, whirlpool tubs, linen storage, laundry rooms or alcoves, cooking islands, food-processing centers, dining counters, and the like.

By way of example, Illustrations 3–1A and 3–1B show several examples of small residential spaces with both typical and non-typical plan arrangements. Both pages of illustrations are drawn at ¼" = 1'-0", with the kitchen plans drawn freehand and the bathroom plans drawn with CADD. Issues of drawing quality, while always important, are not a central issue in this part of the learning process, and discussion related to drawing technique and presentation matters are deferred for consideration until Chapter 7. Note also the lack of concern for three-dimensional issues. For now, it is best to keep the focus on space planning; at the end of this chapter (and at a few additional points beyond) the three-dimensional reality and its relationship to the planning process will be explored.

Most of the equipment-intensive spaces discussed in this chapter involve the use of plumbing fixtures. Whenever plumbing is involved in buildings, knowledgeable consideration must be given to prevailing plumbing codes, as well as to good standards of practice related to piping and economy of construction. These issues will be dealt with in some depth in Chapter 4. For the present, observe the back-to-back plumbing walls, the grouping of fixtures,

and the use of pipe chases in Illustration 3-2 as an example of these factors put into practice.

When some basic skills in planning small residential spaces have been achieved, the same approach should be taken for non-residential uses. Although resource material is not as plentiful for non-residential uses, several adequate sources are available (see "Recommended Reading" at the end of this chapter). Some of the small utility spaces in non-residential settings, such as powder rooms and serving kitchens, are only subtly different from their residential counterparts. The major differences are in restroom facilities, which are significantly more difficult to plan than residential bathrooms and require concerted effort to acquire skill in planning them well. In addition to the usual concerns of functional planning, comfortable clearances, and traffic flow, a few special considerations must be accounted for in public restroom facilities:

1. *Visual privacy.* Use partitions or vestibule spaces to avoid direct views into toilet or urinal facilities.

2. *Special accessories.* In addition to the basic plumbing fixtures, toilet stall partitions and accessories, such as soap and towel dispensers and trash receptacles, must be planned for comfortable use.

3. *Barrier-free design.* Federal law and most building codes require that public restroom facilities be designed for comfortable use by disabled users, including those who are wheelchair-bound.

Because barrier-free design standards are critical in the planning of public restrooms, the suggested planning exercise for restroom facilities (Exercise 3-2) follows the discussion and illustrations of barrier-free standards (see page 54).

In addition to relatively standard restroom facilities, specialized, dimensionally demanding spaces in non-residential settings range from the fairly common (mailrooms, darkrooms) to the highly unique (scientific laboratories, medical treatment rooms). Occasionally space planners become expert in a particular type of specialized facility and do not require the guidance of an outside specialist or consultant. However, in most cases it is customary to call upon a consultant, either formal (paid) or informal (a manufacturer's representative). Consultants will typically provide information in the form of

RESIDENTIAL KITCHEN PLANS

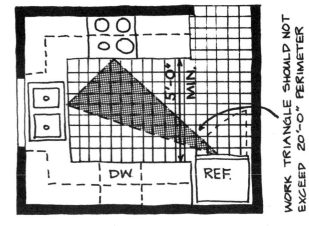

WORK TRIANGLE SHOULD NOT EXCEED 20'-0" PERIMETER

• U-SHAPED KITCHEN, 9'x 11'

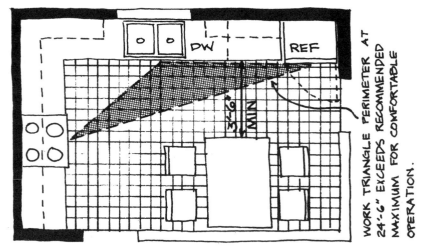

WORK TRIANGLE PERIMETER AT 24'-6" EXCEEDS RECOMMENDED MAXIMUM FOR COMFORTABLE OPERATION.

• L-SHAPED KITCHEN W/ DINING AREA, 10'x 15'

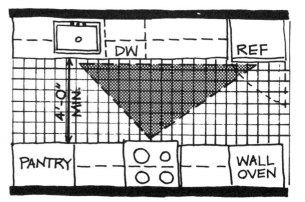

• CENTER AISLE KITCHEN, 8'x 13'

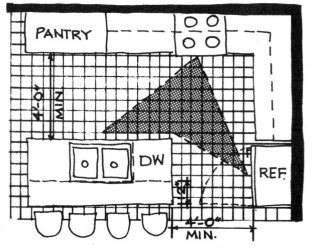

• L-SHAPE KITCHEN W/CENTER ISLAND AND BREAKFAST BAR, 10'x 13'

RESIDENTIAL BATHROOM PLANS

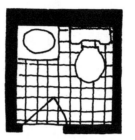

● POWDER ROOM
4'-6" x 4'-6" MIN.

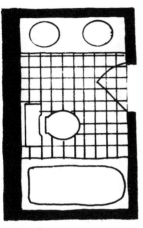

● FULL BATHROOM
5' x 9' MIN.

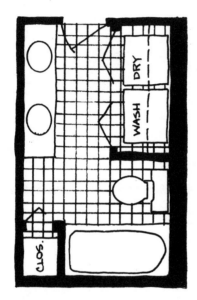

● FULL BATHROOM WITH
LINEN CLOSET AND
LAUNDRY 12' x 7' MIN.

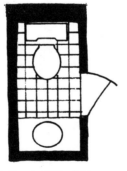

● POWDER ROOM
3' x 6'-6" MIN.

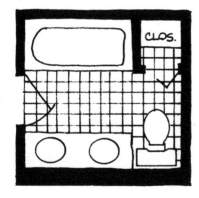

● FULL BATHROOM WITH
LINEN CLOSET, 7'-6" x 7'-0" MIN.

PUBLIC RESTROOMS

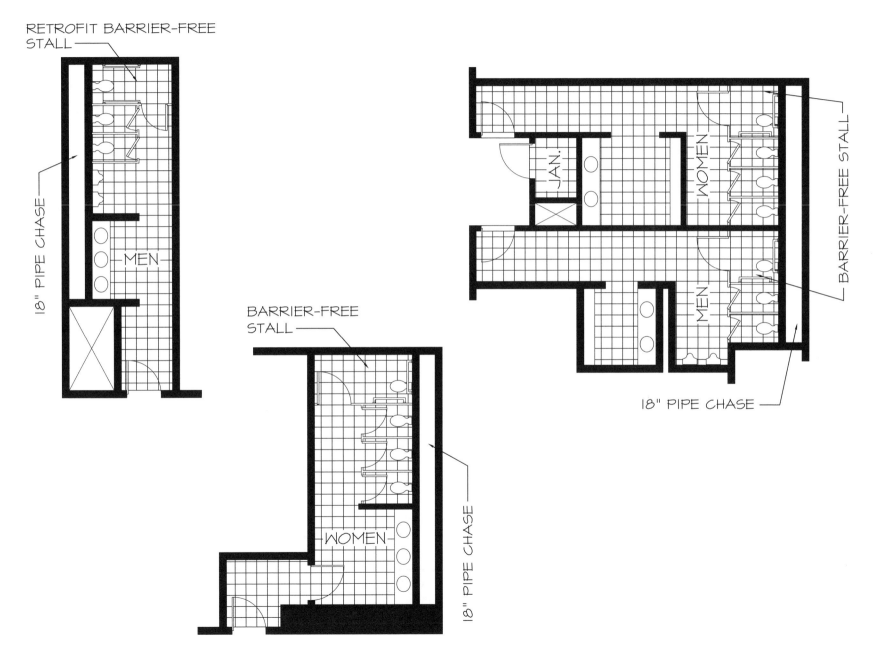

RETROFIT BARRIER-FREE STALL

18" PIPE CHASE

MEN

BARRIER-FREE STALL

WOMEN

18" PIPE CHASE

JAN.

WOMEN

BARRIER-FREE STALL

MEN

18" PIPE CHASE

drawings and published data, as well as personalized direction from the programming phase of a project (square footage requirements, natural lighting needs, etc.) through the detailed completion of the design and documentation phases (equipment size and placement, electric lighting specifications, etc.). Gaining expertise with the more typical small spaces will help to make the planning of specialized spaces easier; but the help of a consultant for facilities such as commercial kitchens, central computer equipment rooms, or commercial laundry facilities is customary. Without any attempt at completeness, a few examples of preliminary plan sketches of specialized, equipment-intensive functions demonstrate the similarities in approach with the more standardized restroom facilities, as seen in Illustration 3-3.

HUMAN FACTORS

Human factors is a broad field of scientific research that has many applications in architectural and interiors planning and design. Many of those applications lie far outside the concerns of space planning, such as the comfort factor in specifying a lavatory faucet handle or the productivity and comfort factors in the lighting design of a computer facility. Conversely, many human factors research applications are directly related to space planning issues within buildings in general, as well as in small and dimensionally demanding spaces. The most obviously applicable of these factors are those related to human dimensions, providing us with the necessary information about planning sizes and clearances. While most human factors research is related to the general adult population at large, some research has been related to special populations such as children and the elderly.

Space planners should be both sensitive to and knowledgeable about human factors, to know when such research data require application and where to find the information. Because of the relative economy or tightness in their planning, these applications are used more frequently in small and dimensionally demanding spaces; but applications exist in most interior spaces, as in the placement of architectural elements such as partitions and doors, as well as in the placement of conventional furniture and equipment.

Some of the issues involved in this area simply require common sense— avoiding the use of projecting sharp countertop corners in a tightly planned

bathroom or restroom, or avoiding the placement of a toilet paper holder beyond comfortable reach. Other issues in this area will require some extensive human factors data gathering, such as the planning of a preschool day-care facility or a patient facility in a health-care setting. An open-minded attitude toward human factors issues will increase the designer's sensitivity to the need for research and broaden his or her knowledge of how to seek out data. The designer's need for human factors information goes far beyond space planning issues, and all professionals in the field should feel some responsibility to have a basic background in this area. The "Recommended Reading" section at the end of this chapter suggests books that provide an introduction to the field, as well as references for resource data.

BARRIER-FREE DESIGN STANDARDS

Accommodating people with physical disabilities, from minor (the early stages of aging) to major (wheelchair-bound), is regularly required of the space planner. This accommodation can be addressed from varying viewpoints: (1) philosophically, in terms of satisfying a human and social need; (2) legally, referring to code requirements that must be fulfilled; and (3) pragmatically, insofar as barrier-free concepts should be seen as a means to plan interior spaces that are more comfortable for all users. The purpose here is not to address the conceptual or philosophical aspects of barrier-free design, but rather to present it as one necessary factor in the space planning process. A great deal of readily accessible resource material is available, as can be seen from the recommended reading at the end of this chapter. For this reason, the related planning standards data illustrated in this text are limited in number and scope, and address only those aspects of barrier-free design that have practical and repeated influence on space planning. In terms of graphic illustrations, several books recommended for further reading provide quite complete illustrations of all barrier-free standards. But designers should be aware that code requirements and enforcement related to accommodations for disabled people are being regularly increased; the impact of the Americans with Disabilities Act will continue for many years to come. These code increases will relate to all categories of disabilities, including those related to sight, hearing, and physical movement and accessibility. Designers will be held accountable for this knowledge and its application.

SPECIALIZED EQUIPMENT — INTENSIVE SPACES

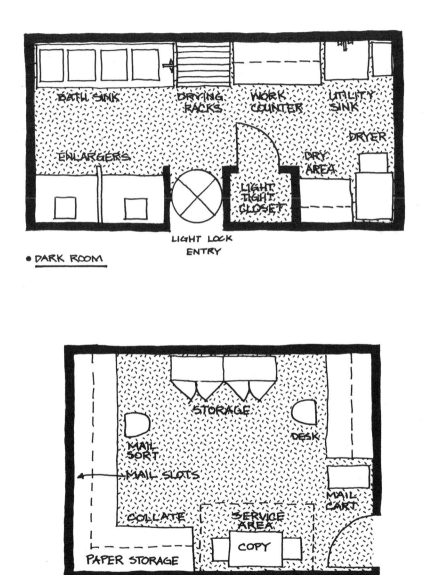

BATH SINK   DRYING RACKS   WORK COUNTER   UTILITY SINK

DRYER

ENLARGERS

DRY AREA

LIGHT TIGHT CLOSET

LIGHT LOCK ENTRY

● DARK ROOM

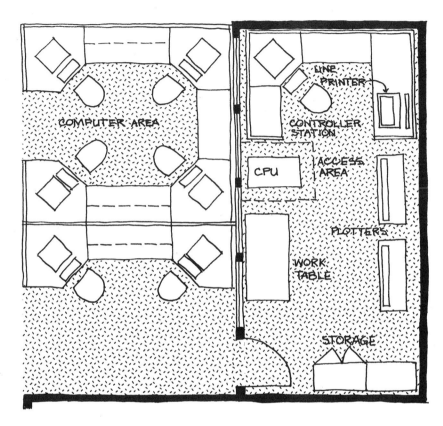

COMPUTER AREA

LINE PRINTER

CONTROLLER STATION

CPU

ACCESS AREA

PLOTTERS

WORK TABLE

STORAGE

● CONTROL ROOM WITH PLOTTERS AND COMPUTER STATIONS

STORAGE

DESK

MAIL SORT

MAIL SLOTS

MAIL CART

COLLATE

SERVICE AREA

COPY

PAPER STORAGE

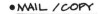

● MAIL / COPY

While barrier-free requirements have bearing on many aspects of space planning, there are four major areas that have particular impact on the planning process:

1. Travel and egress

2. Toilet and bath facilities

3. Residential kitchens

4. Furniture planning and placement

Although all aspects of planning for people with disabilities are important, in space planning terms the controlling dimensional factor is wheelchair operation. It is an extremely valuable practice to place oneself in the position of a wheelchair-bound person moving through and using the spaces that are created, from the major travel and egress routes down to the details of entering rooms or spaces and negotiating one's way through furniture and partition panels. Gaining a personal sensitivity to the potential problems faced by disabled users goes a long way in creating interior spaces that will satisfy all users.

Travel and Egress

Corridors and Aisles
• A 360° turn of a wheelchair requires a 5'-0"-diameter space, as in the end-of-corridor condition shown in Illustration 3–4A.

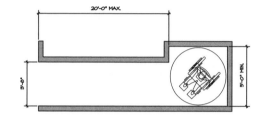

ILLUS. 3–4A

• A straight corridor should be at least 3'-8" wide for comfortable wheelchair operation, but this dimension will not permit a walking person to pass the wheelchair. Two-way corridors should be at least 5'-0" wide. See Illustration 3–4B.

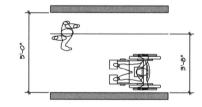

ILLUS. 3–4B

• A right-angle turn requires a 3'-8" radius for comfortable wheelchair operation. See Illustration 3–4C.

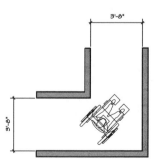

ILLUS. 3–4C

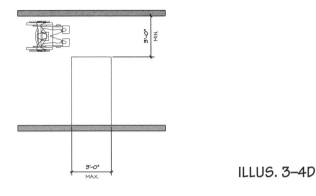

ILLUS. 3–4D

- A narrow passageway requires a 3'-0" minimum opening for comfortable wheelchair operation. See Illustration 3–4D.

Ramps

- The maximum slope of a ramp is 1:12, or a maximum 8.33 percent grade change. The maximum run of a continuous ramp is 30 feet; beyond that length, ramps must have a flat rest area of at least 5 feet in length. Ramps must be equipped with handrails. See Illustration 3–4E.

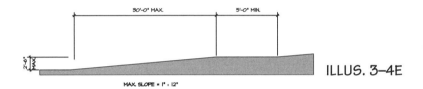

ILLUS. 3–4E

Doors

- A minimum door opening must be at last 2'-8" wide, and 3'-0" is considered optimal. Note that a standard 2'-8" door provides a clear opening of only 2'-7" due to the projection of standard ½" door stops on both sides of the door jamb. Since 2'-10" doors are not a standard size, 3'-0" doors are customarily used where wheelchair access is required. Also note that sliding doors are difficult for wheelchair-bound people to operate. See Illustration 3–4F.

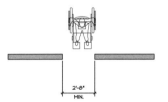

ILLUS. 3–4F

- On the pull side of a door, a minimum distance of 1'-6" must be maintained from the operating handle jamb of the door to an intersecting partition or any other obstruction that will not permit wheelchair access to the door. On the push side of a door, a minimum distance of 1'-0" must be maintained. See Illustration 3–4G.

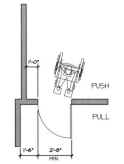

ILLUS. 3–4G

Stairs

- Building codes regulate every detail of stair design, from stair width and tread/riser relationship to nosings and handrails. Obviously wheelchair operation does not play a role in regulating stair design, but ADA requirements do regulate some details of stair design, most particularly in handrail dimensions and configurations. While designers must know how to apply these ADA regulations, they do not affect the space planning process or the dimensional details of interior planning. See Illustration 3-4H

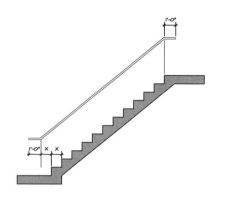

ILLUS. 3–4H

Toilets and Lavatories

- Wheelchair access for toilets require the placement of two handrails of the sizes and positions shown in Illustrations 3–5A and 3–5B.

- Wheelchair access for toilet stalls requires a space 5'-0" wide by 5'-0" deep, with a 3'-0" access door placed diagonally opposite the toilet and hinged to swing out of the stall, as shown in Illustration 3–5A. Note that the wheelchair user must back out of the stall because there is not enough space for the wheelchair to make a 180° turn within the stall.

- The stall access door may swing into the stall when the stall is 7'-0" deep, as shown in Illustration 3–5B. This configuration permits the wheelchair to turn around within the stall. Note that the toilet is wall-hung, permitting the footrest of the wheelchair to pass under the toilet, and that the details of toilet and handrail placement remain unchanged from the 5'-0"-square stall (Illustration 3–5A).

ILLUS. 3–5A

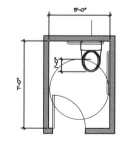

ILLUS. 3–5B

- The handrail positioning shown in Illustrations 3–5A and 3–5B permit the wheelchair user to make a side transfer from the wheelchair to the toilet; this is the preferred handrail configuration. In retrofit situations, where providing a 5'-0"-square stall is unusually difficult, ADA requirements permit the use of a 3'-6"-wide by 6'-0"-deep stall, with a 3'-0"-wide outswinging door, the toilet placed in the center of the opposite (or rear) wall, and handrails placed on both side walls. This is not the recommended configuration for a barrier-free stall because many wheelchair users are not able to turn their bodies around after lifting themselves out of the wheelchair and are forced to sit on the toilet backward.

- Wheelchair access for lavatories requires the center of the fixture be placed at least 1'-6" from a wall or other obstruction and set vertically so that the wheelchair armrest can fit under the front of the fixture; wheelchair armrest height is 30". In addition, hot water supply pipes must be insulated to avoid possible leg burns that might be caused by contact with extremely hot supply pipes under the lavatory. Several plumbing fixture manufacturers make a lavatory specifically designed for barrier-free conditions, as shown in Illustration 3–5C. It is possible for counter-set lavatories to accommodate wheelchair access if the required conditions of lateral and vertical positioning are met. While wheelchair access is not involved, ADA requires that faucet handles be of lever design for those who have difficulty with knob-action faucet controls.

- When toilets and lavatories are placed side by side, the lavatory must be situated so as not to crowd access for the wheelchair. Using a lavatory designed for wheelchair access, the minimum dimension between the centerlines of the two fixtures is 3'-6". When placed in a wheelchair-access stall, the minimum stall width is 6'-6", as shown in Illustration 3–5C.

- The plan drawing in Illustration 3–5D of a typical six-fixture women's room provides an example of the foot of the wheelchair carrying under the open area below the lavatory counter. This allowance of up to 1'-0" of the 5'-0"-diameter turning radius of the wheelchair can be used below any wall-hung fixture, such as a toilet or urinal, as well as a conventional wall-hung lavatory.

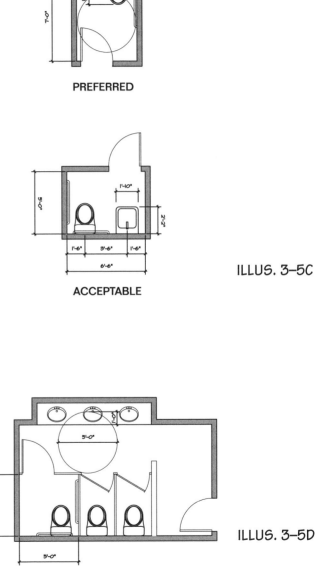

PREFERRED

ACCEPTABLE

ILLUS. 3–5C

ILLUS. 3–5D

• Residential and hotel bathrooms present the need for bathing and/or showering facilities in addition to their customary toilet and lavatory fixtures. The dimensional and placement requirements for toilets and lavatories that are described (and illustrated) above apply to both residential and non-residential settings. With three or four major elements (as well as the possible addition of a linen or storage closet), there are no fixed or standard arrangements (such as a standard toilet stall) for full bathrooms. Keep in mind that a bathtub may be very impractical for some wheelchair-bound people, who may require a roll-in shower stall for unassisted, easily accessible use. One must allow adequate maneuvering space for a wheelchair to have access to a bathtub or shower stall. The floor plan shown in Illustration 3–5E is one of many workable solutions for a universal residential or hotel bathroom. It contains about 75 square feet, which should be considered a reasonable minimum for a four-element bathroom of this kind.

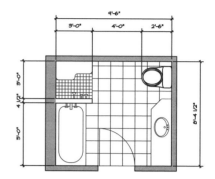

ILLUS. 3–5E

Residential Kitchens

• Residential kitchens for wheelchair-bound users are as varied in size and configuration as all other residential kitchens, ranging in size from as little as 50 to 60 square feet to luxurious kitchens as large as 200 to 300 square feet. They vary in equipment and style depending upon cuisine, the user's interest in food preparation, and the importance of the kitchen in family or social life. Kitchen space planning for the wheelchair-bound resident deals primarily with providing enough space for wheelchair operation. Because typical kitchens are so often designed with minimum clearances and efficient proximity of the "work triangle" (see page 43), they are typically ill-suited for wheelchair users. The modestly sized barrier-free kitchen plan shown in Illustration 3–5F is one of an almost infinite number of plan variations that are useable for someone who is wheelchair-bound. From a plan point of view, it varies from a non-barrier-free kitchen only in the minimum width (5'-0") of the center aisle. It is the detailed differences of counter and shelf height dimensions, pull-out work surfaces and storage units, and open under-counter kneehole space that are so important to the user. Beyond the issues of space planning, a great deal of research is needed to design a truly workable barrier-free kitchen.

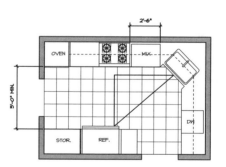

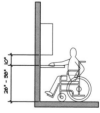

ILLUS. 3–5F

Furniture Planning and Placement

It is not difficult to imagine the almost infinite number of obstacles the wheelchair-bound and other physically disabled people face on a day-to-day basis in terms of maneuvering through typically furnished interior spaces.

Finding an appropriate place at a conference or restaurant table or joining a conversation in a lounge or living room setting is often troublesome, if not impossible. There are countless commonplace situations of this nature. It is the designer's responsibility to know and plan for the dimensional and configuration requirements that make for comfortable use by those who are physically disabled. The examples cited here, a conference room and a lounge or living room, are just two of the many typical planning situations that are common in design practice.

• The conference room shown in Illustration 3–5G provides larger-than-typical passage space at the entrance end of the room and the side of the room that is adjacent to the entrance. The 5'-0" aisle permits a wheelchair-bound person comfortable access to a place at the table without disturbing others, as well as having access to the credenza at the entry end of the room.

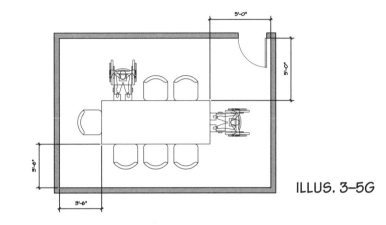

ILLUS. 3–5G

• The lounge/living room shown in Illustration 3–5H provides open access for a wheelchair-bound person to comfortably join in conversation, as well as both enter and exit the space gracefully without disturbing others. Unlike the conference room setting described above, there are no specific aisle dimensions to cite, but leaving enough space for a wheelchair within the conversational grouping, as well as space to turn around and maneuver, should be an integral part of the furniture planning.

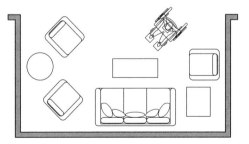

ILLUS. 3–5H

EXERCISE 3-2

To become reasonably proficient in planning public restroom facilities, it is necessary to try one's hand at a broad variety of possibilities, starting with small and simple requirements such as a non-compartmentalized two-fixture restroom and building to larger, more complex facilities for male and female users, imposing special criteria (use in office buildings, theaters, restaurants, etc.) as well. By incorporating specific planning requirements, such as a 160-seat restaurant or a 550-seat auditorium, this exercise can additionally provide some experience in using the prevailing building code to establish the number of plumbing fixtures required to serve the facility. Before starting this exercise, study the examples of such facilities shown in Illustration 3–2, as well as the examples found in the reference books suggested in this chapter's "Recommended Reading" section, paying particular attention to barrier-free requirements. For each planning study, include an accompanying three-dimensional sketch that provides a graphic view of the plan's spatial qualities. If drawing on paper, from a learning viewpoint this exercise is best done in ¼"= 1'-0" scale in order to more fully visualize the dimensional issues.

THE THREE-DIMENSIONAL REALITY

This text has focused and will continue to focus on the development of floor plan solutions. Do good floor plans always make for well-designed interiors? Obviously not. Yet there is a strong inclination for the planner to get so involved in the space planning process and its two-dimensional, jigsaw-puzzle-like qualities that the resulting three-dimensional qualities of the space become an afterthought.

Note was made in Chapter 2 that it is entirely appropriate to include notations concerning three-dimensional or spatial ideas while developing bubble diagrams. But for most designers, the bubble diagram phase is too early in the process to attempt sketches—isometrics, perspectives, sections, or elevations—that develop three-dimensional ideas. This chapter, however, has dealt with specific floor plan arrangements, defining a proposed architectural reality, and whenever a floor plan arrangement emerges in any stage of the planning process, some form of three-dimensional sketch can be useful, no matter how rough or tentative.

It is not necessary to debate here whether a solidly functional floor plan is more important than visually satisfying spaces; both are crucial to good building interiors. As the first rough floor plans emerge on your drawing board or computer screen, they should be accompanied by first rough elevations, sections, perspectives, and/or isometric sketches, which might look like those in Illustration 3–6. One of the major advantages of CADD is the ease with which multiple three-dimensional views can be generated. No matter how well defined one's mental image of a space may be after drawing it in plan, more is seen and understood about that space after it has been visualized three-dimensionally. The meeting of planes and the visual interrelationships that emerge in three-dimensional views crystallize the mental image and permit the spatial concept to be more fully defined.

Recommended Reading

2*, 4*, 7*, 9*, 13*, 15*, 16*, 19*, 20*, 21*, 23*, 24*, 26*

Books marked with an asterisk are also included in the recommended reading for other chapters.

ROUGH THREE-DIMENSIONAL SKETCHES

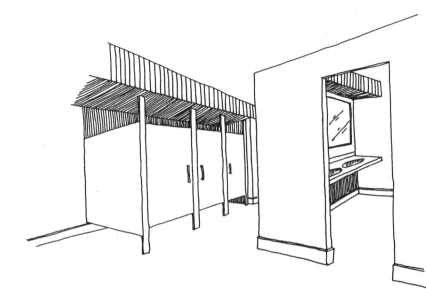

PERSPECTIVE OF RESTROOM

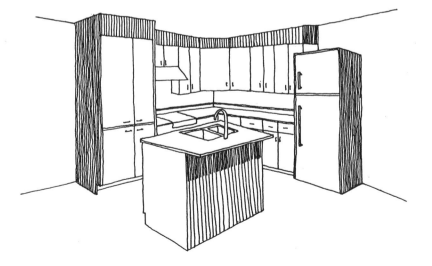

PERSPECTIVE OF KITCHEN

Chapter 4   THE BUILDING SHELL AND MAJOR SYSTEMS

The range and depth of knowledge an experienced space planner brings to a planning project is immense. It is the kind of knowledge that is rarely attained in the classroom, but rather amassed through experience in many and diverse projects over an extended period of time. Textbook or classroom processes cannot fully simulate the learning experience of repeated project research efforts related to the complexities and idiosyncrasies of realistic situations. Throughout the course of any project, the space planner can call upon consultants and/or research information and application techniques related to building codes, acoustics, lighting, mechanical and electrical construction, historic preservation requirements, structural considerations, or interior construction techniques, as well as many others.

This chapter and Chapter 5 are designed to provide an overview of each area of general planning and design background fundamentally important to the space planning process. As part of each overview, a general indication will be provided of the required level or depth of knowledge needed for that area. In addition, specific recommended reading geared to developing that knowledge is identified at the end of the relevant chapter. Each of the areas discussed is complex and deserves separate coursework of its own, but a significant depth of knowledge in each area goes beyond the intent of this book; the focus here will remain on space planning.

A general comment must be made here about the use of consultants in most of the areas discussed in Chapters 4 and 5. Customarily, professional planners make extensive use of engineers and other specialists throughout the planning and design process; the world of building design has become too complex for any single professional to know it all. Put simply, one of the most important facets of professional practice is to know when and how to use consultants. The issues discussed in Chapter 4 would involve structural and mechanical engineers; in Chapter 5, the relevant consultants would be lighting designers, code specialists, acoustic consultants, and furniture and equipment manufacturers' representatives. The important message here is not to feel intimidated by the amount and depth of information required of the space planner, but rather to know that no one is expected to have all the answers and that help is always available from specialized consultants. Once the consultants are at hand, the planner must know enough to intelligently discuss the design issues and convey to the consultants what is expected of them. A great deal of the learning process will happen as one practices in the field during the first several years of professional experience.

THE BUILDING SHELL

Beyond satisfying users' needs, there is no more basic influence on the planning and design process than the intrinsic qualities of the building shell containing those functions. It is extremely important that space planners and interior designers develop a thorough knowledge of and sensitivity to the basic qualities of buildings. Structural systems, construction materials, fenestration types, building shape and configuration, and architectural design and detail have a major effect on space planning decisions. Knowledge of and sensitivity to these aspects of buildings usually begin with school coursework. The "Recommended Reading" section at the end of the chapter is geared to the development of that knowledge. Further knowledge and sophistication can be gained through regular and keen observation of buildings. And over time, varied and repeated project experience in space planning and interior design will bring a full and authoritative knowledge in this area.

Planning within wood frame, masonry bearing wall, or columnar system buildings will determine the freedom with which one can manipulate interior space; interior bearing walls, masonry ones in particular, are often a serious impediment to creating floor plans that work and flow well. A building's basic structural materials—wood, masonry, steel, or concrete—will influence the ease with which wall and floor openings can be made, creating a major influence on the usefulness of a building for its intended new function. The length of a building's structural spans (bay size), often related to the building's age (generally, the more recent the building's structural technology, the longer the span), will determine the degree of flexibility and openness that can be created; obviously, small bays will restrict partition and furniture placement and limit traffic flow. A combination of structural system and materials factors will govern if, where, and how new door and window openings can be

made in both interior and exterior walls. The relative simplicity or complexity of a building's shape or configuration will impact upon its usefulness for a given set of planning requirements; complex exterior wall configurations and peculiarly placed stairwells and elevator shafts can render a building unsuitable for a particular use. All these issues may require consultation with architects and structural engineers, but a basic background on the part of the space planner is necessary to intelligently discuss the issues with the consultants and ultimately make wise space planning decisions. Illustrations 4–1A and 4–1B demonstrate some of the basic aspects of the influence of the building shell on space planning.

Beyond these issues of structure and shell are the subtler but still important ones of building history and design. Buildings of true historic significance are in a special category in which space planning decisions are dominated by architectural factors; this is true whether the historical significance is architectural, political, or social. But every building has its own connection with history—an expression of its time—that warrants sensitivity when re-planning within it. The designer needs to have knowledge of architectural and construction history to exercise appropriate design sensitivity; one should approach a traditional nineteenth-century building shell very differently from a 1930s Art Deco structure. These differences in historical context have relevance across the design spectrum, from major stylistic characteristics to the details of trim and molding. In most buildings of recent vintage, door and window trim have been kept to a minimum; consequently, new partitions can often be made perpendicularly flush with door and window jambs. But in many older buildings, where wide trim elements are carried around doors and windows, it is necessary not only to allow for the existing trim, but also to leave some wall surface adjacent to the trim before placing a perpendicular partition. Similar attention to detail must be given when planning in buildings with bay windows, as "crowding" a bay with a new partition can have a very unsatisfactory result. Many buildings of recent vintage have continuous bands of windows with repeated mullions every few feet; it is often difficult to plan new partitions to line up with existing mullions, requiring "jogging" the partition to meet the exterior wall at a mullion. These examples related to building design detail are demonstrated in Illustration 4–2. These are just three cases in which building design quality will have a significant influence on space planning decisions; almost endless examples can be cited, from incorporating monumental staircases and ornamental ceilings to utilizing decorative floor patterns and traditional wall paneling. The importance of gaining a sophisticated background in architectural and interiors history, as well as in the art of building, cannot be overstated.

BUILDING CONFIGURATION INFLUENCES SPACE PLANNING

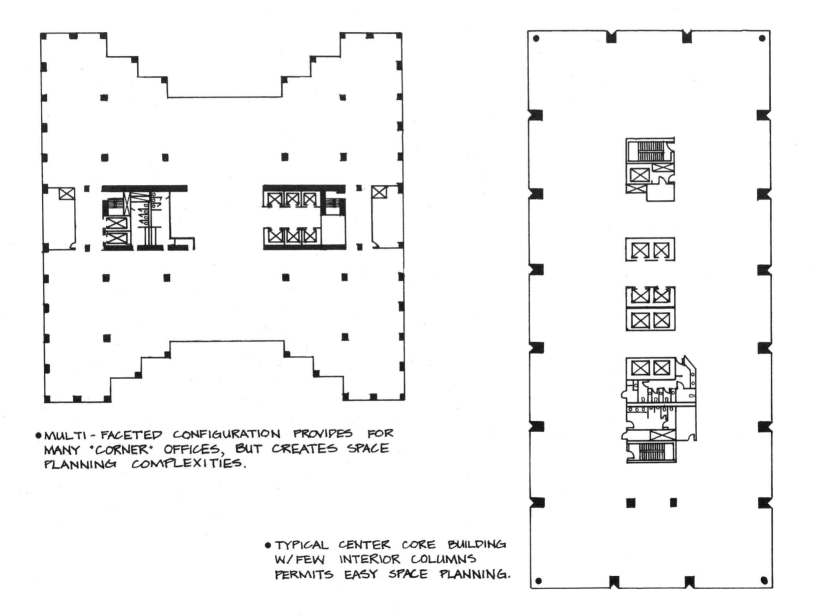

• MULTI-FACETED CONFIGURATION PROVIDES FOR MANY "CORNER" OFFICES, BUT CREATES SPACE PLANNING COMPLEXITIES.

• TYPICAL CENTER CORE BUILDING W/ FEW INTERIOR COLUMNS PERMITS EASY SPACE PLANNING.

BUILDING CONFIGURATION INFLUENCES SPACE PLANNING   ILLUS. 4–1B

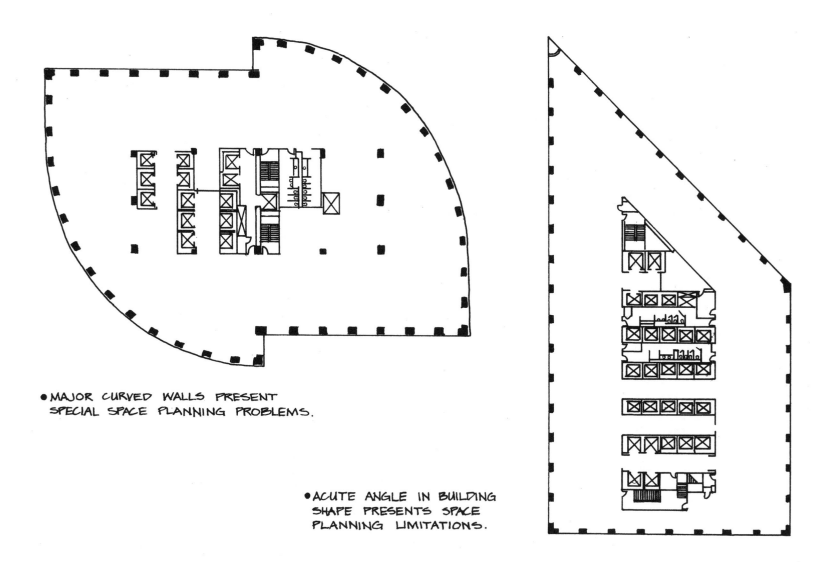

● MAJOR CURVED WALLS PRESENT
SPECIAL SPACE PLANNING PROBLEMS.

● ACUTE ANGLE IN BUILDING
SHAPE PRESENTS SPACE
PLANNING LIMITATIONS.

SPECIAL PARTITION PLACEMENT CONDITIONS

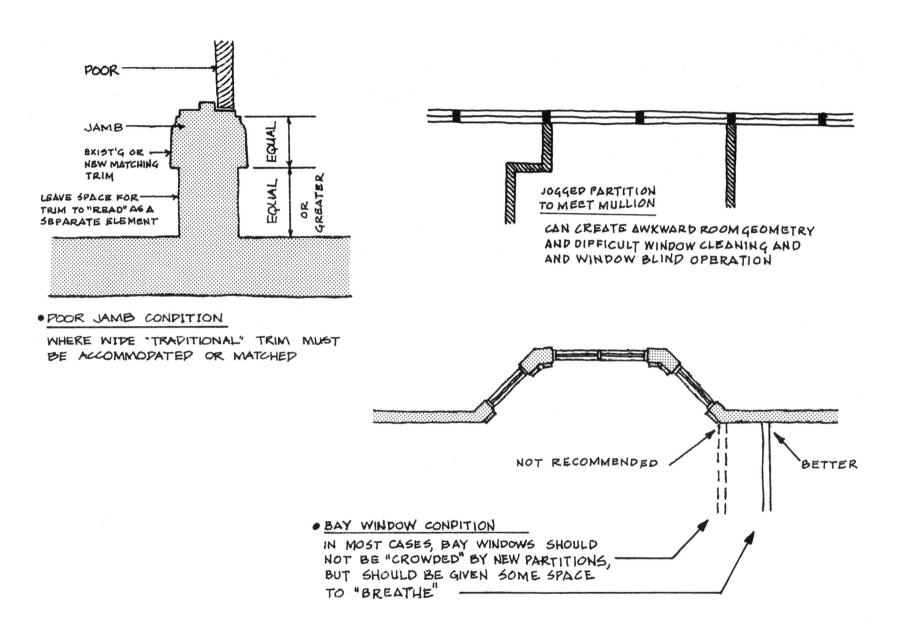

POOR

JAMB

EXIST'G OR NEW MATCHING TRIM

LEAVE SPACE FOR TRIM TO "READ" AS A SEPARATE ELEMENT

EQUAL | EQUAL

EQUAL | OR GREATER

● POOR JAMB CONDITION

WHERE WIDE "TRADITIONAL" TRIM MUST BE ACCOMMODATED OR MATCHED

JOGGED PARTITION TO MEET MULLION

CAN CREATE AWKWARD ROOM GEOMETRY AND DIFFICULT WINDOW CLEANING AND AND WINDOW BLIND OPERATION

NOT RECOMMENDED

BETTER

● BAY WINDOW CONDITION

IN MOST CASES, BAY WINDOWS SHOULD NOT BE "CROWDED" BY NEW PARTITIONS, BUT SHOULD BE GIVEN SOME SPACE TO "BREATHE"

PLUMBING SYSTEMS

The placement of plumbing fixtures presents one of the most stringent constraints in the space planning process. A limited number of situations exist, such as one-story buildings with utility basements or crawl spaces below the floor, in which plumbing fixtures can be placed almost at will.

In the great majority of situations, construction practicalities and cost factors require that fixtures be placed in close proximity to existing vented waste lines, limiting the location of typical rooms or functions requiring fixtures, such as restrooms, kitchens, and laboratories; there are also special situations, such as medical offices, that require the dispersal of fixtures throughout the facility. It should be noted that interior designers very often "inherit" public toilet rooms and consequently have limited experience in planning them. The constraints on fixture placement are threefold:

1. Adherence to good plumbing construction practice

2. Compliance with the prevailing plumbing code

3. Grouping of fixtures for economical piping layouts

Space planners do not have to know as much about plumbing as mechanical engineers or contractors do, but a basic understanding of the three constraints listed above is needed. A great deal of the necessary knowledge is usually gained in the professional office and on the job site. Over time, the space planner should attempt to build that informational background in the following manner:

1. For good plumbing construction practice, become familiar with the terminology and principles of plumbing construction. Through reading, working with mechanical engineers and contractors, and observing piping layouts on the job site before they are covered up by finish materials, the planner can gain an adequate understanding of the relationship between plumbing construction and the practicalities of space planning.

2. For plumbing code compliance, get to know the specific limitations on construction imposed by the plumbing code that has jurisdiction in specific project locations. This information should be sought from code enforcement officials, mechanical engineers, or contractors before definitive space planning solutions are attempted.

3. For construction economy, become proficient with typical planning techniques for the grouping of fixtures. Typically, fixtures are placed along pipe chases to keep construction costs low and for ease of future building maintenance. See the left-hand sketch in Illustration 4–3 for a graphic example of this kind of fixture grouping.

![EXERCISE 4-1]

The recommended exercises in Chapter 3 involving public restroom planning should be studied again from a plumbing systems viewpoint as well as a space planning perspective. Are the original exercise results practical and economical in terms of construction? Rework the plans in terms of construction practicalities; real-world projects will demand it.

In the very preliminary space planning phases of a project, before plumbing code information has been established, many space planners will use a rule of thumb for the preliminary placement of fixtures. For this early phase of planning, a reasonable rule of thumb would place fixtures so that their horizontal waste lines slope at a minimum of ¼" per foot to a vented waste stack, as graphically described in the right-hand sketch of Illustration 4–3. If construction conditions permit the waste piping to run under the floor, there is no limit to the length of the horizontal run, although the depth of a plenum space below the floor may place a very practical limitation on how far the horizontal line may run. In addition to the issue of the plenum depth, basic practicalities such as headroom or structural observations may also limit the length of a horizontal waste line. There are also instances where horizontal waste lines may be concealed above the floor when thickened walls or pipe chases can be created to house them. Like any other rule of thumb, this approach should not be used beyond a very preliminary planning stage.

HEATING, VENTILATING, AND AIR-CONDITIONING (HVAC) SYSTEMS

Broad generalizations are difficult to draw concerning the relationship between the space planning process and HVAC systems, because the basic

PLUMBING CONSIDERATIONS

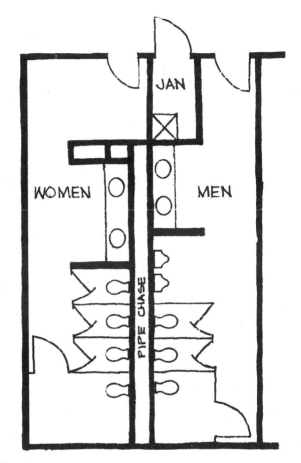

JAN

WOMEN

MEN

PIPE CHASE

- PLUMBING FIXTURES GROUPED ALONG COMMON PIPE CHASE

CONSTRUCTION AND MAINTENANCE ECONOMIES DEMAND THIS TYPE OF ARRANGEMENT

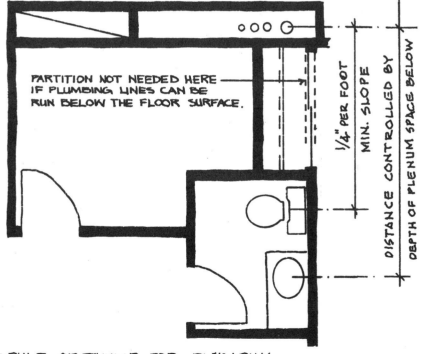

PARTITION NOT NEEDED HERE IF PLUMBING LINES CAN BE RUN BELOW THE FLOOR SURFACE.

1/4" PER FOOT MIN. SLOPE

DISTANCE CONTROLLED BY DEPTH OF PLENUM SPACE BELOW

- RULE-OF-THUMB FOR PLUMBING FIXTURE PLACEMENT

IN VERY PRELIMINARY PLANNING STAGE

HVAC SUPPLY TECHNIQUES IN OLDER AND/OR UNIQUE BUILDINGS

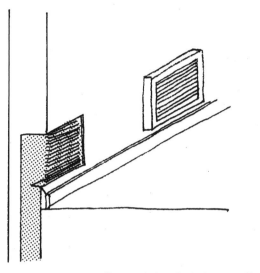

- HEAT BY RADIATION, FORCED AIR OR CONVECTION; SURFACED MOUNTED OR RECESSED.

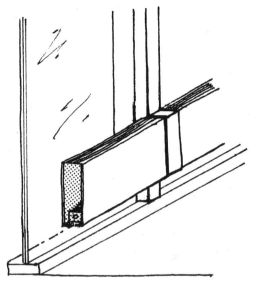

- MULLION OR WALL MOUNTED HEAT BY FORCED AIR OR CONVECTION.

- BASEBOARD UNIT. HEAT BY CONVECTION.

THE PLACEMENT OF NEW PARTITIONS IN THE RENOVATION OF OLDER BUILDINGS WITH SYSTEMS SIMILAR TO THOSE ILLUSTRATED HERE REQUIRES PARTICULAR ATTENTION TO CONSTRUCTION DETAILS AND ACOUSTIC CONTROL BEWTEEN ROOMS.

- UNDER FLOOR CONVECTOR UNIT.

qualities of HVAC systems can vary greatly from building to building. The great majority of modern, non-residential buildings have flexible HVAC systems exclusively contained in ceiling plenum spaces and/or exterior wall units. Because these systems are designed for maximum flexibility, they permit quick and easy changes and have little impact on the space planning process. More specifically, new partitions can be located with almost complete freedom in terms of HVAC requirements. But this is not the case when working within older buildings or ones originally designed for specific or unique functions. Since the replacement of an entire HVAC system is usually very costly and time-consuming, more often than not, existing systems are retained unless they are totally outdated or specialized beyond reuse. When older, inflexible systems are retained, HVAC requirements could place significant limitations on space allocation and partition placement. Older or unique buildings have many variables in configuration and HVAC system design, and no quick and easy rules of thumb or space planning techniques apply. In situations of this kind, it is important to consult with a mechanical engineer as soon as a survey of the existing conditions is available, and certainly before the bubble diagramming process has begun. Illustration 4–4 shows some of the typical and non-typical variables encountered in existing buildings. Pay particular attention to acoustic control in these situations, where it is often difficult to make tight acoustic closure around existing pipes or equipment.

The space planner should strive for an understanding of the basic principles of HVAC systems, with particular emphasis on air distribution. More specifically, the planner should have knowledge of how supply diffusers and return grilles are placed in drywall and acoustic tile ceilings, plus an understanding of the principles that place supply air close to the offending exterior wall surfaces and return grilles as remote from them as possible to provide maximum supply air coverage and minimize short-circuiting of the supply air. Illustration 4–5A demonstrates an appropriate application of these principles. In this one aspect of HVAC systems design, the interior designer is often the best or most appropriate member of the building design team, rather than the architect or mechanical engineer, to decide upon the final placement of such equipment. Detailed knowledge of specific or likely placement of furniture and related equipment permits the intelligent deployment of these HVAC devices within the space, maximizing human comfort. Although much of this placement process occurs long after the space planning has been finalized, a general eye to ductwork and dropped soffit locations during the space planning phase will create a better HVAC system design. Illustration 4–5B shows one of the typical application problems encountered in this placement process. Note also the capacity of HVAC

HVAC/AIR SUPPLY CONSIDERATIONS   ILLUS. 4–5A+B

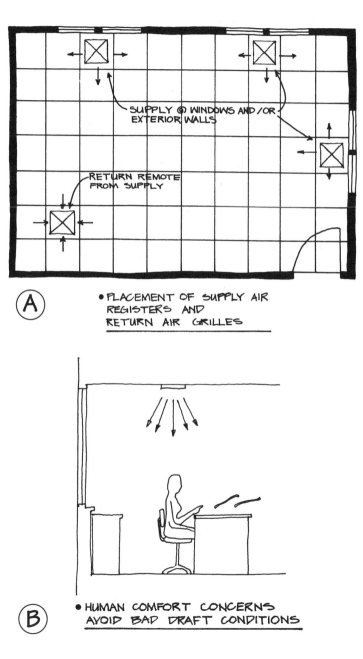

(A) • PLACEMENT OF SUPPLY AIR REGISTERS AND RETURN AIR GRILLES

(B) • HUMAN COMFORT CONCERNS AVOID BAD DRAFT CONDITIONS

ductwork to carry sound and destroy otherwise well-planned acoustic environments. Wherever sensitive acoustic situations exist, HVAC systems must be designed to accommodate those needs.

Again, the interior planner is not expected to be an expert in the complexities of interior environmental control systems, but rather to have enough understanding of basic principles and knowledge of basic terminology to be able to intelligently discuss the matter and ask the appropriate questions of mechanical engineers and contractors. Initially, specific coursework and prescribed reading will build that knowledge base, and the recommended reading for this chapter should be helpful; beyond that, depth of knowledge is built through repeated project experience, both in the professional office and on the construction job site.

Recommended Reading

1*, 3*. 4*, 7*, 9*, 13*, 15*, 20*, 23*, 24*, 26*, 31*

Books marked with an asterisk are also included in the recommended reading for other chapters.

Chapter 5   IMPORTANT INFLUENCING FACTORS

In addition to the building shell and major environmental systems issues discussed in Chapter 4, several other factors have significant influence on the space planning process. The ideas raised at the beginning of Chapter 4 about the planner's depth of knowledge and the complexity of factors bearing on space planning decisions have equal application for the influencing factors discussed in this chapter. Each area discussed deserves a book or course of its own, but that kind of depth in each area goes far beyond the intent of this book. The focus here remains on space planning, and readers may pursue additional knowledge in each area as needs and circumstances require.

BUILDING CODES

Building codes deal with almost every area of building planning, design, and construction; consequently, they are very complex. To compound matters,

their language is very technical, sometimes arcane, and generally difficult to penetrate for the uninitiated. Typically, interior designers' primary code involvements are limited to the sections on use group classification, types of construction, means of egress, and fire-resistive construction, plus the issues of flammability and noxious fumes. During the space planning process, most building code involvement is limited to means-of-egress concerns, but that area will have major impact on most of the basic planning decisions that must be made. Remember the ADA requirements, as discussed in Chapter 3; those requirements are still another set of standards and regulations that will have significant bearing on space planning solutions.

Safe departure from a building during a fire or other panic situations is at the heart of means-of-egress standards. The basic principles and the details of these standards should be thoroughly understood by every interior planner. That understanding begins with reading (and if necessary, rereading) that section of the building code as well as the books cited in the recommended reading for this chapter. Not only should the following code concepts be understood, but their typical forms of applications should also be known:

1. Occupant load

2. Exit capacity

3. Door, corridor, stair width

4. Two remote means of egress

5. Length of exit travel

6. Dead-end corridors

The International Building Code, published for the first time in 2000, presents a universal building code standard. It has been adopted by many state and local governing bodies, replacing the three major regional model codes (BOCA, SBCCI, and UBC) that had been the prevailing codes for many years. From a practical point of view, read and become familiar with the code prevalently used in your region, as well as any state and local variations that may amend it. Real depth of knowledge will come with applying the code concepts to specific space planning problems. With this end in mind, the following exercise is suggested as a first attempt at those applications. As you progress through the space planning exercises provided in Chapters 6 and 7, the building code issues inherent in those design problems must be addressed and solved. As each of those exercises is completed, it should be specifically reviewed and critiqued from a building code perspective.

EXERCISE 5-1

Using the Group 3 building shell plans (approximately 4,000 square feet in size) provided in the Appendix, sketch corridor pattern solutions for each that satisfy code requirements for egress (corridor widths, remote exits, length of travel, dead-end corridors) while maximizing usable (or rentable) square footage. This exercise can be further extended by using the shell plans for any multistory commercial or institutional buildings that can be found in most interior design and architectural publications.

Knowledge of prevailing codes related to the building process is critical to the space planner. Even aspects of zoning codes will have bearing on space planning problems. Despite this, there is a limited number of books available that address these issues comprehensively. The recommended reading for this chapter provides some answers, but there is no substitute for digging into the codes themselves and learning how to use them—and, when necessary, learning whom to call upon for expert advice. When it comes to learning codes, there are no useful shortcuts. To simplify the learning curve, interior designers should focus on six areas related to codes and regulations that require competency: (1) use group classifications, (2) types of construction, (3) means of egress, (4) fire-resistive construction, (5) the issues of flammability and noxious fumes, and (6) ADA requirements.

LIGHTING DESIGN

Both natural and electric lighting play a significant role in the space planning process. Although a sophisticated approach to lighting design would draw strong relationships between the planning of natural and electric lighting for a specific building or interior space, it is not necessary to integrate the two for preliminary space planning purposes, since that integration deals with subtleties of design and lighting technology that will not have bearing on the allocation of space. Consequently, they will be dealt with here as distinct and separate entities.

Natural Lighting

It is difficult and unnecessary to separate the issues of natural lighting, energy conservation, view to the exterior, solar orientation, and natural ventilation as they relate to the preliminary space planning process. In some cases, only one of these issues will be a factor in providing windows for a function or space, while in other cases, all four of these issues will be involved to determine window location. A well-articulated criteria matrix can and should be able to keep all of these issues clear during the planning process. Remember that building codes generally require that all habitable rooms—code-defined as all residentially used spaces (except for mechanically ventilated bathrooms and kitchens)—must have natural light and air, typically requiring window area to be at least 8 to 10 percent of the floor area, and that one-half of that (4 to 5 percent) must be operable for ventilation, as shown in Illustration 5-1. Code issues aside, people psychologically need natural light and a view to the exterior in most rooms they spend time in, residential or otherwise, and these human factors should be the ultimate determinants in window placement decisions. One more factor to keep in mind is energy conservation, indicating that the use of natural lighting be maximized while maintaining an appropriate balance with heating and cooling needs.

NATURAL LIGHT/AIR FOR HABITABLE ROOMS   ILLUS. 5–1

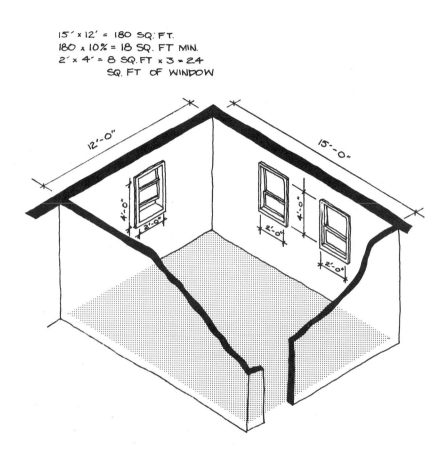

15' x 12' = 180 SQ. FT.
180 x 10% = 18 SQ. FT MIN.
2' x 4' = 8 SQ. FT x 3 = 24
   SQ. FT OF WINDOW

The psychological and esthetic concerns of interior planning will have the strongest influence on the use of natural lighting. For both living and working spaces, the quality of natural light and a view to the exterior, except for unique functions such as presentation rooms, will be seen as highly desirable and often essential. Buildings with an abundance of windows and a minimum of deep interior regions far from exterior walls do not present problems in planning for natural light. But some buildings have limited windows or large interior regions far from windowed exterior walls. In these cases, planning for natural light can be a critical space planning element, in which difficult decisions must be made about which spaces get the windows or choice view and

which go without. Two graphically comparative examples of this space planning influence are demonstrated in Illustrations 5-2A and 5-2B.

Planning for natural lighting begins with the initial space planning analysis, as described in Chapter 1. When organizing user and spatial needs, as in the development of a criteria matrix, priorities should be created for natural lighting needs, identifying those spaces for which natural lighting is essential (habitable rooms, executive offices), desirable (long-term work spaces, student lounges), unnecessary (public restrooms, short-term conference rooms) and undesirable (darkrooms, valuable document storage). When windows are abundant, one may identify the desired direction of view and/or solar orientation for specific rooms or functions. In addition to the criteria matrix, relationship diagrams can easily reflect these needs and priorities. Decisions about natural light are made during the bubble diagramming or block planning phase. The final diagram or block plan must satisfy the natural lighting requirements, because it is usually impossible to reconfigure the building later to admit natural light where it is not already available. Similarly, requirements for solar orientation and direction of view are determined at this very early planning phase, because it is impossible to rotate an existing building to satisfy these needs. Very often the issues of solar orientation and selected views are not given high priority in the criteria matrix, particularly in nonresidential buildings; but when they can be satisfied. a valuable esthetic element has been served.

Note should be made about the use of skylights. Their applications are limited because they can be used only in one-story buildings, on the top floor of multistory buildings, and for atrium spaces in multistory buildings. When skylights can be used, they bring to a space a unique and marvelous quality of daylight that is quite different from the quality of light admitted by conventional windows. Unusually generous, flooding qualities of natural light can be admitted by relatively small skylights. Learning to use them effectively requires observation, research, and project experience.

Planning for natural lighting is not technical or difficult, although as project size and scope increase, the sheer number of factors and priorities that must be kept in mind and satisfied can make natural lighting a complex space-planning task.

Electric Lighting
Unlike natural lighting, electric lighting is complex and highly technical—an area in which every interior designer should have significant background. As with natural lighting, electric lighting can have a significant effect on space planning decisions. From the outset, it should be remembered that most

NATURAL LIGHT/VIEW CONSIDERATIONS in OFFICE BUILDING PLANNING   ILLUS. 5-2

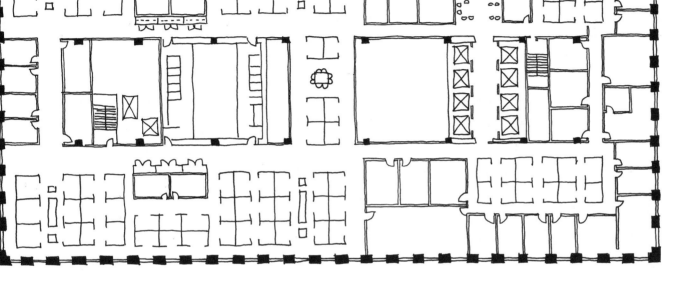

ILLUS. A

BUILDING WITH GENEROUS NATURAL
LIGHT/VIEW AVAILABILITY PROVIDES
DESIREABLE CONDITION FOR
MAJORITY OF EMPLOYEES.

ILLUS. B

BUILDING WITH LIMITED NATURAL LIGHT/VIEW
AVAILABILITY CREATES DIFFICULT DECISIONS
CONCERNING PRIORITIES ON WINDOWED SPACES.

buildings must be planned for nighttime as well as daytime use; therefore, natural lighting has only limited effect upon electric lighting planning and design.

For buildings without existing lighting systems (or when it makes economic sense to entirely remove an existing system), the effects of lighting design on space planning solutions are usually not critical. In these situations, accommodation for lighting can wait until a first rough floor plan is established.

For nonresidential buildings with existing lighting systems (most typically, part of an integrated suspended ceiling system), construction economy will frequently dictate that the system be reused and conformed with. If that is the case, space planning cannot be accomplished without careful coordination with the existing system. More specifically, the complex interrelationship between the existing suspended ceiling grid and window locations and the placement of partitions, luminaires, furniture, and equipment must be coordinated. Once the bubble diagramming or block planning phase is complete, the building shell floor plan and the reflected ceiling plan must be worked with as an integral unit in the development of a rough floor plan. See Illustration 5-3 for reflected ceiling plans that demonstrate these issues of planning and design coordination.

Once a rough floor plan has been tentatively established, a first attempt at a reflected ceiling plan should be drawn. Basic ceiling configuration should be considered, including ceiling height(s), slopes, and soffits. The ceiling, despite its basic importance, is too often the "forgotten surface" in interior spaces. Now is the time to consciously address those design concerns, not after the floor plan has been so well established or refined that ceiling design considerations might be difficult to incorporate without making significant floor plan changes. In most buildings, particularly nonresidential buildings, lighting is implemented through the ceiling construction, and lighting design decisions are integrally tied to the design of the ceiling. For that reason, a rough reflected ceiling plan incorporating a first tentative lighting design solution should be prepared at this critical point in the space planning process. A method to incorporate this procedure in the space planning process is discussed and described in Chapter 6.

In professional practice settings, once the basic ceiling design issues have been considered and sketched, it is wise to consult with a lighting designer. Since lighting design has become very complex and technical, consultation with a specialist is desirable for all but the simplest interior conditions. Under

TYPICAL REFLECTED CEILING PLANS   ILLUS. 5-3

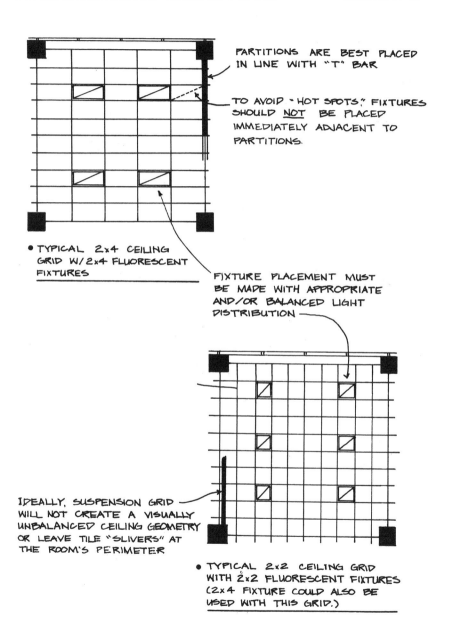

PARTITIONS ARE BEST PLACED IN LINE WITH "T" BAR

TO AVOID "HOT SPOTS," FIXTURES SHOULD <u>NOT</u> BE PLACED IMMEDIATELY ADJACENT TO PARTITIONS.

• TYPICAL 2x4 CEILING GRID W/ 2x4 FLUORESCENT FIXTURES

FIXTURE PLACEMENT MUST BE MADE WITH APPROPRIATE AND/OR BALANCED LIGHT DISTRIBUTION

IDEALLY, SUSPENSION GRID WILL NOT CREATE A VISUALLY UNBALANCED CEILING GEOMETRY OR LEAVE TILE "SLIVERS" AT THE ROOM'S PERIMETER

• TYPICAL 2x2 CEILING GRID WITH 2x2 FLUORESCENT FIXTURES (2x4 FIXTURE COULD ALSO BE USED WITH THIS GRID.)

normal professional practice conditions, it is best to consult with the lighting designer at this very early phase in the planning process, and specifically before the final preliminary floor plan is started, to integrate the lighting design solution into the final design solution.

In a classroom, when the aid of a professional lighting design consultant is not available, it is excellent experience for design students to try their hand at a lighting design solution. Ideally, some lighting design coursework has already been completed, but even if you do not yet have that background, thinking through the lighting design issues is a valuable learning experience.

Lighting design is a field unto itself, requiring much knowledge and expertise. For space planning purposes, the interior designer's depth of knowledge need not be very detailed; only broad-brush concepts and solutions are required. With all factors that require design integration with a consulting specialist, one must know enough to be able to work intelligently with that consultant. If your knowledge in this area needs strengthening, some recommended reading is listed at the end of the chapter.

Note that other aspects of electrical construction are not raised in this text. Although they represent major aspects of interior construction, they usually do not have critical impact on space planning because of the ease with which wiring is placed in chases, partitions, and ceiling plenums.

ACOUSTICAL PLANNING

Although the field of architectural acoustics is complex, with a technology of its own, its application to basic space planning is relatively simple and essentially commonsensical. Except for relatively large performance spaces such as auditoriums, lecture halls, or cabarets, space planning for good or acceptable acoustics involves simple technical knowledge plus some basic interior construction information about what can be accomplished and relative costs.

Good architectural acoustics begin with concepts of zoning and isolation, followed later by insulation and absorption. The planning process for acoustics begins with the initial space planning analysis, as described in Chapter 1. When organizing user and spatial needs, as in the development of a criteria matrix, acoustic needs for privacy, isolation, and absorption should be identified. Creating quiet and noisy zones (often coinciding with private and pub-

lic zones) can be accomplished during the bubble diagramming or block planning phase. Common sense tells one that it is inappropriate to put a school library adjacent to a band practice room or the company president next to a noisy mechanical equipment room. Wherever possible, acoustic conflicts or problems should first be addressed through appropriate and sensitive space allocation, as demonstrated in Illustrations 5–4A and 5–4B. Despite this, many acoustic conflicts cannot be easily resolved through space planning; work function and traffic flow adjacencies often require that acoustic conflicts be ignored, or even compounded, in terms of space planning, as is typically found in the necessary groupings of lawyers' offices, medical examining rooms, or conference rooms. In these cases, the acoustic interference must be dealt with through means other than zoning and isolation.

The transmission of sound through walls and partitions, except in the most extreme cases, can be limited to acceptable levels through established construction techniques. The greater the decibel level generated, the heavier, more complex, and costly the construction solutions. For unusually noisy functions (banquet halls, music practice suites, etc.) when space planning cannot zone them away, buffer spaces (storage rooms, filing rooms, etc.) can be used if space planning adjacencies will permit, as demonstrated in Illustration 5–4B. If it is difficult or inappropriate to use a buffer space for this purpose, the cost of a dense isolating wall must be accepted.

Conventional groupings of rooms or spaces in which acoustic interference is common (offices, classrooms, conference rooms, etc.) require the space planner to have knowledge of the sound levels generated and the construction techniques needed to limit transmission to acceptable levels. Although space planners are not required to have detailed knowledge of those construction techniques, they should be familiar with the levels of acoustic control that can be accomplished with those techniques. Basic information on these construction techniques is readily available in many reference sources (see "Recommended Reading" at the end of the chapter). Illustration 5-5 indicates a sampling of information one needs to solve acoustic transmission problems through construction techniques. Detailed involvement in construction techniques to limit sound transmission or to absorb ambient sound within spaces goes far beyond the issues of space planning and is generally dealt with during the subsequent project phases of design and construction documentation. As mentioned in Chapter 4, HVAC construction can also play a critical role in achieving good acoustic results. An acoustic consultant's advice is often valuable in addressing those HVAC construction detail issues.

SPACE PLANNING FOR GOOD ACOUSTICS

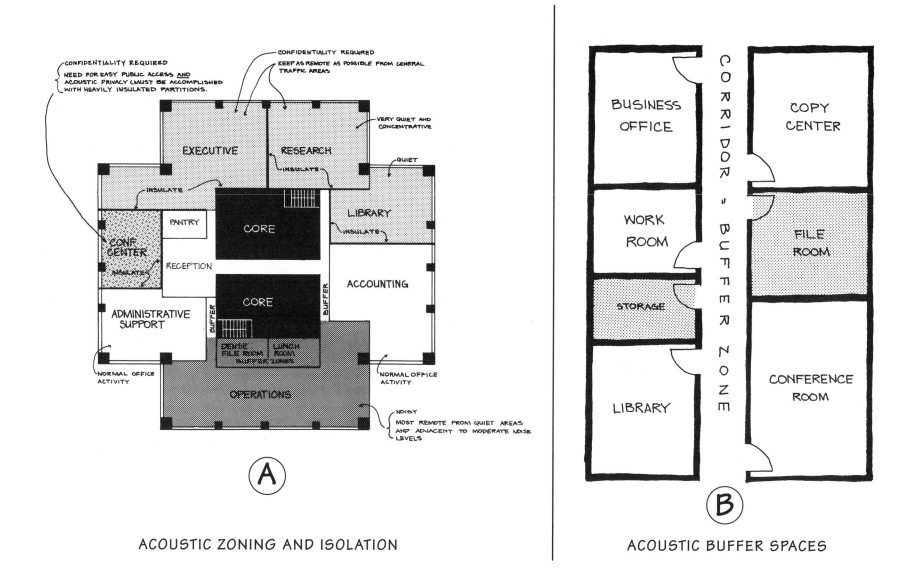

ACOUSTIC ZONING AND ISOLATION

ACOUSTIC BUFFER SPACES

PARTITION CONSTRUCTION

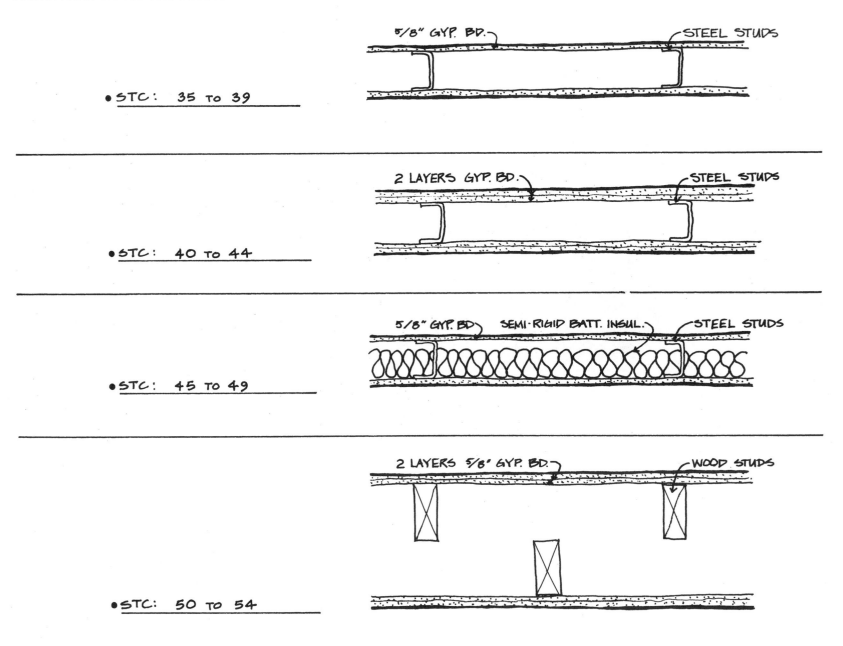

5/8" GYP. BD.   STEEL STUDS

• STC: 35 TO 39

2 LAYERS GYP. BD.   STEEL STUDS

• STC: 40 TO 44

5/8" GYP. BD.   SEMI-RIGID BATT. INSUL.   STEEL STUDS

• STC: 45 TO 49

2 LAYERS 5/8" GYP. BD.   WOOD STUDS

• STC: 50 TO 54

When relatively large performance spaces are part of a planning project and the shape, height, and configuration of the performance space are affected by acoustic considerations, an acoustic consultant should be brought into the project at its earliest phases. Most designers and architects are not well enough versed in performance acoustics to design such spaces without the help of an experienced consultant who is able to provide design direction that will ensure acceptable acoustic results. In these cases, the unique shape of a performance space may have a profound effect on the spatial organization of the entire project. The acoustic consultant's help is also invaluable in designing the details of those spaces and in the development of construction detailing when acoustic privacy and acoustic absorbency are needed. These more detailed issues are usually addressed at later stages in most planning and design projects.

The need for multiple uses of interior space occurs so frequently that space planners should also have general knowledge of the achievable sound transmission ratings of the several types of moveable partitions available and the approximate costs involved in their installation. Multiple uses of space are most common in classrooms, conference or meeting rooms, and banquet facilities but are not uncommon in many other types of interior uses. Surprisingly high acoustic ratings are achievable with these construction techniques, but usually at very high cost. Illustration 5-6 diagrams the most commonly used types of moveable partitions to separate spaces Multiple space use is discussed again in this chapter, but from a perspective much broader than acoustic planning. (See "Flexibility/Multiuse" in this chapter.)

PLANNING RULES OF THUMB

Knowing the approximate size of typical rooms and spaces makes the preliminary space planning process easier and more efficient. It is impossible for the space planner to commit to memory square footage rules of thumb for every type of interior facility, but recurring spaces in most buildings have typical square footage requirements. It is for these spaces and functions that rules of thumb are worth developing and remembering.

Without any attempt at completeness but keeping barrier-free needs in mind for nonresidential settings, here is a beginning list of spaces and functions for which every space planner should attempt to remember an approximate space requirement:

Typical powder room (two-piece)	20–30 sq. ft.
Typical barrier-free powder room (two-piece, non-compartmented)	45–55 sq. ft.
Typical apartment bathroom (three-piece)	35–45 sq. ft.
Typical barrier-free apartment bathroom (three-piece)	65–75 sq. ft.
Typical apartment kitchen (not studio or efficiency)	65–80 sq. ft.
Typical Apartments	
Studio/efficiency	400–600 sq. ft.
One bedroom	550–800 sq. ft.
Two bedroom	750–1,200 sq. ft.
Lounge (hotel lobby, student center)	25–35 sq. ft./person
Waiting/reception room (doctor's office, school registration center)	20–25 sq. ft./person
Conference Room (business and professional offices, institutions)	25–35 sq. ft./person
Assembly Rooms (stack chairs for lectures-schools, hotels)	10–15 sq. ft./person
Auditorium (fixed seating)	8–14 sq. ft./person
High school cafeteria	10–15 sq. ft./person
Midpriced restaurant	18–25 sq. ft./person
Elegant restaurant	30–40 sq. ft./person
Systems furniture, work stations (minimum)	35–40 sq. ft./person
(average)	50–70 sq. ft.
(generous)	80–100 sq. ft.
Private offices typically w/ full-height partitions (standard work and consulting space)	120–150 sq. ft.
Private offices typically w/ full-height partitions (executive office w/ lounge seating)	200–300 sq. ft

Rule-of-thumb square footages are best thought of as approximations or a size range, rather than as specific numbers; perceptive judgment must be used to match the desired spatial quality with the appropriate part of the range. Keep in mind that rule-of-thumb figures apply only to typical sit-

TYPICAL MOVABLE PARTITIONS

• PAIRED PANEL
STC: 30-50

• CONTINUOUS PANEL
STC: 30-50

• ACCORDION
STC: 15-40

• COIL
STC: 15-30

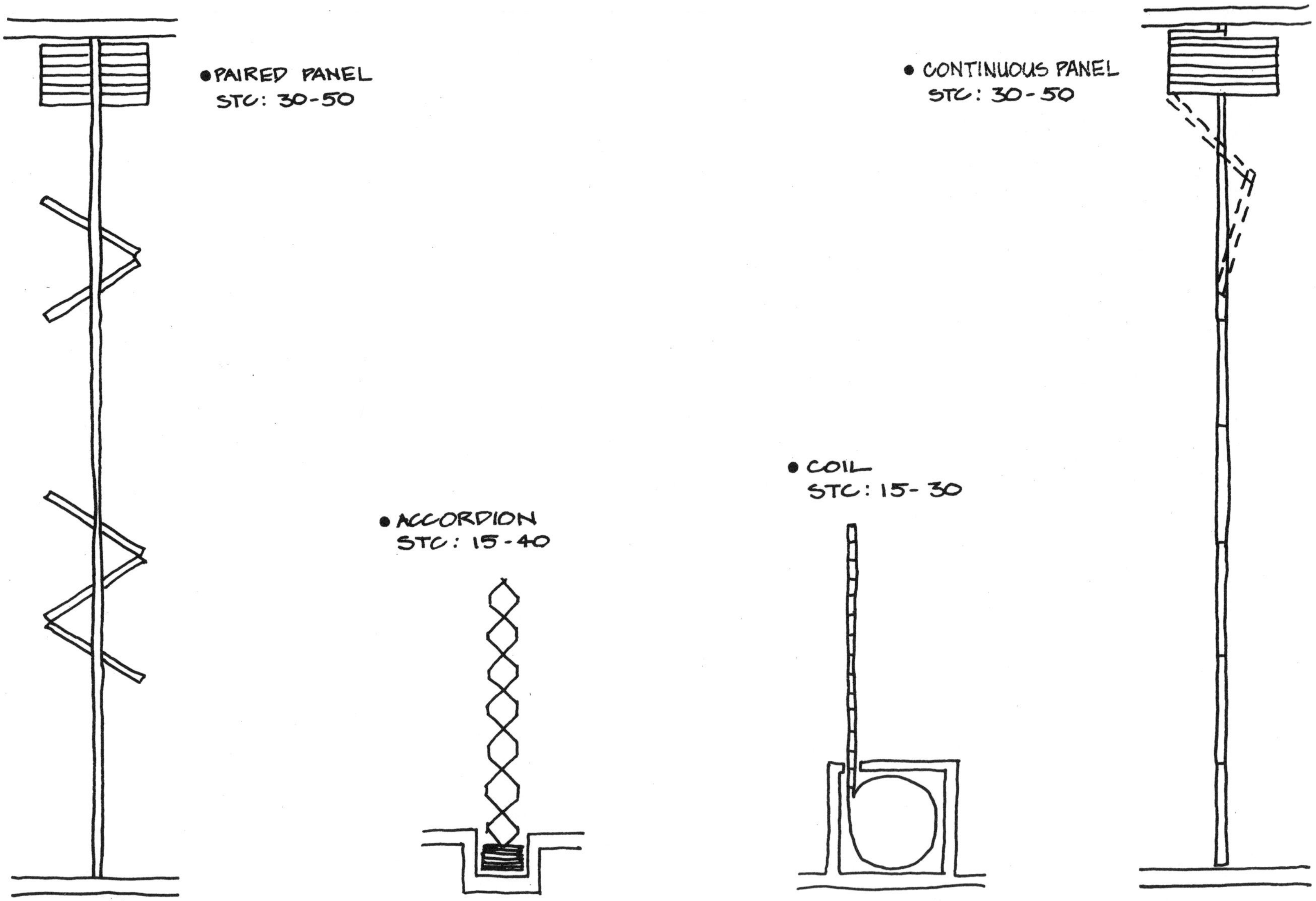

uations; if a conference room requires a significant guest or spectator area, the rule-of-thumb figure will not work. One should not try to store too much of this in their head; the prototypical plan sketch technique described in Chapter 1, an integral step in preparing a criteria matrix, will always provide an adequate preliminary square footage figure if the specific requirements of a given space are known. When unique or special spaces require unconventional or specialty equipment, such as a dental operatory, it is time to get out the appropriate reference sources or call in the specialist or consultant.

Reference sources are available (see "Recommended Reading" at the end of this chapter) to help develop a store of useful square footage rules of thumb. Rote learning has severe limitations; rather than memorize numbers, work with the resource materials by sketching floor plans for a variety of situations and verifying the resource data. In this manner, the information will be more meaningful and long-lasting.

FLEXIBILITY/MULTIUSE

With the increasing cost of buildings, there is increasing pressure on interior designers to provide functional facilities that maximize the use of interior space and permit it to serve more than one limited programmatic requirement. For example, in conference centers, classroom buildings, and banquet facilities the ability to change room sizes is essential. Similar kinds of flexible space are often required in less typical or less obvious situations. Through in-depth knowledge of programmatic needs, the space planner can often suggest space-saving planning techniques, such as combining two functions in one space when functional needs are not seriously compromised. For example, a combination of library and conference rooms for smaller law firms is common. When traffic and use is frequent, time-use studies for specific planning situations will often reveal scheduling techniques that can eliminate unnecessary treatment, conference, or practice rooms when large numbers of such spaces are planned within one facility.

The space planner should know the conventionally available building products and techniques to open and close spaces, including their approximate installed cost, their approximate sound transmission qualities (discussed in "Acoustical Planning" earlier in this chapter), and the relative ease with

which they can be opened and closed (are maintenance personnel required, and for how much time?). Sometimes esthetic qualities are important in these decisions, since some products frequently used in institutional settings are not acceptable in commercial or professional settings, or vice versa. As an example, the nuts-and-bolts appearance of a gymnasium's moveable partition may be entirely appropriate for that use but inappropriate for a high-profile law firm's conference room.

In addition to construction techniques, the planner should develop an awareness of programmatic situations that present possibilities for multiple use and space-saving scheduling of facilities. Professional planners can more than earn their fee through just one space-saving "discovery" of this kind. Many valuable scheduling techniques are used by professional facilities managers, some of which are available in commercial computer software packages.

FURNITURE

Although the space planning specialist does not have to possess the same depth of knowledge about the furniture marketplace as the more typical specifying interior designer, basic knowledge about typical furniture and equipment sizes and characteristics is essential. To some extent, this issue has already been discussed in Chapter 1 in relation to prototypical plan sketches, and it will be raised again in Chapter 6, which recommends exercises to strengthen furniture planning skills. The space planner needs to have, or needs to know where to find, information on space requirements for specific furniture and furniture uses. It may be necessary to know how much space is required for a given number of seats in an airport lounge, the size of the storage space required to stack chairs and folding tables in a banquet facility, the size and capacity of filing cabinets for a law firm's central files, and so on. Nothing is complex about this planning factor; a personal store of dimensional information and/or access to manufacturers' furniture and equipment catalog information, either online or with a conventional catalog library, is all that is needed. The development of that store of information usually comes quickly when one is space planning or furniture planning on a regular basis. The actual selection of furnishings is a complex and artful skill developed after much trial and error and is usually done after the space planning process has been completed.

SPATIAL QUALITY

Space planning has a natural consequence that is too often ignored or not given appropriate importance. As the space planner allocates and subdivides interior space, the basic spatial and esthetic qualities of that interior environment are determined, either consciously or unconsciously. There is a very strong tendency for the space planner to get so involved with the jigsaw-puzzle-like qualities of the planning task that the three-dimensional experience of the people using the space is given little priority. Once the partition locations are established, the interior's basic three-dimensional design quality is essentially determined.

The experienced space planner keeps an eye on spatial quality while the rough floor plan emerges on the computer screen or drawing board and will often make decisions about the general plan organization based on the perceived three-dimensional qualities inherent in the plan. The experienced planner is regularly testing the concepts of entrance impact, room shape, spatial order, symbolic qualities, and interior space and time experience of the users while making planning decisions. One of the best techniques to test spatial quality is the regular production of spatially revealing 3-D drawings or sketches (elevations, sections, isometrics, perspectives), whether drawn by hand or computer-generated, while going through the planning process (shown in Illustration 3-6). If a planning solution looks promising, one should quickly sketch room shapes, travel or corridor vistas, view to the exterior, coordination of structural and internal details, and the like. As the space planning solution develops, the basic spatial and esthetic qualities of the completed interior are in the planner's hands.

It is not uncommon for a rough study model to be built immediately following the establishment of a rough floor plan to better visualize the realities of the three-dimensional experience. This rough study model, usually constructed from illustration board or foam core, is much more time-consuming than developing 3-D views, but the rewards are considerable, since so much more of the basic three-dimensional quality of the space can be visualized through this technique.

Regardless of the techniques employed, it is important to have a fairly accurate sense of the resulting spatial quality before final plan decisions are made. The most inventive decorative and detailed treatments cannot compensate for the opportunities lost in a basically unsatisfying spatial experience.

Interior Design Specialties

This book on the basics of space planning does not focus on any particular type of interior facility or function. The demonstration project, Design Program 25, has a mix of office, residential and meeting functions. The nine design programs in the Skill Development Exercises in the Appendix involve a variety of interior functions. All of them have some element of office use, and there are several meeting/assembly spaces, as well as some involvement in business, health care, dining and exhibit spaces.

It is rare to find an interior designer or architect who designs every type of interior facility or building. There are two primary reasons for this. First, most interior and building types are complex and require specialized knowledge and experience to provide high quality professional service. Being fully knowledgeable and experienced in more than one or two specialized areas is both difficult and unusual. Second, the great majority of clients expect to hire a design professional who is highly experienced in the type of facility that they plan on completing. One would expect a restauranteur, planning to open a new restaurant, to engage a professional designer who has previously designed at least a few restaurants.

Recommended Reading

Building Codes: 2*, 4*, 13*, 25, 31*
Lighting Design: 1*, 3*, 11, 14
Acoustic Planning: 1*, 7*, 10
Planning Rules of thumb: 9*, 15*, 20*
Flexibility/Multiuse: 9*, 15*, 24*, 26*
Furniture: 6*, 15*, 20*, 24*, 26*
Spatial Quality: 6*, 8*, 12*, 23*, 27*

Books marked with an asterisk are also included in the recommended reading for other chapters.

Chapter 6 DEVELOPING A ROUGH FLOOR PLAN

After the pre-design process has been completed and bubble diagrams have produced a basic spatial organization, it is time to get to the heart of the matter and develop a floor plan that satisfies client or user needs. It should be restated at the outset that the planning process involves a series of compromises between conflicting criteria. The process regularly involves the weighing of pros and cons of many varied configurations in which all user needs are rarely, if ever, satisfied. In simpler terms, the space planner would be unrealistic to expect a perfect solution satisfying all the program requirements in detail.

Even relatively small space planning problems are full of complex and often conflicting requirements, plus many demands for subtle and sensitive design judgments by the planner. Consequently, space planning skills are best developed in a progressive manner, starting with the relatively small and simple and slowly building to larger, more complex problems. This chapter takes a step-by-step process in the development of a rough or first-phase floor plan. The approach presented here makes a distinct separation between this first-phase plan and the subsequent development of a final preliminary floor plan, described in detail in Chapter 7. The distinction between these two stages identifies the rough floor plan as an interim "design tool" phase, and the final preliminary plan as one that, after a refining process, develops into the presentation form, either for the classroom or for the client. At the end of this chapter, planning exercises using 1,500-square-foot programs and shells in the Appendix are recommended. Planning exercises for the larger 2,500-square-foot and 4,000-square-foot sizes are reserved for Chapter 7.

As stated at the outset, the progressive learning experience presented here assumes that the reader is reasonably proficient in furniture planning within single spaces—living rooms, bedrooms, private offices, conference rooms, and so on. If those skills are lacking or have not been used for some time, a methodical series of furniture-planning exercises in typical residential and non-residential spaces is essential before proceeding further. Experience with larger, more complex furniture arrangements, while not essential, is quite valuable in the process of acquiring space planning skills. The larger arrangements include public lounges or waiting rooms, restaurant or club dining rooms, multiple desk or workstation offices (both conventional and systems furniture), and large-scale or multiuse conference and meeting rooms, among others. If your competence in any of these areas is limited, it is very important to systematically go through a series of large-scale furniture arrangement studies before venturing into the development of a rough floor plan. The following exercise is strongly recommended for that kind of skill development experience.

EXERCISE 6-1

Draw at least one (and possibly more) plan sketch for each of the spaces listed below, including each of the size variations suggested. Although this may seem a laborious process, the plan sketches themselves may be quickly drawn with reasonable accuracy, and the gain in skills can be considerable. Drawing quality is not of much importance in this learning experience, and this exercise can also be used to improve drawing skills, if desired. One can experiment with a variety of drawing techniques, both hand drawn (freehand, hard line) or on the computer (using varying line types and weights). Scale with the smaller size variations should be at ¼" = 1'-0", while scale with the larger size variations should be at ⅛" = 1'-0"; every planner should feel comfortable working at both scales. Approach these exercises from a two-dimensional viewpoint; though you may keep an eye on three-dimensional implications, the floor plan context should be the dominant focus.

- A corporate headquarters reception area with a reception desk to seat 6 people. Then try 10-, 15-, and 20-person spaces. Assume a ground floor location, with the entrance door in a floor-to-ceiling glass wall.

- A law firm's conference room to seat 6 people, followed by one to seat 10 people, with modest accommodation for audiovisual facilities (front-projection slides and film, large-screen video); then try one for 20 people. Assume a windowed wall opposite the entrance door.

- An executive dining room (waiter service) to seat 16 people. Then try similar rooms for 24 and 40 people. Assume a corner space with windows on two sides, and identify the kitchen door location.

- A university conference suite for 40 people in a lecture setting, which can be divided by a moveable partition to create two seminar rooms to accommodate 8 and 12 people, respectively. Then try a similar facility with lecture seating for 100 and seminar rooms for 12 and 24, respectively. Assume entry from a corridor, with a windowed wall opposite the corridor.

- A secretarial pool for 6 people at workstations, each equipped for word processing and containing 9 linear feet of letter files plus three box storage drawers and 8 linear feet of book or catalog shelves. Then try secretarial pools with 12 and 20 workstations with the same requirements. Assume a column-free space on an upper floor of a typical center core (elevators, toilet rooms, etc.) office tower, with 40'-0" between the core wall and the exterior wall, which has a continuous band of windows and a 3'-0"-high sill.

- A public utility customer service facility with a central receptionist, waiting area for 8 people, and 6 interview stations (each station to contain a CRT with keyboard, 4 linear feet of letter files, and two box drawers, plus two guest chairs). Try it again with waiting areas for 12 and 20 people and 8 and 15 interview stations, respectively. Assume a ground-floor location, with the entrance door in a floor-to-ceiling glass wall.

The situations described above are just a sampling of many possible furniture arrangement exercises. Try some others as well, using reasonably typical non-residential settings; it shouldn't be too difficult to improve on many of the design results of existing facilities seen in design publications.

Useful rules of thumb are often developed from furniture arrangement studies, including the prototypical plan sketches described and recommended to establish square footage requirements in the development of a criteria matrix. Their value is not only numerical (how many square feet are required for specific uses), but also visual and geometric (what room configurations are best for specific uses). The experienced space planner slowly compiles a mental list or vocabulary, sometimes recorded in notes and sketches, of space standards that will help solve future planning problems more easily and efficiently. Many designers develop a personal computer file or library of drawings, figures, and notations that can be used again and again. Although some standards of this kind are published (auditorium seating, cafeteria dining, etc.), hands-on development of these rules of thumb provides the planner with a more flexible and useful working tool.

GETTING STARTED

Regardless of drawing medium or technique, the process for developing a rough floor plan is primarily the same. After bubble diagrams or block plans have been completed and the best diagram (as described in Chapter 2) has been selected for the development of a rough floor plan, the two essential tools are that diagram and a base plan of the building shell at matching scales. The decision to work on paper or a computer screen is one of personal familiarity and comfort; the space planning outcome will not be influenced by that decision. For those new to the space planning process, it is probably best to experiment with both approaches before deciding on one technique or the other.

If working with pencil or pen on tracing paper, place a tracing paper version of the diagram over the base plan. If a tracing paper or Mylar film version of the shell plan is available, place the diagram under the shell plan, so that the shell plan is more visually dominant than the diagram. Place a fresh sheet of tracing paper over the combined shell/diagram plans, using a better quality paper than used for the diagram, because a lot of erasing is likely to occur in the development of a rough floor plan. (It is not necessary to use the best quality tracing paper for this process because it is unlikely that this will become the final or presentation preliminary floor plan). Use a fairly bold line when drawing the rough floor plan, so that your rough scheme becomes the visually dominant element on the drawing board; this will help to focus on the newly developed plan, rather than the shell on the sheet below.

If working with a computer program, place layered images of the diagram and the base plan on the screen, using a light gray or other pale color for the diagram and black or other bold tone for the base plan. A bubble diagram or block plan can be generated with a stylus and digital pad or can be scanned from a previously developed paper drawing. A block plan can easily be generated as an original CADD drawing on its own layer. Once the combined shell and diagram plans are visible on the screen, the development of the rough floor plan, on its own layer, should be done in a bold and colorfully dominant line, in order to make it the strongest visual element on the screen.

Still another useful drawing strategy is to start with traditional pencil and tracing paper and work with this method until a spatially recognizable rough plan can be seen (probably at the point where basic furniture placement is needed), and then convert to a new computer-generated plan, completing the rough plan with CADD. Moving from hand drawing to digital drawing, as described above, is demonstrated in the step-by-step illustrations that follow in this chapter. Just as there are no "perfect" space planning solutions, there are no "perfect" drawing techniques for developing a rough floor plan; each designer must find a personalized approach that is best suited to his or her own thought processes and work habits. In addition, there are no approaches that seem best for today or that one can be sure will be the best in a few years; the rapid change and growth in digital technologies are sure to bring unforeseen new tools and techniques.

For the sake of continuity, the same design program, 2S (page 179), and building shell, 2S (page 204), used for descriptive illustration in Chapters 1 and 2 will continue to be used for illustrative purposes in this chapter, with bubble diagram D in illustration 2–2B (page 33) used as the best diagram.

As the rough plan emerges and divergences from the diagram multiply, as they usually do, it may become desirable to remove the diagram (either tracing paper or layer image) completely, since it is no longer very relevant and may be more of a distraction or nuisance than a help. Unlike the preceding bubble diagramming/block planning process, which is so strongly intuitive in nature, the development of a rough floor plan, while still requiring spontaneity and intuition, is decidedly more methodical and predictable. Although one can vary from the step-by-step process described below and shown in Illustrations 6–1 through 6–11, the process through this phase of plan development should be highly organized. To stay on track, keep the criteria matrix within view throughout the process and make frequent reference to it; do not rely upon your memory.

CONSTRUCTION REALITY

From the outset, the rough floor plan drawing should be realistic rather than diagrammatic. If it isn't, it is likely that dimensional inaccuracies will make the plan impractical or unworkable at a later stage. Partitions should be drawn with appropriate thickness; 4" is a good nominal dimension for most preliminary floor plans, with 8" thickness for partitions containing plumbing waste lines and 1'-6" to 2'-6" for complex or multiuse pipe chases.

START WITH PLUMBING

The previously completed diagramming process established the point of entrance to the space and a basic circulation path. Because those planning decision have already been made, the best approach is to start the planning process with the dimensionally demanding and plumbing-system-bound spaces, such as kitchens, bathrooms, and restrooms, since their sizes and possible locations within the shell are least flexible. Occasionally there are existing conditions that permit unrestricted locating of plumbing fixtures, but those cases are rare. And remember to adhere to the increased square footage demands of barrier-free requirements. Illustration 6–1 demonstrates this first step. Note that the 10'-0" limitation on the placement of plumbing fixtures from the north wall and the wet column has been graphically identified on the plan.

MAJOR SPACES NEXT

In most cases, one or two unusually large or functionally dominant (heavily used) spaces exist. It's a good idea to work with these next, since they are of critical importance to the functioning of the whole and may only fit in a limited number of locations within the shell, based on existing structural or building configuration conditions. A fairly accurate room size and shape, plus the location of access doors and other planning details, such as required equipment, built-ins, or storage closets, are important to establish at this early stage. See Illustration 6–2, in which the seminar room, the interview stations, and the guest apartment have been hard-lined.

CIRCULATION STUDIES

Look next to the circulation spaces—those defined by partitions (corridors and required exit stairs) and those that are traffic aisles within larger spaces. Circulation paths are often not well defined in bubble diagrams or block plans and can be deceptively space-consuming. There are also very demanding building code requirements concerning paths of circulation and means of egress, which are discussed in Chapter 4; these code requirements should be kept in mind throughout the rough plan development phase. More specifically, check your plan for two remote means of egress, maximum length of

travel to an exit, corridor widths, dead end corridors, corridor obstruction, and so on. It is also a good idea to check at this point on the efficiency of the circulation space and determine the percentage of space consumed by corridors and other pathways. See Illustration 6-3, in which the total circulation space consumes 21.7 percent of the total space.

A common error made by inexperienced space planners is the unnecessary continuation of dead-end corridors, as shown in the "right" and "wrong" sketches of Illustration 6–4. In general, efficient use of circulation space should be a high-priority planning criterion so that valuable square footage is not wasted and to make traffic patterns within the space convenient for its users.

BASIC ROOM ALLOCATIONS

Proceed with the remainder of the basic room allocations. Continue to keep program requirements in mind, including appropriate priority for spaces that demand light and air, privacy, and acoustic control (quiet zones). Don't lose sight of door swing conflicts in this early planning phase, because as the plan solidifies, it becomes more difficult to rectify those conflicts. The best way to guard against this is to draw door swings as the plan develops, rather than wait until later. See Illustration 6–5.

FURNITURE AND EQUIPMENT

As tentative decisions for partition locations are made to form rooms and spaces, the placement of basic furniture and equipment should follow shortly; if too much time goes by, it may be discovered that in one or more spaces, due to size and/or configuration (room shape, door and window locations, etc.), it is impossible to meet program requirements. It is not necessary or desirable to finalize furniture placement to the last detail at this stage, but it is very important to know that basic furniture arrangements will work well. In Illustration 6–6, demonstrating the first incorporation of furniture, the bubble diagram has been removed; as suggested earlier, the diagram becomes more hindrance than help as the rough plan progresses. In the previous rough plan illustrations (6-1, 6-2, 6-3, and 6-5), the plan development was drawn with pencil on a tracing paper overlay. In Illustration 6-6,

ROUGH PLAN, STAGE ONE: PLUMBING USE SPACES

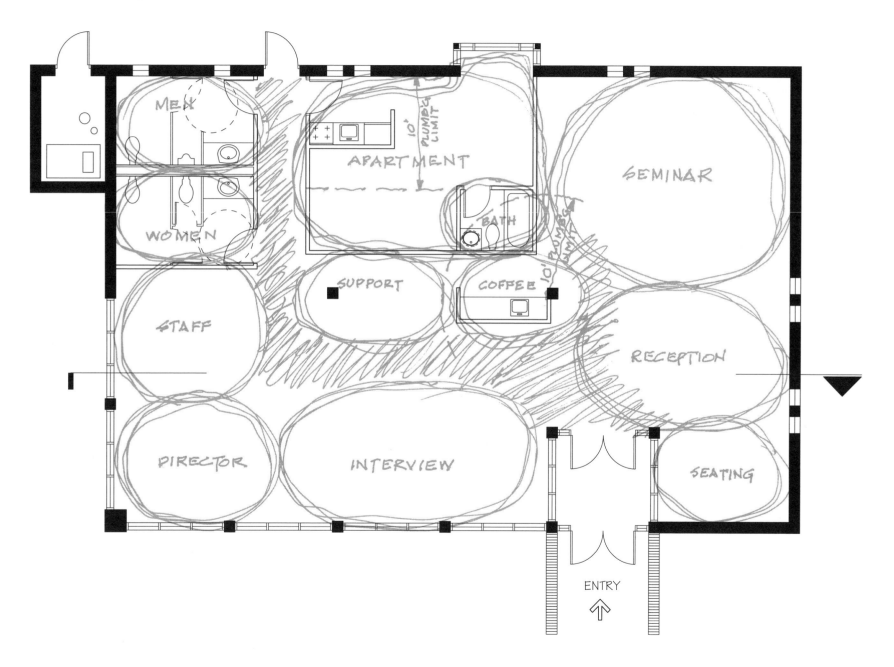

ENTRY

ROUGH PLAN, STAGE TWO: INCORPORATE MAJOR SPACES

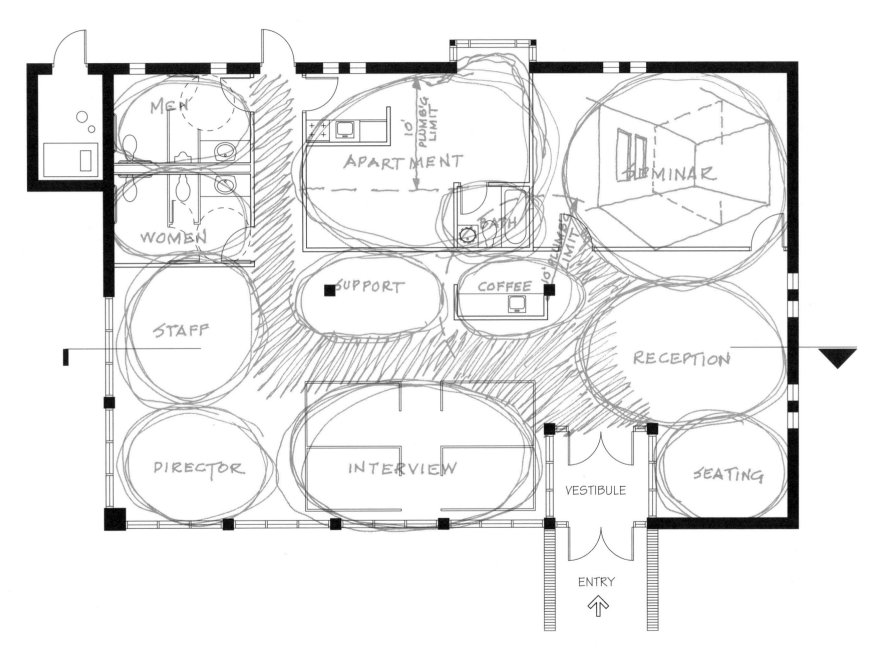

ROUGH PLAN, STAGE THREE: INCORPORATE CIRCULATE SPACES

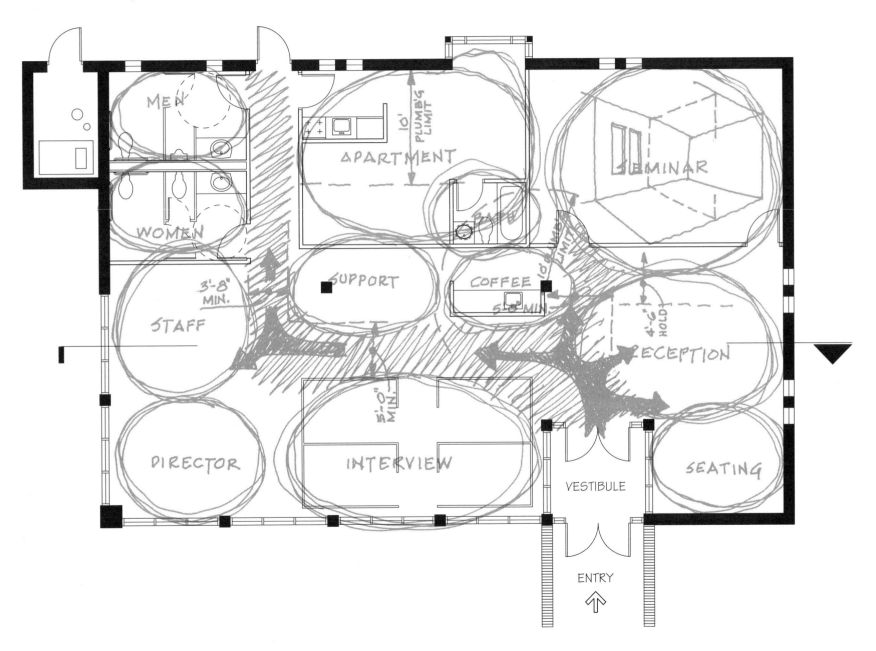

EFFICIENT CORRIDOR PLANNING

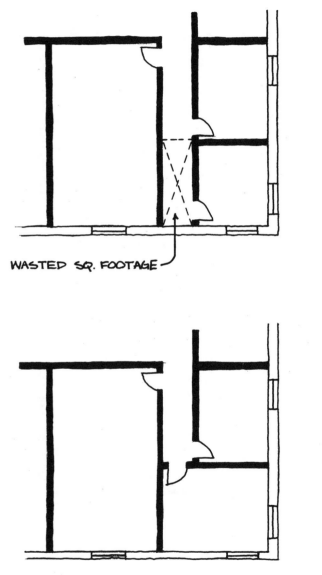

WASTED SQ. FOOTAGE

CORRECTED

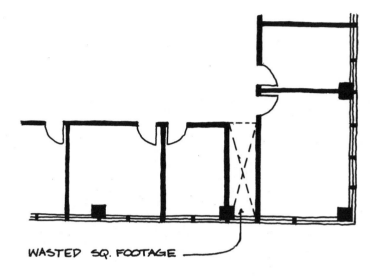

WASTED SQ. FOOTAGE

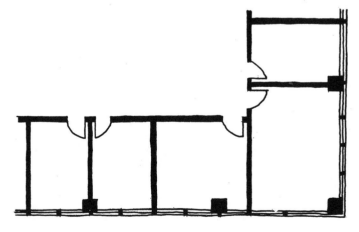

CORRECTED

ROUGH PLAN, STAGE FOUR: BASIC ROOM ALLOCATIONS

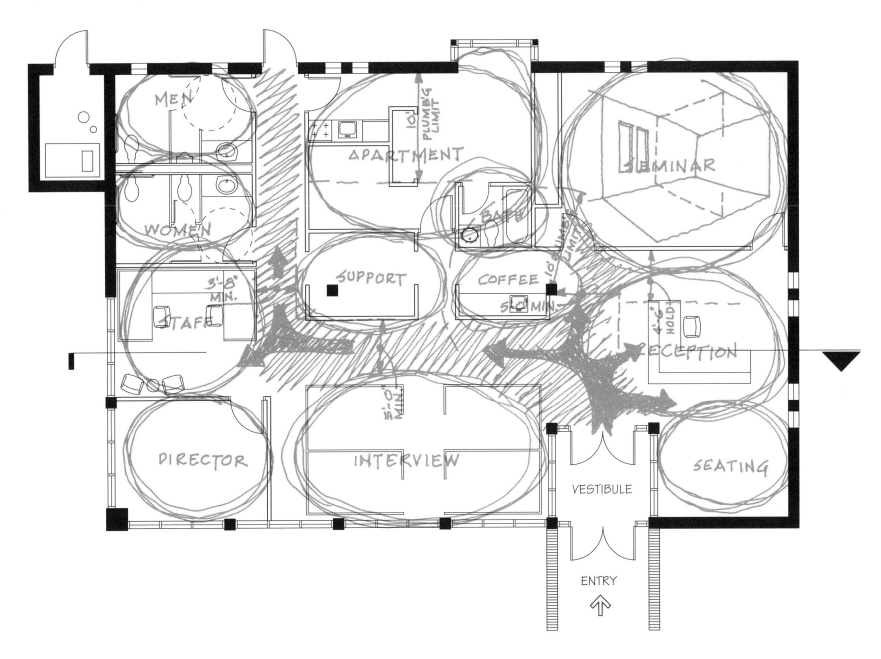

MEN

WOMEN

APARTMENT

10'

PLUMB'S LIMIT

SEMINAR

BATH

3'-8" MIN.

STAFF

SUPPORT

COFFEE

5'-0 MIN.

10' LIMIT

4'-0" HOLD

RECEPTION

5'-0" MIN.

DIRECTOR

INTERVIEW

VESTIBULE

SEATING

ENTRY

ROUGH PLAN, STAGE FIVE: INCORPORATE FURNITURE

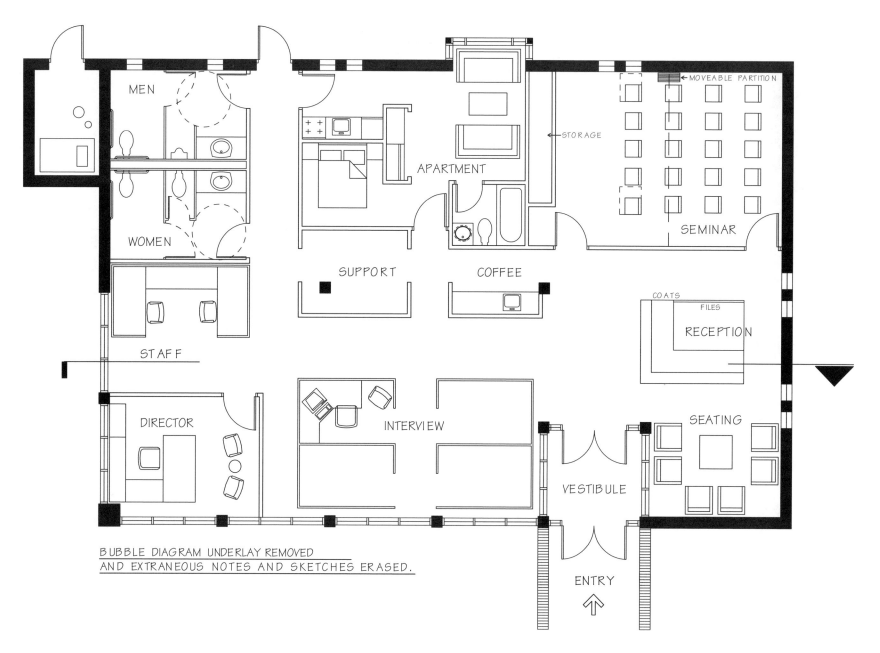

MEN

WOMEN

STAFF

DIRECTOR

APARTMENT

SUPPORT

COFFEE

INTERVIEW

STORAGE

← MOVEABLE PARTITION

SEMINAR

COATS

FILES

RECEPTION

SEATING

VESTIBULE

ENTRY

BUBBLE DIAGRAM UNDERLAY REMOVED
AND EXTRANEOUS NOTES AND SKETCHES ERASED.

the drawing mode is CADD. As mentioned earlier, choice of drawing medium is usually based on personal factors; if CADD has not been used in the plan development to this point, and if the finished plan is to be CADD-drawn, this is a good point at which to make the switch in drawing method. Note that the furniture should be drawn on its own layer.

Remember that most furniture and equipment require adjacent space for appropriate use; too often these basic dimensional issues are forgotten— for example, when a conference table is too close to an adjacent wall to permit comfortable seating, when a sofa is too close to a coffee table for comfortable access, or when a bed is placed so that it is almost impossible to be made easily. Some furniture and equipment have moving parts (such as drawers) or required servicing space (such as copying machines) that demand spatial accommodation. To forget these factors could result in poorly functioning rooms. A common example is not to provide proper allowance for the opening of file drawers, described in the "right" and "wrong" sketches in Illustration 6–7.

STORAGE AND FILING

Storage and filing requirements are often deceptive; make sure that program requirements for filing cabinets, storage closets, coat hanging space, storage for stacking chairs and folding tables, and the like have been met. See Illustration 6–8, in which chair and table storage for the seminar room has been refined, leaving room for a bookshelf and TV niche in the guest apartment sitting area; required lateral files and coat storage have been incorporated in the reception area, and the work area and coffee station have been rearranged to provide for the required files, storage cabinet, and copier.

SPATIAL QUALITY

The issues related to the importance of deliberately testing the three-dimensional consequences of the evolving floor plan early in its development have already been raised in Chapters 3 and 5. How do the spaces feel to people moving through them? Are the size, scale, and proportions of a space appropriate to the number of people who will pass through it? Spatial use runs the gamut from intimate (a bedroom) to public (a theater lobby). Does the scale

FILE DRAWER ACCOMODATION ILLUS. 6–7

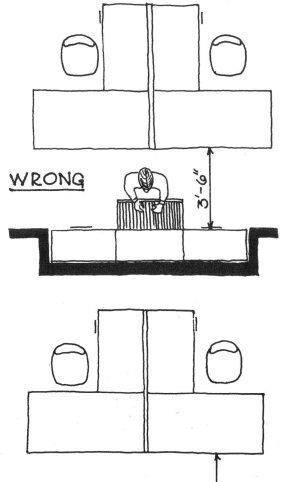

WRONG   3'-6"

RIGHT   5'-0"

ROUGH PLAN, STAGE SIX: INCORPORATE FILING STORAGE

ILLUS. 6-8

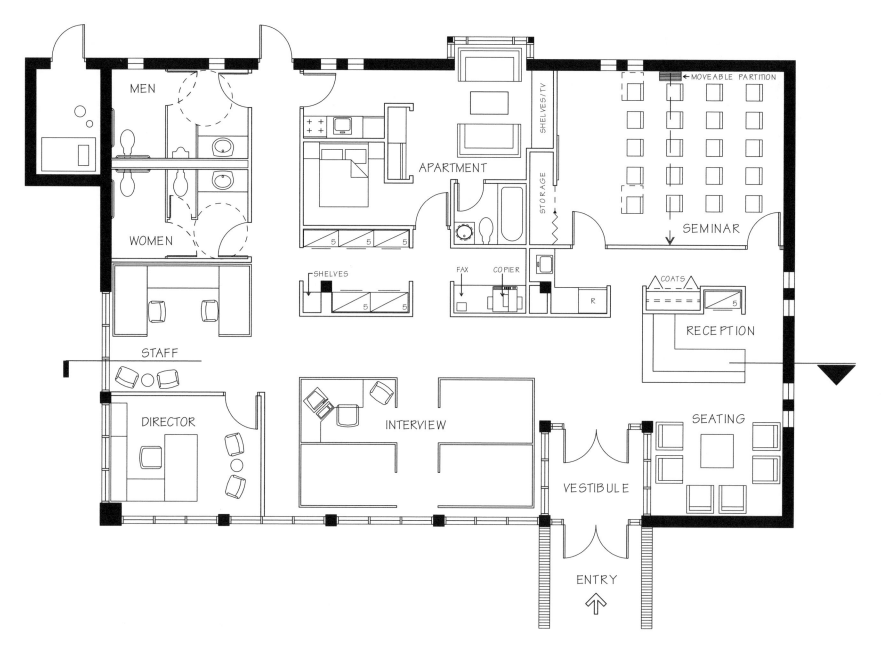

of each space appropriately reflect its use in this sense? Has the potential of spaces with high ceiling height been taken advantage of? Have spaces been made visually varied and interesting, using changing ceiling heights and soffit areas? When appropriate, are rhythmic or sequential spatial experiences provided? Are the proportions of walls and spaces pleasing? With the rough floor plan nearing completion, now is the critical moment to test and evaluate its three-dimensional potential. Look at the main entrance area, travel paths, major spaces, special spaces, and other elements. There is still plenty of time to adjust the plan to better satisfy spatial quality. See Illustration 6–9, in which the two reduced rough sketches, the one on the left hand-drawn and the other CADD-drawn, demonstrate this type of preliminary spatial testing.

REVIEW

A basic review is extremely valuable at the point when an entire floor plan can first be seen, no matter how sketchy it may be. This is a self-review in which the designer's skills in objective criticism should be called upon and exercised. Get out a bold or colored pencil or marker and a roll of sketch tracing paper for an overlay, or a print of the plan, and make note of all the plan's qualities that are lacking or ways in which it fails to meet the requirements established in the criteria matrix. Check the plan for the following points.

Program Requirements

Does the plan satisfy the program requirements? Now is the time to catch a forgotten space or function or a miscount in the number of people or operations to be served, rather than after a great deal more time has been spent in the further development and refinement of the plan. The criteria matrix technique for problem analysis, recommended in Chapter 1, is an excellent tool at this point to see if the program requirements have been fulfilled, not just in numbers but in basic issues of function and aesthetics as well, such as space adjacencies, acoustic isolation, or spatial quality.

Code Requirements

Are building code requirements complied with for safe egress from the building? Although code issues should be kept in mind throughout the rough plan development process, as the plan comes together as an entity for the first time, a basic overview for code compliance should be made. Now is the time

to catch such things as unacceptable lengths of travel, unnecessarily long or dead-end corridors, or unsuitable corridor and stair widths, rather then after significant plan refinement has been accomplished.

Barrier-Free Requirements

Is there compliance with barrier-free design standards required by law or by user needs? It is difficult, if not impossible, to try to adjust a refined floor plan that has not accommodated barrier-free needs to one that meets those needs well. Now is the time to make the plan conform with these requirements.

Detailed Requirements

Do conflicts exist in the detailed aspects of planning—door swings, tight clearances between pieces of furniture, inclusion of required equipment (appliances, fixtures, communication devices), windows for habitable rooms, dimensions between plumbing fixtures and waste lines, and so on? Although one has time to catch these details at a later point in the process, the more that can be accomplished now, the greater the savings in time and effort later.

As this review process comes to an end, the tracing paper overlay or marked-up print of the rough floor plan probably looks something like the marked-up plan in Illustration 6–10. Revise the rough floor plan now, to correct as many of the planning flaws or inconsistencies found in the review process as possible. Keep in mind that not all the program requirements can be met; if all the major issues and most of the other basic requirements are resolved, the plan may come as close to a successful problem resolution as possible. Illustration 6–11 shows the rough floor plan revised to address most of the flaws noted in the previous illustration.

REVISIONS

After going through the long and often difficult process to arrive at a revised rough floor plan, the planner may look at the result and believe that the present solution is too far removed from the best possible solution to consider it acceptable. The only recourse is to begin again with another of the refined bubble diagrams or block plans developed earlier. Despite this difficult decision, the second development of a rough floor plan will take much less time than the first. At the outset of a second start, the original plan development will provide insights about what will and won't work, and the selection of a

TWO THUMBNAIL PERSPECTIVE SKETCHES

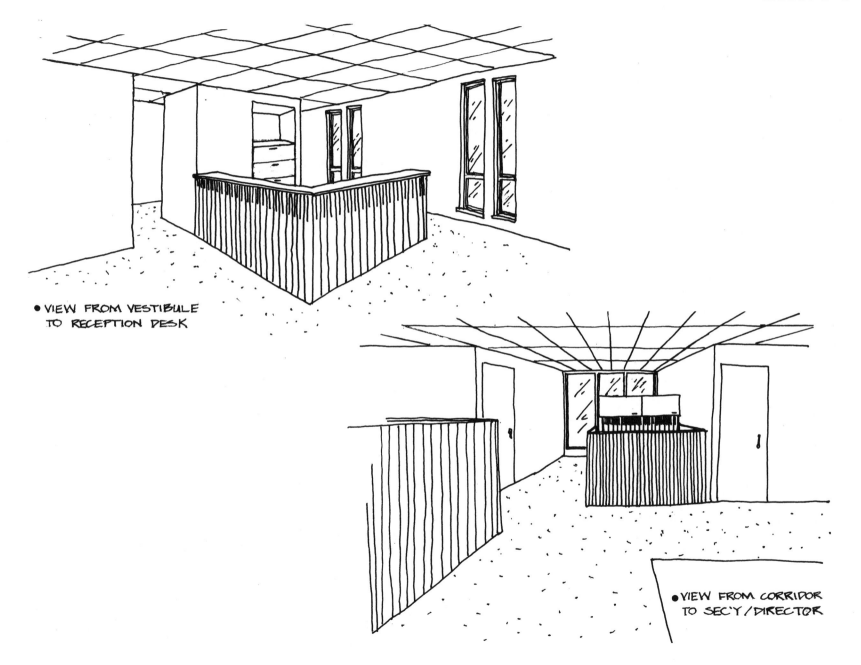

● VIEW FROM VESTIBULE
TO RECEPTION DESK

● VIEW FROM CORRIDOR
TO SEC'Y / DIRECTOR

ROUGH PLAN — MARKED-UP CORRECTIONS

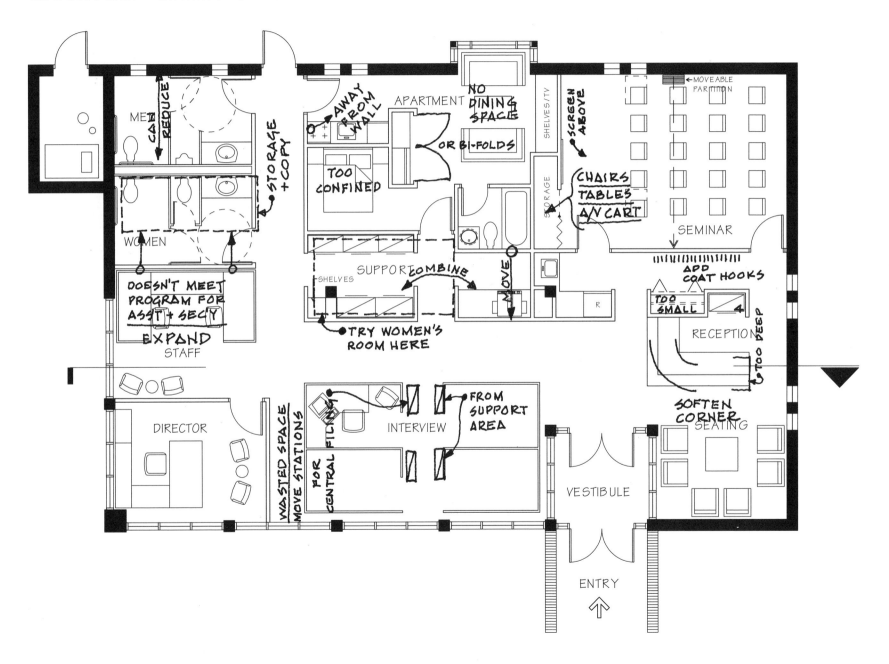

ROUGH PLAN REVISED (BASED ON MARKED-UP CORRECTIONS)

ILLUS. 6–11

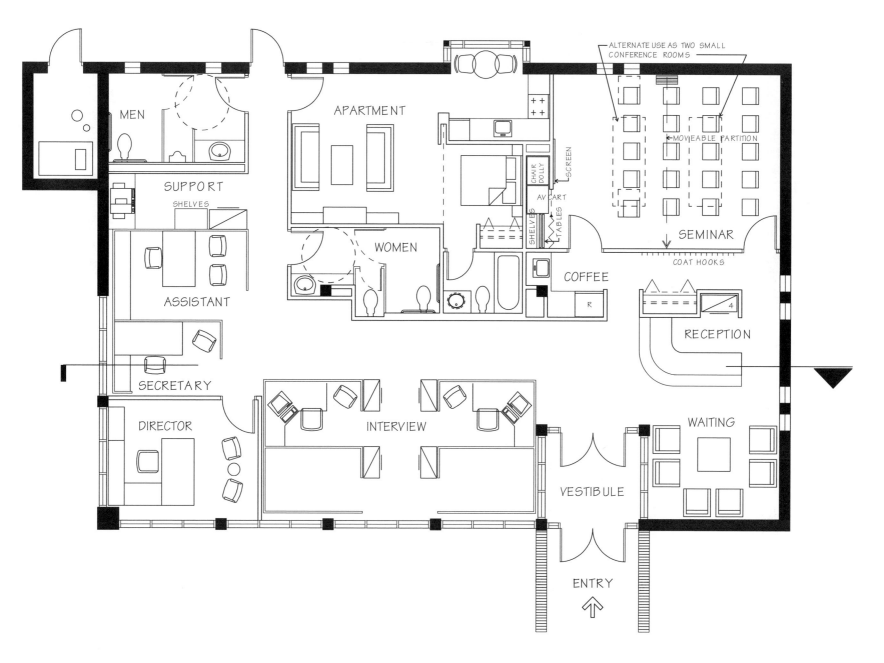

second refined bubble diagram or block plan will be done with much more knowledge than the first. More importantly, the time-consuming thought and data search efforts that went into the first try will not have to be repeated. These comments about a second attempt at a rough floor plan are not meant to be discouraging; the basic process recommended here is usually successful, but one should not fear making the tough judgment to repeat the process. The fundamental success of an interior planning solution lies in the workability and aesthetic qualities of the spatial arrangements contained in the rough floor plan; your design solutions deserve your best efforts in this critical phase of the design process.

It is early in the planning process to consider non-space-planning issues, but once a workable rough plan has been developed, it is extremely valuable to develop a rough reflected ceiling and lighting plan. The ceiling configuration has such great potential to create sculptural quality that this aspect of the reflected ceiling plan should be given major priority while the three-dimensional characteristics of the space are still malleable. From a lighting design perspective, simple or standard rooms or functions can be given rudimentary attention at this point, but more complex spaces or functions requiring multiple lighting systems or multilevel ceilings can and should receive design attention. All aspects of the ceiling configuration (soffits, sloping surfaces, skylights, acoustic tile grids, etc.) and the use of luminaires (recessed, surface, pendant, wall-mounted, etc.) may clearly suggest revisions in the rough floor plan that are best made now, before the plan becomes solidified and difficult to change. Illustration 6–12, which can be accomplished as a tracing paper overlay or a separate CADD layer, shows the kind of rough reflected ceiling plan appropriate at this stage of planning development.

In a typical professional setting, this is the ideal time to have the first discussions with appropriate consultants, such as engineers, contractors, and specialists (acoustic, food service, etc.), to get their first input concerning spatial needs, adjacencies, accommodation of equipment, and any other issues bearing on space allocations, while it is still easy to make changes to the rough floor plan. The details of these issues can wait until after the final preliminary floor plans and other design development drawings have been approved by the client. Beyond that point, the next round of meetings with consultants is usually scheduled, but a first meeting with consultants during the rough floor plan phase can reduce the need to revise plans after the design development documents have been completed.

The suggestion that the designer should develop a rough reflected ceiling plan and consider specialized space and equipment needs (with or without consultants) at this early point in the space planning process may seem to pull the designer away from the primary task of developing a preliminary floor plan. Despite the step-by-step space planning process suggested here, do not forget that the entire design problem-solving process is highly creative and cannot appropriately be confined to a simple deductive reasoning process. As discussed in Chapter 1, designers must learn to think in a lateral (rather than vertical or hierarchical) manner, permitting complex, divergent, and sometimes conflicting factors to bear appropriately on the solution. Although the complexities presented by the consideration of these non-space-planning issues may be difficult to deal with because they introduce new sets of factors to an already formidable tangle of factors. it is best to raise them now, rather than have them come as a surprise later.

The classroom presents a unique opportunity for evaluation and critique rarely encountered again in professional practice. The experience of having peers working on similar design problems at the same time is not likely to be repeated. In addition to the valued insights and critique that the studio instructor has to offer on a one-to-one basis, many other forms of feedback, both formal and informal, are offered in the classroom. Particularly at this rough floor plan stage, major insights are to be gained from discussion and comparison of the planning process, the drawing tools and techniques, and the interim results of this first tentative plan. Such an exchange of ideas can occur in one-to-one conversation with another student, small group discussions and comparisons, or classwide critiques or pinups of work in progress. Learning opportunities of this kind will be hard to find in the professional setting; make maximum use of them now. Chapter 7 will include follow-up discussion of critiquing the final preliminary plan and critiques in the real world beyond.

The rough floor plan process described in this chapter must be put to work and experienced before it can have real meaning or value. The exercises following are geared exactly to that purpose. Before reading Chapter 7, in which the next and final step in the space planning process is described, it is important to try at least two or three rough floor plans without attempting to refine or finalize them beyond a rough sketch drawing stage. If put to proper use, these exercises are the most valuable aspects of the entire process presented here.

ROUGH REFLECTED CEILING PLAN

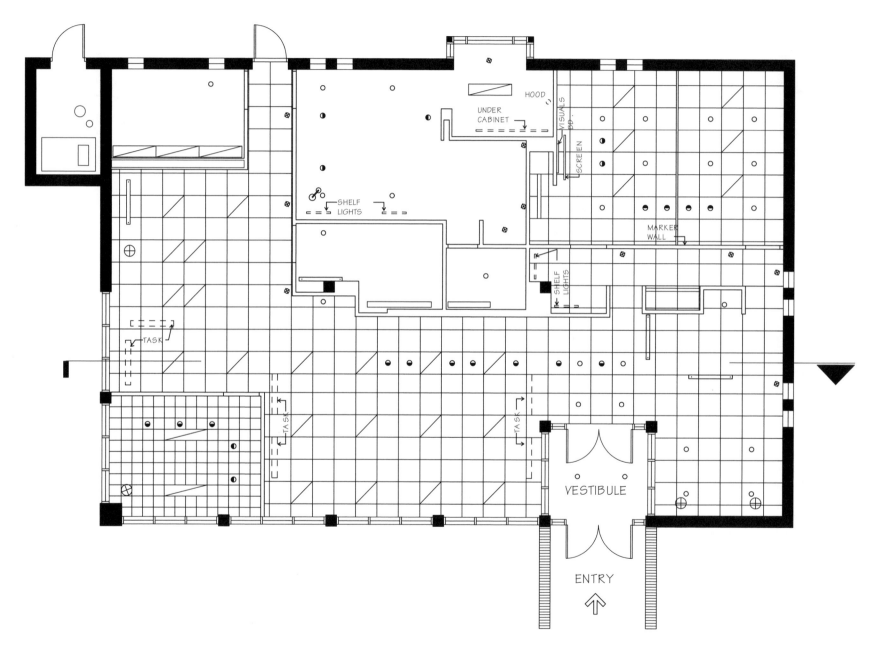

To this point, no mention of time has been made. How long should it take to develop a rough floor plan? Ultimately, the time it takes to complete a task is of importance to all professionals because of the economic factors inherent in professional practice, but during the learning process, trying to hurry the development of a plan can be counterproductive. Speed will come with experience; for now, without wasting time, be more concerned with solving these problems well, not fast. Take the same attitude in the overall development of professional-quality space planning skills. In general, if the exercises provided within the text are performed thoroughly over several weeks to a few months, a reasonable level of professional skill will be attained. Professional project experience is necessary for the full development of space planning skills. For those still in the learning process, growth and sophistication will happen in the not-too-distant future. Diligent application of energy to the solution of these exercises is critical to gain professional competence.

EXERCISE 6-2

The criteria matrixes and bubble diagrams or block plans developed for the exercises in Chapter 1 and 2 may be used now for the rough floor plan exercises recommended here; or new matrixes and diagrams can be developed. With this material in hand, develop and draw a rough floor plan for at least three of the 1,500-square-foot program/shell combinations provided in the Appendix. It is best to experiment with both hand and CADD drawing techniques in order to get a first sense of what works best for you. Most importantly, work with the process at this small scale until it feels comfortable. Ideally, both informal and formal critiques should be part of the process in order to put one's best efforts to work in the final preliminary plan development described in Chapter 7.

One could immediately move on to develop rough floor plans for the 2,500-square-foot and 4,000-square-foot program/shell combinations, but it is recommended that the development of final preliminary floor plans at the 1,500-square-foot size be accomplished first. Exercises for rough and final preliminary floor plans at the larger sizes will be recommended in Chapter 7.

It should be noted that the aggregate of program and building shell exercises provided in the Appendix are planned to give you experience with as broad a variety of interior uses and spaces as is practical. The programs run the gamut from intimate residential plans and typical office and working uses to public settings used by large numbers of people. The building shells range from residential wood-frame construction and typical low-rise, steel-frame commercial or institutional structures to high-rise office building shells. In addition to solving the mechanics of the problems presented, be aware of and sensitive to the issues of usage, scale, and architectural context when working with the exercises of this chapter and Chapter 7. As a professional, you will be called on to appropriately respond to these issues, and to a lesser degree the NCIDQ examination will also test your competence in these areas of customary professional concern.

Recommended Reading

2*, 4*, 5*, 6*, 13*, 19*, 31*

Books marked with an asterisk are also included in the recommended reading for other chapters.

Chapter 7   REFINING THE SOLUTION

Chapter 6 left the rough floor plan in an almost complete but unpresentable form. In terms of presentability, even the most informal preliminary plan expectations, such as a first-phase critique in the classroom or an in-house staff review in the professional office, would anticipate something more finished. (The rough floor plan pinup suggested in Chapter 6 would rarely happen outside of a classroom; sketchy plans of this nature would seldom, if ever, be shown at a staff review session or to a client in a professional office.) Preliminary floor plans can be completed in a simple, unpretentious manner or in a complex, flamboyant style, with possibilities ranging from one extreme to the other, depending on the requirements of the setting or situation.

The manner of completion is usually determined by the nature of the project. In the classroom, project assignments are usually given in a variety of forms, from the quick sketch problem to the full-blown design project requiring a range of presentation techniques from basic black-and-white drawings to a large set of fully rendered, colored, exhibit-quality display boards. The professional setting also demands the same broad range of techniques, from the simply drawn preliminary plan presented informally to the client across a desk to the large, formal, complex presentation of a major project in a conference room with many client representatives evaluating the design solution.

The primary concern of this text is space planning, not design presentation. Despite this, the language of space planning is the floor plan, and its graphic qualities cannot be entirely ignored. One of the premises of the planning methodology presented here is that the transition from the rough floor plan to the preliminary or presentation floor plan is part of the planning process, not just a graphic refinement. The transition phase of the process will be described first and in full detail; some comments on drawing quality and presentation technique will be added and interjected as a natural supplement to the planning process.

REFINING THE ROUGH PLAN

The development of the rough floor plan, as described in Chapter 6, suggests significant review and evaluation within the plan development process. Assuming that has been done, the concluding phase of the space planning process, the development of a "final" preliminary plan, should begin now.

Discussion of the issues related to drawing method become increasingly less important as this text proceeds. For planners who work through the rough floor plan process entirely with pencil or pen on tracing paper, it is likely (but not necessary) that they will continue to work in that mode through the refinement process. For planners who begin with or transition to working digitally through the rough floor plan process, it is likely (again, not necessary) that the refinement process will continue in digital mode. The drawing process employed should not affect the space planning results. Students are encouraged to experiment with both hand and computer drawing in order to find their best personal working method. The choice of selecting hand or digital drawing methods for final presentation drawings has other implications and is discussed later in this chapter.

If working on paper, tape down the latest revision of the rough floor plan, and then tape down a reasonably high-quality tracing paper over it (high quality because there may be a lot of erasing during the refinement process). Work with a few types of pencil leads, from soft to medium to hard, to more easily express visual importance with line weight; a door swing should read differently than a full-height partition. Basic drawing technique can range from a meticulous hard-line drafted style to a fairly loose freehand style, keeping in mind that reasonable dimensional accuracy is important; a conventional stud and drywall partition should not be mistaken for an 8" plumbing wall. Remember that this is a plan refining process and that the drawn product is not meant for presentation, except for the possibility of a classroom or in-house pinup for critique and discussion.

If working on the computer screen, copy the latest revision of the rough floor plan, and work with the copy so that a record of the latest revision has been saved. Dimensional accuracy is not an issue when working digitally; if anything, the computer's accuracy is a bit of overkill at this point. While maintaining focus on the refinement process, it is practical to make the refinement revisions with an eye to the future desired style of the finished presentation drawing. Decisions about basic drawing elements, such as type of line, line weight, poché graphics, door swings, and so on, are appropriate and time-efficient at this early stage of floor plan development. Unlike the hand-drawn product of the refinement process, the digitally drawn product can often become the basis for the presentation plan drawing.

Later in this chapter there are several illustrations of refined rough floor plans employing various drawing methods. Regardless of the drawing method employed, this refinement process presents an opportunity to see the rough floor plan from a fresh vantage point, almost demanding a closer look at the plan details for the first time in the space planning process. This opportunity should not be wasted. Although major plan changes at this point would be counterproductive, minor changes—refinements rather than revisions—are both possible and productive. Use this fresh vantage point to discover plan refinements that enhance the solution without requiring you to rethink the basic plan arrangement. This process is not unlike the final editing technique one uses with written material when moving from first to final draft. The kinds of plan refinements appropriate at this point are:

• The addition of incidental furnishings, such as an end table or floor lamp

• The change of a closet door from sliding to bifold

• The minor relocation of a partition by a few inches to, for example, better accommodate furniture or improve access

• The relocation of a door to provide better access to a room or appropriate wall space for an anticipated signage system

• The creation of a niche to accommodate a built-in unit or a decorative element

• The expanding of a pipe chase to better accommodate the plumbing system

If time pressures do not exist, this refining process can be done in a slow, methodical manner, but even if time is short, one can make several small but significant changes at this time. As suggested before, during the learning process it is best to avoid the highly pressured time frame to get the most out of each planning step. It is recommended here that you incorporate this refinement phase into your basic approach to space planning and assume that it will become an integral part of your personal space planning process.

THE PRELIMINARY FLOOR PLAN

As the plan refinement process comes to a close, the planner is ready to start a final preliminary or presentation plan drawing. That drawing is usually the fundamental or central element of a typical interior design project presentation. If you are working digitally, the only cautionary note is to be careful to avoid smearing the wet ink as the print emerges from the plotter. If you are working by hand, there are several cautionary notes that should be considered. Start at the top of the drawing and work down in order to minimize working over completed portions of the drawing, making it easier to maintain sharp and clean pencil lines or avoid going over wet ink or marker lines. Some designers have a difficult time keeping a pencil drawing sharp and clean; if this is the case, try using pounce or a crumbled eraser compound, or keep finished portions of the drawing covered with inexpensive tracing paper while completing the balance of the sheet, to avoid rubbing over lines with hands or drafting tools.

DRAWING QUALITY AND TECHNIQUES

The subject of drawing quality warrants some basic comment here. The original end product of space planning is a floor plan, which can only be expressed in graphic form, making the connection between planning and graphic quality inescapable. The quality of one's planning efforts is expressed not in words but in a unique drawing language universally understood by designers, architects, engineers, contractors, and others who work in the world of building environments. It follows that the planner should know

that language well, and that working on the exercises presented here should be seen as an opportunity to concurrently develop drawing skills and a repertoire of techniques.

Good drawing quality will provide a readable floor plan and create a positive impression on critics in a classroom or clients in a professional practice setting. Remember that a floor plan is really a horizontal section taken through a building (normally assumed at 4'-0" above the floor) and should present a good pictorial view of the building from above, after the portion of the building above the section line has (in theory) been removed. Good and consistent line quality should be maintained, and line weights should appropriately express the degree of importance of the building or furnishing element being drawn. More specifically, the architectural elements being cut through by the drawing plane section line (walls and partitions) should be drawn with the darkest and boldest line, major items of furniture and equipment (such as plumbing fixtures) should be drawn with a medium-weight line, and minor elements of the plan such as door swings, area rugs, floor tile patterns, or wood grains should be drawn with the lightest lines. The experienced designer, over time, develops drawing techniques with a broad range of graphic subtleties that represent a complex and articulate language rivaling all of the intricacies and shadings of verbal language.

When drawing with pencil, varying line weights can be accomplished primarily by using a relatively soft lead for the darkest lines, a medium weight for the middle-value lines, and a relatively hard lead for the lightest lines, although the degree of pressure exerted by one's hand is also a factor in controlling line weight. It's impossible to recommend specific lead weights, because the type of paper being used and the personal tendency to apply hand pressure when drawing are unknown variables. Generally, when using conventional pencil leads on good-quality tracing paper, an F or HB lead should work well for the darkest lines, a 2H or 3H is appropriate for the middle-weight lines, and a 4H or 5H usually works well for the light lines.

The greatest value in using ink is its boldness and clarity; the negative factor is the lack of varying tones of gray. Line weight must be controlled by line thickness only. Although conventional wisdom often advises against mixing pencil and ink techniques, no absolute rule exists against it. That combination can be very effective, particularly if the final product is to be reproduced. Similarly, despite conventions to the contrary, a combination of drafted or hard-line and freehand techniques is often quite effective, particularly when the hard line is used for the architectural elements and the freehand line is used for furnishings, equipment, and other graphic notations, such as material indications. Clearly, the development of drawing skills requires repeated experimentation over considerable time.

A note about drawing templates: On floor plans, they are normally used for door swings, plumbing fixtures, and furniture. They are invaluable, in terms of time expended, for uniquely shaped furniture (a specific chair), equipment (a toilet or bathtub), or repetitive items (auditorium seating). Despite this, one should be selective in their use and generally opt to draw the item rather than use a template. In addition to providing visual consistency in the drawn quality of the plan, drawing these items by hand will avoid the amateurish or unsophisticated look too often lent by oversimplified or inappropriately shaped template forms, such as a rectangle for a sofa or an obviously traditional furniture shape in a nontraditional setting. Remember that beds and most upholstered furniture have soft or round corners.

When drawing digitally, all of the issues related to good graphic quality in a hand-drawn floor plan also apply to CADD-produced drawings. Many of the graphic elements, such as line weights and tones of gray, are programmatically and easily controlled. Instead of templates, there are generic and manufacturers' libraries of symbols and blocks, most of which are graphically appropriate. And conventional CADD drawings can be enhanced with hand-drawn sketches or images, as well as with other software programs, such as Adobe's Photoshop and Illustrator.

Illustrations 7–1 and 7–2, of a refined and completed preliminary floor plan (developed from the rough floor plan shown in Illustration 6–11), represent a very simplified and bare-bones approach to the final step in the initial planning process. Note that the first example (7–1) uses a conventional drafted technique and was CADD-drawn, although the same graphic result could easily be accomplished with a conventional hand-drafted technique. The second example (7–2) was drawn freehand except for the use of templates for the seminar room and office chairs, plumbing fixtures, and door swings; because it was originally drawn at ¼" = 1'-0" scale, the hand-drawn quality is not very noticeable in this reduced image.

Although you should ultimately strive for a more developed drawing product, these drawing techniques are reasonably communicative and should be adequate for many informal purposes, from classroom presentations to professional settings. Many occasions call for this kind of simple plan drawing, particularly when something more descriptive or complex would be inappropriate.

Make note of several detailed aspects of these two drawings:

- Each drawing is consistent in using one technique exclusively. Another quite successful approach is to use the hard line of Illustration 7–1 for the architectural elements and the freehand style of Illustration 7–2 for furnishings and other non-architectural elements.

- Line weights vary in relation to their building and furnishings use and importance, as described earlier.

- A few plan refinements have been made, following the rough floor plan revision of Illustration 6–11. The men's room is a little smaller, the door to the guest apartment bathroom has been relocated to create a more comfortable use of the bathroom space, and a few table and floor lamps have been added.

- Except for a few standard items, furniture and equipment have been drawn without the use of a template in the hand-drawn plans of Illustrations 7-2 and 7–4.

- The low partition behind the receptionist's filing cabinet has been furred out to accommodate the actual depth of the cabinet.

- The positions of the conference tables in the seminar room are shown with a dotted line to indicate that the varying program requirements have been met.

- Storage space for seminar room tables and chairs has been refined.

- Room names are boldly lettered and underlined in each room to clearly identify each space.

- Several small lettered notations have been added to clarify the use of the space and its furnishings. Some designers may argue that these notes are not necessary on a preliminary drawing, tending to ruin the visual simplicity of the presentation. Strong arguments to the contrary state that the

MINIMAL PRESENTATION TECHNIQUE — COMPUTER DRAWN

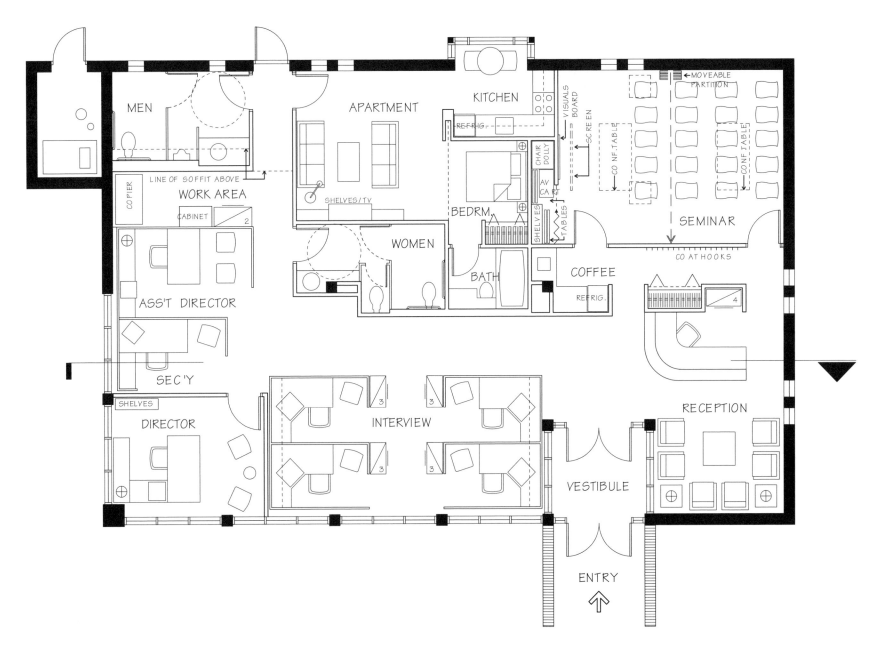

MINIMAL PRESENTATION TECHNIQUE — FREE-HAND

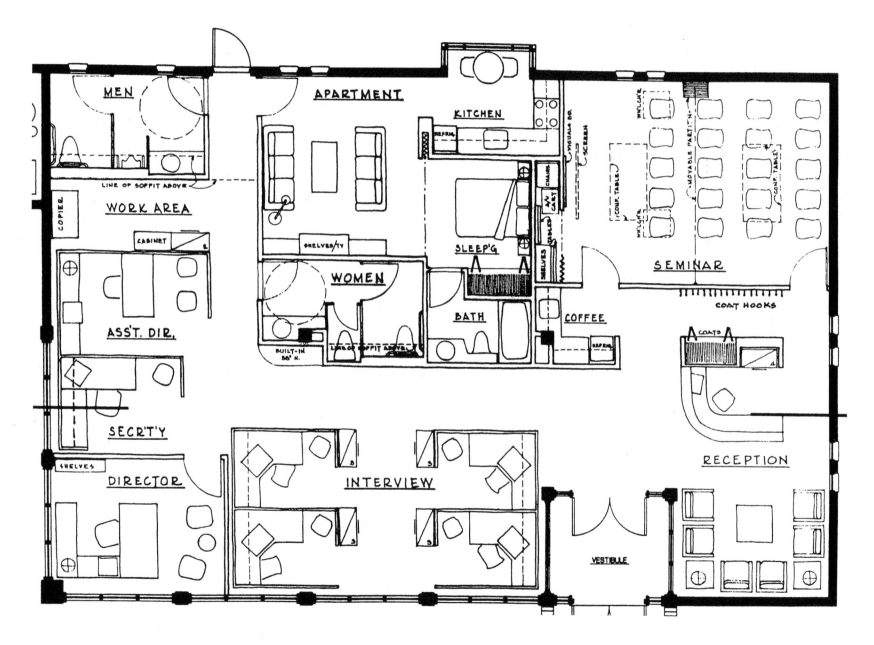

MEN

APARTMENT

KITCHEN

LINE OF SOFFIT ABOVE

WORK AREA

COPIER

CABINET

SHELVES/TV

SLEEP'G

SEMINAR

MVL'CHR.

MOVABLE PARTIN.

CONF. TABLE

CONF. TABLE

MVL'CHR.

A/V CART

CHAIRS

VISUALS DR.

SCREEN

SHELVES

COAT HOOKS

WOMEN

ASS'T. DIR.

BATH

COFFEE

COATS

REFRIG.

BUILT-IN 36" H.

LINE OF SOFFIT ABOVE

REFRIG.

SECR'T'Y

RECEPTION

SHELVES

DIRECTOR

INTERVIEW

VESTIBULE

visual language of the floor plan is not complete without them and requires augmentation with verbal notes. This issue can be decided by the designer either as a general rule or case by case. The approach presented here favors a judicious use of verbal notations.

The bare-bones approach of Illustrations 7–1 and 7–2, while adequate and appropriate for many classroom and professional purposes, is far from the most articulate graphic language available. It is quite reasonable to strive for a descriptive and readable drawing quality that will create a more positive impression of one's professional skills to critics, jurors, clients, or anyone else making evaluations or judgments. A presentation enhanced beyond this bare-bones level will have many appropriate classroom and professional applications. It takes little time to add the elements shown in Illustrations 7–3 and 7–4, and the added degree of readability and professionalism is quite significant. Make note of the added elements:

• The partitions have been filled in with a tone; this technique is usually referred to as "poché" (pronounced "po-SHAY"). In the computer-drawn plan (Illustration 7–3), the pochéing process is easily accomplished, and many variations of poché are typically available, with solid tones of many colors to choose from (including a full gray scale) as well as a variety of textures and patterns. Note that the full-height partitions are pochéd with a dark or bold tone, and the partial-height (workstation) partitions are pochéd with a lighter tone, differentiating them from the full-height partitions and implying their portable and less permanent nature. In the hand-drawn plan (Illustration 7–4), the pochéing technique is applied with a lead pencil or, better, a hard wax colored pencil, using a black, gray, or essentially neutral tone. (Occasionally a situation may call for a distinct. or even bold color poché, but in most cases, the bold color is too distracting in terms of drawing content.) The poché can be done on the front or back of the tracing paper; if the tracing paper is the final presentation medium, apply the poché to the back of the paper for a more even appearance of the tone. If the tracing paper drawing is to be printed for presentation purposes, such as a black-line Ozalid print, neither the color nor the side of application is of any consequence. The darkness of the tone can vary from very light to black, depending on the pressure with which the poché is applied; a middle-depth tone is recom-

mended for most purposes. Broad- or chisel-tipped markers are often used for presentation poché, but remember that they (and other wet media) are not erasable.

• Floor tile patterns are shown in the kitchen, bathroom, and restroom spaces to better identify them in a graphic manner. In most cases, an 8" to 12" grid is appropriate for kitchens, and a 3" to 6" grid is appropriate for bathrooms and restrooms. Use a very light line for this purpose.

• Wood grain patterns are shown on items of built-in and conventional furniture to separate the plane of the item from the plane of the floor below. Make these the lightest lines of the drawing.

• Area rugs, shown in the reception area and in the guest apartment living room, provide a greater sense of scale and detail. Again, these should be drawn very lightly.

• Dotted lines are drawn *and noted* to indicate dropped ceiling soffits in the otherwise uniform ceiling height, as seen in the men's and women's rooms and the corridor between the men's room and the guest apartment. A light to medium-weight line should be used for this purpose.

• Additional lettered notations describe and clarify detailed elements of the plan. As noted earlier, it is possible to overdo such notations. Allow the circumstance to dictate this decision. Keep in mind that in many classroom and professional office situations, the drawing will be left behind, and no verbal explanation of the drawing or its details will be available for an instructor or client.

A major factor in presenting a design project is the selection and application of reproduction methods and techniques. The range of available digital techniques is vast and evolving rapidly, from multicolor images employing several software programs to PowerPoint and animated walk-throughs. Despite the extraordinary array of electronic media tools that have been developed over the past several years, the hand-drawn presentation retains a great deal of value and appeal. Some major design firms that are fully CADD-oriented continue to use hand-drawn work in major preliminary design presentations, believing that drawings "touched by human hands" make a more positive impression on many clients than the typically mechanical appearance of most CADD drawings. This is true of both plan drawings and perspective sketches.

ENHANCED PRESENTATION TECHNIQUE — COMPUTER DRAWN   ILLUS. 7-3

MEN

LINE OF SOFFIT ABOVE

COPIER

WORK AREA

CABINET

2

ASS'T DIRECTOR

SEC'Y

SHELVES

DIRECTOR

APARTMENT

SHELVES / TV

WOMEN

BATH

INTERVIEW

3   3

3   3

KITCHEN

REFRIG.

BEDRM.

VISUALS BOARD

SCREEN

CHAIR DOLLY

AV CART

SHELVES

TABLES

COFFEE

REFRIG

VESTIBULE

← MOVEABLE PARTITION

CONF. TABLE

CONF. TABLE

SEMINAR

COAT HOOKS

4

RECEPTION

ENTRY

ENHANCED PRESENTATION TECHNIQUE — FREE-HAND

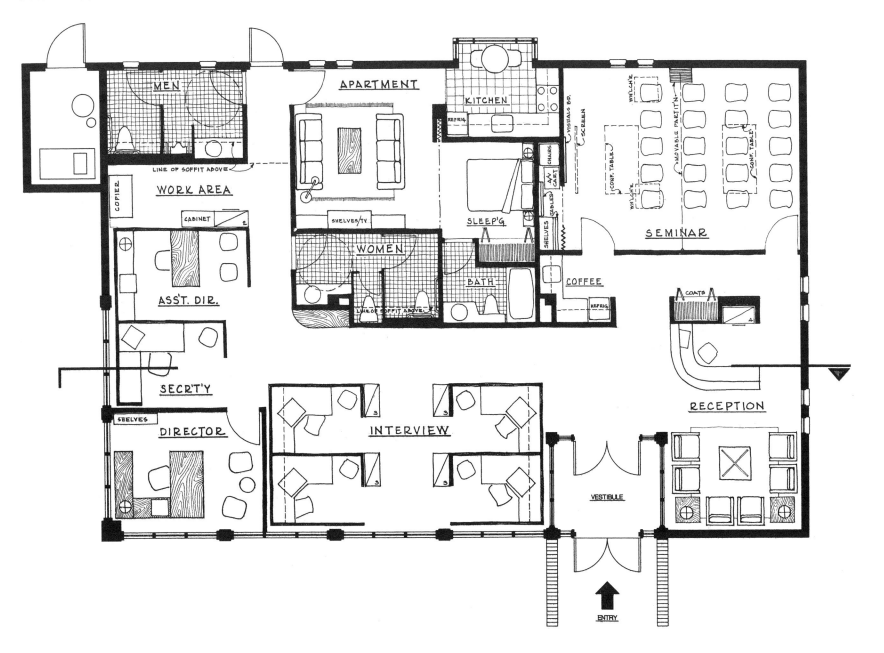

There are many reasons why hand drawings are reproduced for use in final presentations. Original drawings are often perishable and the use of copies is more practical. Very often, more than one set of presentation drawings is required. It is not unusual for detail, notation, and color to be excluded from the original drawings, so copies of the original can have varying added elements, such as color coding, a finish schedule, or a perspective sketch (just to identify a few), giving each copy a special focus. Color on hand drawings is often applied to copies rather than the original, particularly so that color hues and tones can be experimented with. For these reasons, reproduction techniques of many kinds, on several kinds of paper or film, from inexpensive Ozalid techniques to costly photographic and digital processes, have become a part of the designer's presentation repertoire. Within the limits of affordability, students should be encouraged to learn about and experiment with these additional and valuable presentation tools.

How long should it take to accomplish this combined plan-refining and presentation-drawing process? Many factors are involved, such as project size, presentation complexity, deadline, and the varying ways in which individuals work and produce. As suggested in Chapter 6, it is counterproductive to rush while learning. If possible, leave enough time to accomplish this last phase in the space planning process in an unhurried and deliberate manner. The fact that both student and professional designers often procrastinate by putting off design decisions and project completion until the last hour is a reality that cannot be dealt with here. But real-world pressures are often as stringent as these self-imposed pressures; it is not uncommon for the essential work of a consultant to arrive days to weeks late and force a hurried completion of a project or for a client to plead for an unreasonably tight completion date because of an external business pressure. Every designer must learn to work quickly and efficiently and sometimes at breakneck speed. For now, in the process of learning how to refine a floor plan and how to present it well, take enough time to learn these tasks thoroughly.

Some practice for those hurried professional situations can be valuable; one-day sketch problems based in space planning are an excellent learning experience. The NCIDQ exam, now required for entrance to professional societies as well as to obtain most professional licensing, has become a reality for most interior designers; the time pressures of the space planning portion of that exam are quite stringent, and practice exams should be taken several times before the actual examination.

The issues of plan evaluation must be dealt with again. This is true for both classroom and professional settings, although their modes are vastly different. Is the plan a good one? Does it work well? Although one may feel far removed from the original problem analysis by the time the final presentation plan is completed, it can be valuable to go back to the criteria matrix for one last self-critical look at the space planning results. The designer should know a plan's shortcomings before someone else points them out. Beyond this self-critical look, the classroom and professional processes vary greatly. Criticism can be difficult to accept, but students should benefit from the learning opportunities presented by individual and classroom critiques, remembering that one often learns as much, or more, from the critique of other students' work. In most cases, student projects are terminated after the presentation of final preliminary drawings. The professional process is basically different because real-world projects are carried beyond this drawing phase to include construction and furnishings installation, so that the consequences of presenting final preliminary drawings to a client are very different. Whether presented to an individual or a group of non-professionals (such as a building committee or a board of directors) or to other professionals (such as an in-house designer or facilities manager), the results of the presentation must be acted upon. It is unusual in real-world situations to come away from a first presentation without some direction for revisions (sometimes many revisions). One of the greatest advantages of using CADD is the relative ease with which revisions are made, compared to the normally laborious task of revising a hand-drawn presentation. And in the professional setting, the CADD-drawn preliminary documents usually become the basis for the construction documents that follow. Learning to work with clients is a skill normally learned after one's formal education, but students should have some awareness of what the professional designer faces in client relationships and its relevance in the assessment and revision of space planning solutions.

EXERCISE 7-1

To get started with this final phase of the space planning process, use three of the rough floor plans of the Group 1 planning exercises recommended in Chapter 6 and go through the specified refinement and presentation steps with each of them. If necessary, complete more of these Group 1 exercises, to the point when the full execution of planning problems of this scale feels familiar and comfortable. With each project, some form of individual or classroom critique should be incorporated, so that constructive criticism can be used to improve skills at each step along the way. It is recommended that you try one exclusively drawn by hand, one exclusively in CADD, and one in which there is either a mix of hand and CADD or a transition from hand to CADD.

EXERCISE 7-2

Now move on to the Group 2 planning exercises, using the criteria matrix and bubble diagram material from the exercises developed in Chapters 1 and 2. First go through the development of a rough floor plan with each program/shell combination, and then move directly into the refinement and presentation phase, allowing this last step in space planning to become routine. During this exercise, experiment with drawing and presentation techniques in order to begin to develop a personal style; again, work with both hand drawing and CADD. The number of exercises performed before moving on to the final group (Group 3) is a matter of individual judgment — feeling familiar and comfortable with problems of this scale should be the primary measure. Critiques are invaluable to the learning process and should be made an integral part of each exercise at the critical pre-design, diagramming, and rough plan turning points, as well as at the completion of the exercise.

EXERCISE 7-3

Finally, starting from scratch, work on the Group 3 exercises, which present the greatest planning challenge of this text. It would be misleading to imply that mastering these 4,000-square-foot planning exercises will prepare one for any other space planning challenges that may be encountered. A 20,000-square-foot space will probably bring complexities requiring additional growth of one's skills. Specialized interiors with unique equipment or operational procedures will require research and special know-how not covered by these exercises. And the idiosyncrasies of real-world spaces and client problems will bring new challenges. However, these new challenges will not require a basically new methodology or planning process different from what was learned in these exercises.

A few final comments on drawing and presentation skills are appropriate at this point. The learning process described in this text demands many hours at the drawing board or the computer screen. If your presentation skills are not at a level that is personally satisfying, it would be a shame to pass up this opportunity to sharpen those skills. There is an issue of personal aptitude involved with the development of these skills. Some designers have inherent hand-drawing and craft skills, while others must work hard to achieve comparable results. Similarly, some designers have a natural affinity for computer proficiency, while others come by the same level of skill with some difficulty. Regardless of one's personal aptitude, the development of professional quality presentation skills usually takes considerable time with repeated practice in each of the detailed aspects of design presentation.

The drawing skill development process is primarily one of emulation. Whenever you come across a plan drawing you admire, experiment with its techniques — not once, but a few times. It may involve techniques beyond the normal conventions of floor plan drawings, including photography, a variety of computer graphics software, or reproduction techniques. Your result will probably not be identical to the original, but rather a combination of the original and your previously gained techniques. Each time this imitating process takes place, your range of skills will expand. Sources of good-quality floor plan drawings include the monthly interior design magazines; books related to interior design and architecture; and the work of colleagues, other designers, and architects. Purely by way of showing some additional preliminary floor plan drawing techniques, Illustrations 7–5A (hand-drawn) and 7–5B (CADD-drawn) demonstrate a few high-quality drawings by the hands of other designers.

ADDITIONAL DRAWING TECHNIQUE

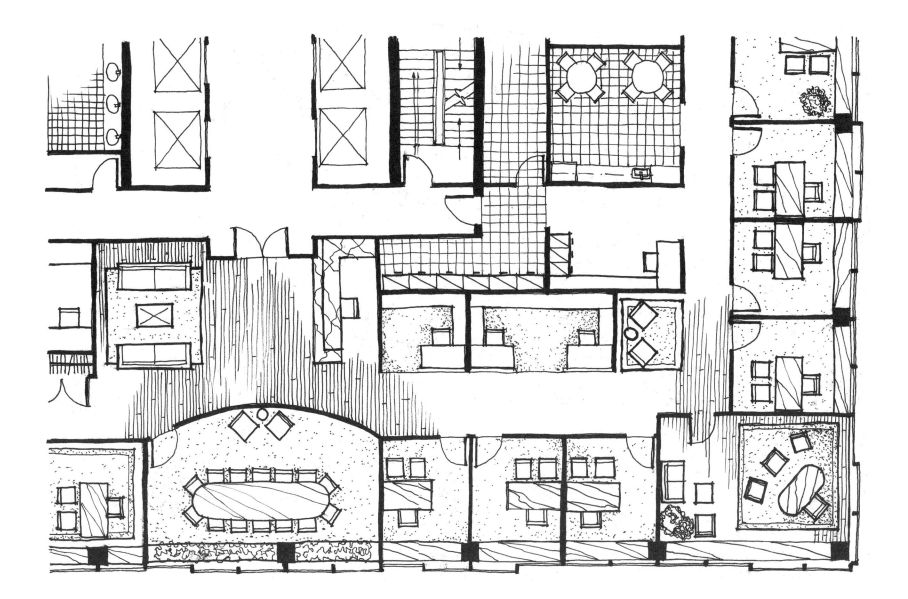

ADDITIONAL DRAWING TECHNIQUE

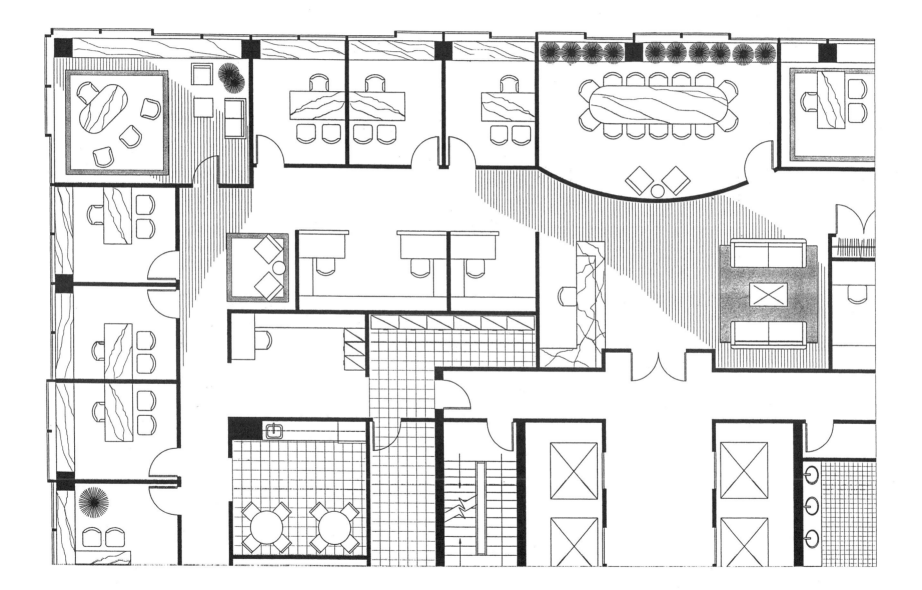

The use of three-dimensional simulation presentation techniques (rendered perspectives, animated walk-throughs, etc.) has not been discussed in this chapter, not because they are unimportant, but because they serve as a selling tool, not a design tool. The development of presentation-quality three-dimensional simulation skills is a complex and time-consuming process to which many texts have already been devoted. These skills should be encouraged in all design students but are essentially unrelated to acquiring space planning skills.

Recommended Reading

5*, 17*, 19*

Books marked with an asterisk are also included in the recommended reading for other chapters.

Chapter 8   DEVELOPING SKILLS BEYOND THE BASIC LEVEL

From a learning viewpoint, the 4,000-square-foot space planning exercises are a practical point of achievement. Although space planning problems of larger size may be more complex and take more time to solve, the methods and techniques for their solution presented here are fundamental and will serve you well as project demands become larger in scale and programmatically more complex. Once a basic approach to this kind of problem solving has been mastered, hands-on experience will be the best way to expand your skills to comfortably deal with larger, more complex spaces. This final chapter is presented with the intent to provide basic ideas and directions to develop skills beyond the basic level of achievement called for in the program/shell exercises presented here.

BASIC IMPLICATIONS

To understand the scale of the 4,000-square-foot space in appropriate perspective, a typical floor in most new mid-and high-rise speculative office buildings ranges from 15,000 to 25,000 square feet of rentable floor space. The typical business or professional firm usually requires from 125 to 250 square feet per person to accommodate its personnel; the variables that create that range of square footage are the programmatic needs of the personnel employed, the number of outside visitors, the amount of equipment space needed, and the degree of spaciousness desired. The program/shell exercises presented here intentionally deal with typical or common functions and do not involve specialized equipment or building systems.

It is not uncommon to find a relatively large facility, accommodating many people, that performs only a few simple functions. The space planning for that kind of project may be no more difficult or time-consuming than it is for a much smaller but relatively complex project. Typically, space planning for the larger user is more complex and difficult, but it should be understood that programmatic complexity or uniqueness can have as much or more bearing on the degree of problem-solving difficulty as size does.

113

Generally, larger spaces serve a greater number of functions, and the complexities of interfunctional relationships multiply. These complexities are compounded when large numbers of both employees and outside visitors are involved, particularly when outside visitors must be isolated to specific areas. Often, specific work-flow processes must be accommodated, requiring exacting spatial adjacencies between functions and departments. It is interesting to note that with the increased use of computer data storage and retrieval, paper flow has become decreasingly important. With some users, the accommodation of large, permanently placed equipment becomes as important as the accommodation of people, not only in occupied space, but also in adjacency to mechanical and electrical services.

Special planning challenges are presented by unique facility functions, such as in television production, specialized medical treatment, or scientific laboratories. In addition to the fact that their detailed functions are beyond most people's experience, they often require the use of specialized equipment; these issues of function and equipment normally require a significant amount of research prior to and during the space planning process. Probably the most difficult and complex building type to plan is the large hospital. It incorporates all the elements that contribute to complex and potentially problematic space planning: large numbers of staff and visitors, separation of staff and visitors, many diverse functions, specific functional processes demanding specific adjacencies, and a great deal of large equipment that must be exactingly placed in specific proximity to mechanical and electrical services. For these reasons, hospitals are always planned with the assistance of specialized consultants. Most specialized facilities require the involvement of at least one consultant, and often several. The comments in the introductory paragraphs of Chapter 4 about the use of consultants apply equally well to the planning of specialized buildings and facilities. Getting out of mainstream design practice and into specialized facilities provides the potential for an interesting and challenging professional career.

Learning to plan larger, more complex spaces can only be accomplished through real project experience. As pointed out earlier, the uniquenesses and eccentricities of real projects cannot be simulated by planned exercises. It would take many long, detailed case study documents to begin to explain the variables that the designer must deal with in planning projects of even moderate size. Existing building conditions may present an unusual floor or ceiling construction assembly, a peculiar door detail, or an HVAC system that is particularly inflexible. Local building and zoning code requirements will often place limitations on space planning options. Even without considering

the problems of personal communication with clients or those created by the typical client's lack of understanding of the design process, the variables and uniquenesses of each client's operating procedures will often be difficult to uncover, understand, and analyze. Ideally, you will have the opportunity to learn progressively, to plan facilities of gradually increasing size and complexity. That way you can adapt and modify the basic planning methods and techniques presented here, until you have developed a personal repertoire of methodologies that can meet the variety of challenges and opportunities available to interior designers.

PROGRAMS WITHIN PROGRAMS

When faced with the problems of planning a facility to accommodate many people who perform a large variety of functions, it is impractical to account for every person and task when you start the planning process. The well-worn analogy of not being able to see the forest for the trees is quite applicable to that situation. With any large, complex problem-solving task, it is important to first break down the problem to a manageable number of parts.

If a particular problem calls for accommodating 156 people in 14 departments on a 23,500-square-foot high-rise office building floor, start with planning the departments, not the individual offices and workstations. The 14 department elements can and should be manipulated in relationship diagrams, and later in bubble diagrams, in the same manner that rooms are manipulated when planning smaller facilities. Even a criteria matrix for departmental needs and interrelationships should be made as a separate and distinct analytical tool; the issues of adjacency, square footage requirements, traffic circulation, work process, privacy, acoustics, and so on apply to departments in a manner very similar to individual rooms and spaces. Illustration 8–1 shows a relationship diagram and a bubble diagram for a departmental arrangement of spaces. Diagrams of this kind are very much like zoning diagrams, in which a spatial zone is set aside for each departmental function. An intentional "zoning concept" is a valuable first step with large-scale facilities.

Accommodating one organization on a number of floors within the same building is a common occurrence. In that situation, a vertical bubble diagram, often referred to as a stacking diagram, is best used to graphically identify the functions and/or departments to be located on each floor, as shown in

DEPARTMENTAL RELATIONSHIP AND BUBBLE DIAGRAMS

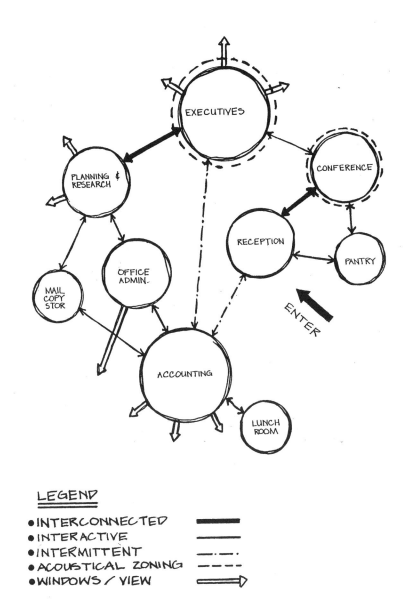

LEGEND

- INTERCONNECTED
- INTERACTIVE
- INTERMITTENT
- ACOUSTICAL ZONING
- WINDOWS / VIEW

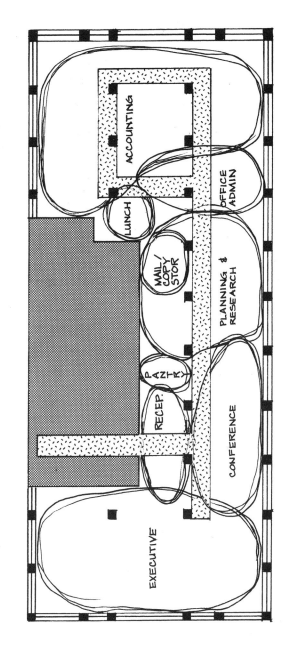

Illustration 8–2. Multifloor facilities are not related to the size of the organization involved; many relatively small organizations are housed in traditional urban town houses or older, multifloor small commercial buildings. Determining the functions to go on each floor must be accomplished before the space planning on individual floors is begun. It should be pointed out that the stacking diagram could be graphically misleading, because the bubbles are not a proportional indication of the size of each function; correct proportions cannot be seen without the use of a conventional bubble diagram for each floor. To compensate for this shortcoming, stacking diagrams should include square footage figures, as shown in the illustrated example.

Generally, large space planning problems are fairly unique; despite some similarities, it is difficult to find two that are the same. As problems become larger and more complex. it is often necessary to devise or invent new problem-solving techniques to cope with new problems. In most cases, remember that the basic technique of breaking down a large problem into smaller, more manageable parts is of great value. This process can also be seen as developing "programs within programs." Although it is necessary to eventually analyze and accommodate each person and task, it can be helpful to separately analyze the department-to-department or zone-to-zone relationships.

OPEN PLAN/SYSTEMS FURNITURE

It is unusual to find a large business or institutional office facility that does not use systems furniture. By way of definition, systems furniture can be described as an integrated combination of partition panels, work surfaces, storage elements, and wire management raceways that can be combined in a variety of configurations to accommodate most functional office use requirements. Because the space planning problems presented in this text are of relatively small size, they do not touch significantly on major uses of systems furniture.

Although systems furniture is often used in small office situations for as few as two or three workstations, its essential purpose is to spatially articulate office areas accommodating several to many workstations. In addition to their spatial organization qualities, these systems are well geared to solve the complex problems of wire management for today's electronic office and offer its users some degree of flexibility. Such flexibility can permit reconfig-

uration of workstations to change functional needs at relatively low cost compared with the demolition and rebuilding of new conventional partitions. In addition to these practical advantages, the proponents of systems furniture also claim that significant benefits exist in the human and personal aspects of open planning by encouraging interaction among people who work together.

Three major office-planning concerns not adequately treated with systems furniture are:

1. A high degree of acoustic control and privacy

2. Security/confidentiality of documents

3. The conventional image of prestige or status offered by the private office

Clearly, it is difficult to imagine the acoustic privacy needs of a lawyer's office, medical examining room, or executive conference room being met by systems furniture. Payroll offices, personnel records management, and research and development staffs, to cite just a few, require confidentiality and security not offered by systems furniture. Regardless of the amount of space allocated, few important executives are satisfied with the privacy, image, or status provided by systems furniture. For these reasons, most office facilities use a combination of systems furniture and conventionally constructed partitions to solve their space planning needs.

Many interior designers' professional involvements are normally related to non-office facilities, such as the hospitality industry or health care facilities. In these situations, the need to learn to plan with systems furniture may not be of primary importance. But most designers who work in settings other than residences need to know how to plan and design with systems furniture. Planning and designing with systems furniture is a process more akin to space planning than to furniture placement or planning.

Ideally, one should start with relatively small spaces and numbers of stations and gradually increase in size and numbers to large office facilities, including several non-workstation functions such as informal conference areas (huddle spaces) or filing and storage areas. The fact that so many systems are being manufactured can make learning to plan with them both trying and difficult. Although most tend to be very similar to one another, each system has its own unique module, panel connections, or configuration potential, making planning generalizations elusive for the uninitiated.

STACKING DIAGRAM   ILLUS. 8-2

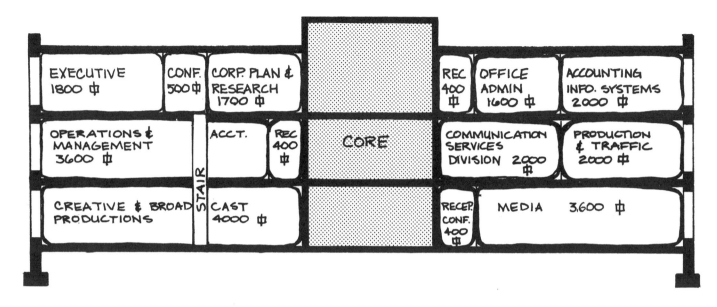

It is not possible to bring a systems planning solution to completion without detailed knowledge of the dimensions, details, and configurations of the particular system being specified. After one has worked in detail with several systems over time, it is possible to do some general space planning without having selected a specific manufacturer's system; even then, however, the final space planning must wait until the specific system has been chosen. The implication here is clear: it will take several projects and detailed investigation and planning with several systems before one can easily and confidently manipulate systems elements within a space with reasonable assurance that the scheme will work well in the final detailed plan.

The manufacturers of systems furniture are interested in having designers become fully familiar with their products. Many of them offer planning manuals and/or seminars on the use of their systems to encourage designers to learn to use them. Particularly for the uninitiated, these learning tools can be very helpful. In addition, most manufacturers provide an easily accessible (on disk or online) CADD library of parts to facilitate planning within their system. Contacting manufacturers or manufacturers' representatives can bring a great deal of valuable planning information.

THE SPECULATIVE OFFICE BUILDING

Large volumes of office planning and design work are the bread-and-butter projects for a major segment of interior design professionals. A great deal, if not most, of that work is performed in multitenant, developer-built buildings in settings from suburban office parks to urban high-rises. Despite the major professional involvement within such buildings, this text and its planning exercises have dealt very little with those kinds of interiors, for the same reasons of scale that systems furniture has not been fully addressed. Every designer who expects to work with office interiors should become thoroughly familiar with the speculative office building, from its general plan configurations to its details of construction, including HVAC and plumbing.

Some buildings are designed and constructed with little accommodation for future change. Hotels, hospitals, and most institutional buildings are in this category of relatively fixed interiors, as are some buildings intended for specific business uses. Planning new interior uses within these buildings usually presents many limitations on the planning process because many elements are relatively fixed and expensive to adjust or relocate.

Speculative buildings are the antithesis of fixed-use buildings. Within the limitations of economical construction techniques, they are designed for maximum flexibility and adaptability, to accommodate as broad a variety of functions and users as possible over many years and tenants.

For these reasons, standardized and modular component systems are used for ceilings, exterior wall and window construction, lighting, electrical distribution, and HVAC control. (The one exception is the major use of steel stud and gypsum drywall partitions because of their low cost and the ease with which they are demolished.) Learning to work with this unique building type is essential to significant involvement in office planning and design. This learning should include the unique building code requirements for egress and compartmentalization, as well as the economics and practicalities of leasing policies devised by the buildings' developers and their rental agents.

Space planning within the speculative office building is quite often done in two stages. The first establishes a general space plan or feasibility plan to confirm the appropriateness of the space for the tenant and to bring the tenant to the point of lease signing; this phase is sometimes referred to as tenant planning. The second stage refines the general space plan and completes the design process down to its final details. Some design firms and some in-house design departments specialize in the first stage, general space planning; these firms or departments are often excellent training grounds to develop professional space planning skills.

FUTURE EXPANSION

Planning for the future is usually a significant factor of most space planning problems, regardless of their size. It has not been dealt with to this point because it involves many conditional or indeterminate elements and is difficult to specify in the kind of pre-planned programmatic exercises presented here. Ideally, it should be a basic planning factor from the first phases of problem data gathering and analysis and should be included as an element in a criteria matrix (see Illustration 1–7A) and other pre-design programming documents, such as relationship diagrams.

Despite its importance, many clients have great difficulty in dealing with future planning, to the point where they resist discussing it in concrete terms. This is understandable, because no one really knows what the future will bring; equally important, planning for the future usually contains major elements of financial commitment.

If the client can identify, quantify, locate, and place a time frame on future growth or change (leasing additional floor space, setting aside land for a future addition, etc.), the space planning problem is usually not too difficult. Too often however, clients are absorbed in current problems and are not interested in or sensitive to the need for addressing future space planning requirements.

Despite the discomforts of specifying needs for an unknown future, most clients are better served if the designer will be assertive and press for an articulated future direction of the organization. Even if the programmatic information for the future is rather vague, a general sense of the functions likely to change or grow will permit the current placement of functional units in a manner that could make future re-planning immeasurably easier. In addition to these space planning issues, many designers believe that an involvement in programming for the future will help to cement a long-standing client/designer relationship.

It should be pointed out that planning for future needs is as important (and difficult) for the small client organization as it is for the large client organization; it is probably most difficult for the relatively new organization, regardless of size. Generally, there are no easy resolutions for these issues, since the difficulty lies in making economic decisions, not space planning ones. Again, real project experience is the best learning mode; designers who have grappled with these future planning issues with a few clients can be a valuable consultant to their clients in this unique area of decision making.

PLANNING NEW BUILDINGS

The process of designing a new building is quite similar to designing a new interior in an existing building. Despite the similarities in process, the design of a new building involves several major and complex considerations not part of the interior space planning process. Without attempting to enumerate the myriad of details related to each of those considerations, the elements of site, exterior form and image, building structure, and the placement of basic environmental control systems demand knowledge and expertise not involved in the typical interior space planning project.

The reasons for the separation in both training and practice of architects and interior designers are many, including the magnitude and complexity of the architect's task. It is relatively unusual to find a fundamental integration of the building design and interior design processes. With architectural firms usually in control of the building design process, the interior designer is too often brought into the process at such a late point in the planning phase that his or her expertise in interior space and detail is relegated to secondary importance, rather than being integrated into the whole of the building design, as would be more functionally useful.

Skillful interior space planning is accomplished only with great attention to detail, both in program development and in the physical planning process itself. The task of designing buildings has become more complex, and it is unlikely that most architects will be able to devote the time to develop well-honed interior space planning skills. Likewise, the design of building interiors has become extremely complex, and it is equally unlikely that most interior designers will acquire architectural expertise or credentials. Ideally, a more productive coming together will happen, both in thought and in practice, between these two interdependent specializations in the field of creating the built environment. This coming together requires greater knowledge and understanding of interior programming and systems, as well as furniture and interior materials, on the part of architects and an equal growth of knowledge and understanding of site, structures, and environmental control systems on the part of interior designers. Clearly, the result will be better buildings.

An interdisciplinary approach should go far beyond the interaction of architects and interior designers. Most design professionals have broad concerns for environmental issues, from intelligent use of our planet's natural resources to the detailed components that determine the day-to-day quality of contemporary life. Making a meaningful effort to implement these concerns will require a knowledgeable global view and a willingness of all design disciplines to work together. It is this kind of professional interdisciplinary collaboration that will support the creation of a more sustainable built environment.

A FINAL NOTE

Becoming professionally proficient in interior space planning is a challenging enterprise. Although a major time investment is required, the rewards are commensurate. Not only is one prepared then to take on the full range of interior design projects, but the basic problem-solving skills in organization, analysis, and synthesis are adaptable and useful lifelong tools for a profession and a world that will surely change.

STAIR DESIGN BASICS

STAIR DESIGN

Successful design of stairs is not a simple task and cannot be learned by reading reference books. The learning process for most experienced designers has occurred in a mentorship mode, with a teacher or experienced professional helping to guide the learner by correcting mistakes or errors in judgment. This chapter will help the fledgling stair designer through the initial phases.

The primary purpose of stairs is connecting pedestrian travel from one level to another. Depending upon the circumstances, that task can be very simple or quite complex. The task becomes increasingly difficult when more than two levels are involved, and even more difficult in the case of a "grand" or "sculptural" stair, or fitting stairs into irregular and/or complex building configurations. For most people, the use of stairs is an everyday occurrence; in most cases, the experience is taken for granted and not given special attention. However, when a poorly designed stair is encountered, the experience is, at best, annoying, and at worst, dangerous. When a particu-larly well designed stair is encountered, its designer has given a moment of pleasure to its users.

As you proceed with using this resource be aware of these three issues:

- There are some basic differences between designing stairs within an existing building and stairs within a new structure that is in the process of being designed; both of these conditions are addressed in this resource.

- Knowledge of building codes and standards for providing for disabled users are critical to realistic and workable stair design.

- Terminology related to stairs can lead to some confusion or misunderstanding of design or construction issues. A brief glossary of stair-related terms is provided on page 215.

This resource is not only meant to be read, but also to be worked with through the use of the Skill Development Exercises provided in the Companion Web site. A great deal of additional knowledge and design inspiration is there to be gained. As one's stair design skills develop, it is inevitable that greater appreciation for the subtleties and nuances of stair design will be developed, including experiencing the significant pleasures of serendipitously coming across a great stair.

Function, Purpose, and History

Beyond the obvious purpose of getting people from one level to another, stairs serve many varied functions. Briefly, those functions include:

Sloping Terrain From gentle slopes to very hilly sites, changes in grade have created the need for stairs and ramps, as seen in the photos of changes in garden levels using shallow risers (Illustration S1-1) and winding hillside paths using combinations of ramps, stair ramps, and steps (Illustration S1-2). Sloping terrain can create the need for entering a building at different levels and then connecting those levels with an interior stair, as demonstrated in the sectional drawing (Illustration S1-3). Unique sites have taken advantage of inclined sites, as seen in the photo of the stepped seating of an ancient open-air amphitheater (Illustration S1-4).

Cultural Issues In centuries long past, ladders and stairs were used as a primary defensive device to thwart advancing invaders by restricting passage to a single-file entry, as seen in the photos of ladder access in native southwest American settlements (Illustration S1-5), and very narrow winding stairs in medieval castles. The accelerating growth of urban centers in the Middle Ages created the need for larger public buildings, and space limitations called for buildings to go up instead of out. As building technologies became more sophisticated, the use of stairs became prevalent and stair design began to grow in variety and complexity, as seen in this 17th century example (Illustration S1-6). Until the advent of the elevator in the second half of the nineteenth century, stairs were the only means of vertical access in multi-story buildings, and the need for larger and taller buildings accelerated with the growing impact of industrialization and urbanization.

Human and Social issues play a role in how we have designed and used stairs. In many traditional buildings, a grand monumental stair is the centerpiece, leading to honored events or ceremonies above, as well as providing the opportunities for an impressive or theatrical descent to a waiting audience (Illustration S1-7). Multiple levels offer many possibilities for separating and/or compartmentalizing functions within buildings serving needs for privacy, confidentiality, or security. Beyond a primary entrance level for public functions, privacy and security are more easily provided on other levels, above or below. So much of our home building traditions place bedrooms on second and third floors, offering a removed or private quarter for sleep and

ILLUS. S1–1 *Shallow riser garden stairs*

ILLUS. S1–2 *Garden step-ramp path*

ILLUS. S1-3 Accommodating sloping terrain

ILLUS. S1-4 Roman era amphitheatre utilizing the sloping terrain

ILLUS. S1-5 Ladder access to south-west American Pueblo settlement

ILLUS. S1-6 Blois Chateau—famous 16th century spiral stair

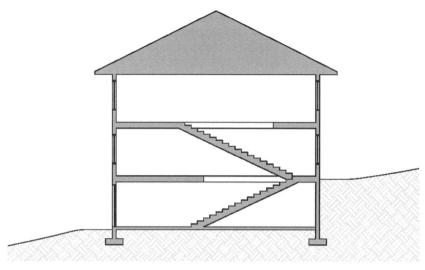

ILLUS. S1-7 Paris Opera House—famous late 19th century grand stair

ILLUS. S1–8 Stair to a contemporary penthouse

ILLUS. S1–9 The Louvre, Paris—20th century addition (I.M.Pei, architect)

ILLUS. S1–10 TWA Terminal, JFK Airport, NY—(Eero Saarinen, architect)

ILLUS. S1–11 KPMS Building, courtyard stair, Munich, Germany

personal space. In addition to these practical human and social issues is an essentially universal human wish for being in a position of status or control; the glamorous associations with penthouse living is certainly an element of this desire (Illustration S1-8).

Aesthetic Issues cannot be overlooked in understanding the role of stairs in our buildings. Even in their most basic form, stairs are dynamic visual elements in any interior space. Just the fact that they do not structurally conform to our conventional, perpendicular building elements and that they introduce a typically sharp, angled plane gives them a unique presence. Beyond the typical stair configurations are dramatic winding stairs

(Illustration S1-9), distinctively detailed stairs (Illustration S1-10), structurally acrobatic stairs (Illustration S1-11), and purely eccentric stairs. For the designer, stairs present special opportunities to make a singular aesthetic statement about a building's character and purpose.

On History

The importance for designers to know and understand the history of buildings and their interior components is generally understood. Within the limitations of this relatively brief "how-to" supplement, this is not the place for a meaningful discourse on the history of stairs and stair design. There are several good discourses on the history of stairs; they are noted in the recom-

ILLUS. S1-12 Rudimentary rough hewn stone stair

ILLUS. S1-13 Roman era ruins in Morocco

ILLUS. S1-14 Pompidou Center, Paris—exterior escalator—(Renzo Piano, architect)

mended reading list on page 219. From a purely visual point of view, the continuum of stair design growth can be seen in the at-a-glance series of photographs in Illustrations S1-12 through S1-14, from the very rudimentary rough hewn stone stairs typical of many early cultures to the hi-tech sophistication made possible with today's building technologies.

Despite the universal use of elevators and escalators in modern multi-story buildings, stairs will continue to be a basic component in today's buildings, as (1) the primary mode of vertical access in small low-rise buildings; (2) means of emergency egress in all multi-story buildings; and (3) as a significant sculptural element in many buildings, large and small.

Human Behavior on Stairs

Understanding how people behave on stairs can provide insights related to the subtleties involved in designing stairs. Surprisingly little research has been devoted to how we behave on stairs. The two primary areas of stair research have been related to (1) the routes people take, and (2) reaction to stairs and their surroundings. Most of the research studies have been performed in high-volume situations, such as subway stations and transportation terminal path-

ways. These are far from typical design situations and obviously not basic to stair design concerns. If one is faced with designing stairs with these complex factors, it may be necessary to consult the related research data.

There are two fundamental facts related to how people behave on stairs:

- Peoples' behavior on stairs is both consistent and predictable, regardless of gender, age, and race.

- In North American settings, people stay to the right side of the stair in both ascending and descending. Most variations to this convention occur when someone wants to pass a slow-moving person, or when there is no handrail on the right.

In addition to these two fundamental facts, it should be noted that despite the convention of staying to the right, when people-bumping seems imminent, as is often the case with a very slow-moving or hurried user on the stair, most people are able to twist, duck, bend, or sharply turn—in the last few milliseconds—before impending impact, in order to avoid a bump, or worse, an accident.

The simpler stair patterns, such as a basic straight run, provide the least opportunity for conflict, accidents, bumping, or discomfort. As stair patterns become more complex, there are increasing opportunities for those kinds of conflicts. "U" shaped stairs have greater potential for conflicts than straight run stairs, and zigzag or other complexly configured stairs are more conflict prone than "U" shaped stairs. Curved or helical stairs are the most conflict prone; despite this, they do not present unusual or unique problems when they conform to building code requirements.

Handrails have influence on how people use stairs. Most people will use them for at least part of their journey, particularly for the first few steps in descending stairs. The classic case is one in which a stair has a wall on one side without a handrail, and a handrail on the open (to below) side of the stair. If the handrail is on the left when descending, most people will break with convention and stay on the left when descending, in order to use the handrail.

In general, an understanding of how people use stairs is valuable background information as one approaches a stair design problem, keeping in mind that peoples' response to stairs is the designer's first responsibility.

Stair Falls and Accidents

Stairs cannot be used without some risk, and the consequences of a stair accident are potentially serious. There are extensive statistics on stair accidents, but just some basic numerical data provide an adequate picture for the stair designer's purposes. In the United States, there are more than 12,000 deaths each year from falls from one level to another, and more than 12 million injuries each year serious enough for at least one day of restricted activity or medical attention. Stair injuries result in more than 1 million cases requiring emergency room treatment each year, and more than 50,000 of those cases required hospitalization. Put in economic terms, stair falls in the U.S. workplace are one of the major causes of compensation claims and lost work hours.

A few basic factors related to stair accidents should be noted:

- Because the effort to lift one's foot is proportional to the riser height, the higher the riser, the greater the likelihood of a trip.

- User behavior, such as hurrying, running, slow gait, carrying things, or not paying attention, is a major cause of stair accidents.

- Stair design and construction factors, such as a single riser, narrow treads, dimensional irregularities, inadequate lighting, no handrail, or slippery tread material, are significant causes of stair accidents.

- Age is a particularly significant factor. The elderly are the most prone stair accident victims; 75 percent of those who die in stair falls are over 65, and 84 percent of those who die in home stair falls are over 65.

- Ice, snow, and water cause a disproportionately greater number of stair falls on exterior stairs, particularly in cold climates.

Design Quality

Stairs can be beautiful, exciting, adventurous, and even inspire designers to exceptional stair designs of their own. A few of the books on the recommended reading list (page 219) are primarily photographic studies, and a few also contain detailed drawings of how the pictured stairs were built. The aesthetic aspects of stairs deal as much with their construction details as they do with their overall form. When possible, experience those stairs which you find particularly appealing by walking up and down the flights in order to viscerally experience their comfort and tactile qualities, as well as examining their materials and means of construction. Also, use the many published examples of well designed constructions to inspire you to make exceptional stairs.

SECTION 2

CODES, DIMENSIONS, AND CONFIGURATIONS

A great many of the dimensional requirements for stairs are regulated by building codes. In addition, some of the dimensional requirements are regulated by the Americans with Disabilities Act (ADA). Rather than repeating all of the International Building Code's (IBC) detailed requirements for and related to stairs in its chapter on Means of Egress, the critical code issues are dealt with in this section, leaving the application of those details to case studies in Section 3.

Riser/Tread Relationships

There is no perfect riser/tread relationship. The IBC regulates maximum/minimum dimensions for residences and nonresidences, as described in Illustration S2-1.

Safety and comfort are always important issues when designing stairs. Assuming that appropriate riser/tread proportions are complied with, the lower

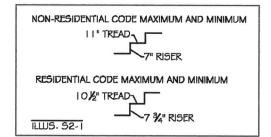

the riser, the safer and more comfortable the stair. There are several published tables and charts that provide prescribed riser/tread dimensions; they vary very little from one another. The riser/tread charts in Illustration S2-2 are recommended here and are used in the case study examples in Sections 3 and 4.

Note that when applying the rule-of-thumb formula for good riser/tread proportions—two risers plus one tread equals 25 (2R + T = 25)—the results stay between 25 and 25½ for all riser heights from 5¾ to 8½ inches. While the code does not state a minimum riser height, a riser height of less than 5 inches is impractical in most interior situations, typically due to excessive length-of-run dimensions.

RISER/TREAD RELATIONSHIPS

RISER	TREAD	2R+T
5"	16"	26
5 1/4"	15 1/2"	26
5 1/2"	14 3/4"	25 3/4
5 3/4"	14"	25 1/2
6"	13 1/2"	25 1/2
6 1/4"	13"	25 1/2
6 1/2"	12 1/4"	25 1/2
6 3/4"	11 3/4"	25 1/2
7"	11"	25
7 1/4"	10 1/2"	25
7 1/2"	10"	25
7 3/4"	9 1/2"	25
8"	9"	25
8 1/4"	8 1/2"	25
8 1/2"	8 1/4"	25 1/4
8 3/4"	8 1/8"	25 5/8
9"	8"	26

CHARTS OF RISER / TREAD RELATIONSHIPS
ILLUSTRATION: S2-2

NOTE: EACH CHART DOES NOT EXCEED RUNS OF GREATER THAN THE MAX. PERMITTED HEIGHT OF 12'-0"

NUMBER OF RISERS & TREADS

	7" RISER		11" TREAD	
1	7"	7"	11"	11"
2	14"	1'-2"	22"	1'-10"
3	21"	1'-9"	33"	2'-9"
4	28"	2'-4"	44"	3'-8"
5	35"	2'-11"	55"	4'-7"
6	42"	3'-6"	66"	5'-6"
7	49"	4'-1"	77"	6'-5"
8	56"	4'-8"	88"	7'-4"
9	63"	5'-3"	99"	8'-3"
10	70"	5'-10"	110"	9'-2"
11	77"	6'-5"	121"	10'-1"
12	84"	7'-0"	132"	11'-0"
13	91"	7'-7"	143"	11'-11"
14	98"	8'-2"	154"	12'-10"
15	105"	8'-9"	165"	13'-9"
16	112"	9'-4"	176"	14'-8"
17	119"	9'-11"	187"	15'-7"
18	126"	10'-6"	198"	16'-6"
19	133"	11'-1"	209"	17'-5"
20	140"	11'-8"		

NUMBER OF RISERS & TREADS

	6 1/2" RISER		12 1/2" TREAD	
1	6 1/2"	6 1/2"	12 1/4"	1'-0 1/4"
2	13"	1'-1"	24 1/2"	2'-0 1/2"
3	19 1/2"	1'-7 1/2"	36 3/4"	3'-0 3/4"
4	26"	2'-2"	49"	4'-1"
5	32 1/2"	2'-8 1/2"	61 1/4"	5'-1 1/4"
6	39"	3'-3"	73 1/2"	6'-1 1/2"
7	45 1/2"	3'-9 1/2"	85 3/4"	7'-1 3/4"
8	52"	4'-4"	98"	8'-2"
9	58 1/2"	4'-10 1/2"	110 1/4"	9'-2 1/4"
10	65"	5'-5"	122 1/2"	10'-2 1/2"
11	71 1/2"	5'-11 1/2"	134 3/4"	11'-2 3/4"
12	78"	6'-6"	147"	12'-3"
13	84 1/2"	7'-0 1/2"	159 1/4"	13'-3 1/4"
14	91"	7'-7"	171 1/2"	14'-3 1/2"
15	97 1/2"	8'-1 1/2"	183 3/4"	15'-3 3/4"
16	104"	8'-8"	196"	16'-4"
17	110 1/2"	9'-2 1/2"	208 1/4"	17'-4 1/4"
18	117"	9'-9"	220 1/2"	18'-4 1/2"
19	123 1/2"	10'-3 1/2"	232 3/4"	19'-4 3/4"
20	130	10'-10"	245"	20'-5"
21	136 1/2"	11'-4 1/2"	257 1/4"	21'-5 1/4"
22	143"	11'-11"		

NUMBER OF RISERS & TREADS

	6" RISER		13 1/2" TREAD	
1	6"	6"	13 1/2"	1'-1 1/2"
2	12"	1'-0"	27"	2'-3"
3	18"	1'-6"	40 1/2"	3'-4 1/2"
4	24"	2'-0"	54"	4'-6"
5	30"	2'-6"	67 1/2"	5'-7 1/2"
6	36"	3'-0"	81"	6'-9"
7	42"	3'-6"	94 1/2"	7'-10 1/2"
8	48"	4'-0"	108"	9'-0"
9	54"	4'-6"	121 1/2"	10'-1 1/2"
10	60"	5'-0"	135"	11'-3"
11	66"	5'-6"	148 1/2"	12'-4 1/2"
12	72"	6'-0"	162"	13'-6"
13	78"	6'-6"	175 1/2"	14'-7 1/2"
14	84"	7'-0"	189"	15'-9"
15	90"	7'-6"	202 1/2"	16'-10 1/2"
16	96"	8'-0"	216"	18'-0"
17	102"	8'-6"	229 1/2"	19'-1 1/2"
18	108"	9'-0"	243"	20'-3"
19	114"	9'-6"	256 1/2"	21'-4 1/2"
20	120"	10'-0"	270"	22'-6"
21	126"	10'-6"	283 1/2"	23'-7 1/2"
22	132"	11'-0"	297"	24'-9"
23	138"	11'-6"	310 1/2"	25'-10 1/2"
24	144"	12'-0"		

ILLUS. S2-2 These three charts are convenient at-a-glance dimensional time savers for preliminary stair planning

There are several additional factors involved in making design decisions related to riser/tread dimensions:

- While lower risers are safer and more comfortable for all users, in facilities with a large or predominant number of elderly users, the use of lower risers (5¾ to 6¼ inches) is particularly important.

- *Length-of-run is* often a critical factor in designing stairs. While lower risers are usually more desirable, they require deeper treads, resulting in a longer stair. In situations where adequate space is available, the greater length is not problematic. However, in situations where space is limited, the designer is often restricted to using a maximum allowable height riser in order to get the stair to fit into the available space. One brief example is described in the following sidebar:

> In a nonresidential building with a floor-to-floor height of 9'x10", a stair using code requirements for riser/tread dimensions would result in a 17 riser stair with 6.94" risers (118" ÷ 17 = 6.94") and 16 treads of 11" depth, resulting in a run of 176" (11 x 16) or 14'-8". If a lower, but still reasonable riser height is desired, a 20 riser stair would result in a 5.9" riser (118" ÷ 20 = 5.9") coupled with treads of 13¾", resulting in a stair length of 21'-9¼" (19 x 13¾). The difference of 7'-1¼" in length-of-run could be the determining factor in deciding on riser/tread dimensions if the amount of available space for the stair is limited. See Illustration S2-3.

- *Nosings* are strongly recommended by code for all interior stairs, because they increase the foot's landing depth for each step taken. They do not affect the riser/tread dimensions because the nosing extension is ignored when considering those dimensions, as shown in Illustration S2-4. Typically the nosing extension is from 1 to 1½ inches.

- *Single-riser* level changes are permitted by code, but a change in level of only one riser is not easily perceived by people approaching the step from either direction, potentially resulting in a trip or fall. For elevation or level changes of less than 12 inches, a ramp is recommended. Good practice dictates that stair runs should have a minimum three-riser run, as shown in Illustration S2-5.

- *Riser/tread* dimensions must remain constant within a stairway, not just within a single run, but for runs of stairs that are contiguous. While the code permits a variation of up to ⅜ inches in riser or tread dimensions within a given flight, a variation of as little as ⅛ inch in riser height, or ¼ inch in tread depth, is usually felt by users and can be the cause of repeated accidents.

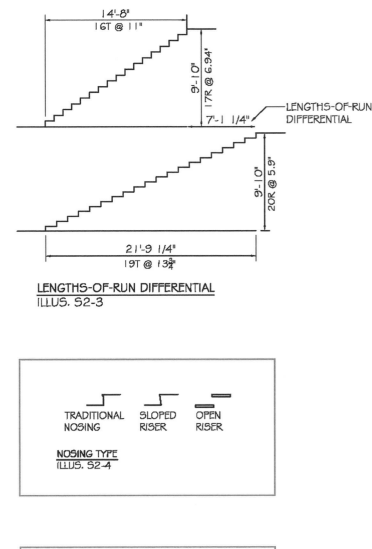

LENGTHS-OF-RUN DIFFERENTIAL
ILLUS. S2-3

NOSING TYPE
ILLUS. S2-4

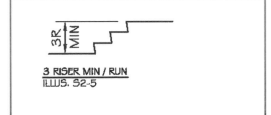

3 RISER MIN / RUN
ILLUS. S2-5

• *Using decimals,* rather than fractions, for riser heights is common practice. Very often, particularly for new stairs within an existing building, risers do not calculate to even inches or convenient fractions of an inch, such as quarters or eighths of an inch. For stairs built on the job site, as well as for those constructed in a shop or factory, experienced stair builders can and will make risers of equal height, regardless of the specific decimal dimension. Tread dimensions are not as ergonomically sensitive, and their dimensions can be conveniently adjusted to easily workable fractions of an inch.

• *Curved stairs* present a specific condition in terms of riser/tread dimensions because the tread depth varies over the width of the tread. Establishing riser height dimensions for curved stairs does not vary from the process used for non-curved stairs. Code requirements on the tread depth for curved stairs are quite specific and are fully described in Case Study 3, on page 149.

• *Winder treads* are not permitted in required exit stairs. The pie-shaped treads of the typical spiral stair, or the triangular treads of winders used in place of a landing, are unsafe and should only be used for personal, secondary, and/or infrequently used situations or locations. Stairs with winders for nonrequired stairs are shown in Illustration S2-6, including some dimensional requirements. Note that the maximum riser height for spiral stairs is 9½ inches, and that minimum tread width, measured from the central pole, is 30 inches.

• *Exterior stairs* also present a special condition in terms of riser/tread dimensions because peoples' gait when walking outside is different from their indoor gait, and because the hazards of dealing with water, snow, and ice on steps demands a different set of dimensional standards. Further in this section, see page 138 for detailed information on exterior stairs.

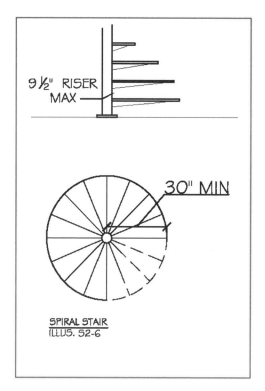

Stair Width

Residential stairs must be at least 3 feet 0 inches wide. While that width is quite common in many houses, an additional 4 to 6 inches of width makes a surprisingly more gracious stair. In very large residences where a luxurious ambiance is desired, widths of 4 to 5 feet may be appropriate.

Stairs in public buildings must be at least 3 feet 8 inches wide, based on the concept that a narrower stair will not permit two adults to comfortably pass one another. Again, an additional 4 to 6 inches of width makes a surprising difference in users' perception of comfort, and even wider stairs, up to 5 feet in width, make two-way traffic feel even easier to manage. In buildings of very high occupancy loads, such as theaters, lecture halls, and classroom buildings, wider stairs are generally required; their width is based on occupancy requirements and must be calculated with the use of code occupancy standards. Note that stairs narrower than 3 feet 8 inches wide are permitted in special (non-egress) utility stair situations.

Stairs over 5 feet wide require a center handrail in addition to the handrails on either side. For many users, unusually wide stairs create a sense of trepidation, particularly for infirm or elderly users, who prefer to feel that a handrail is comfortably nearby. The plan diagram in Illustration S2-8 clarifies the details of this requirement.

Stair configuration or shape and stair width are unrelated. What is true for the width of a straight stair is equally true of an "L" shaped, "U" shaped, or curved stair, including code and human response issues.

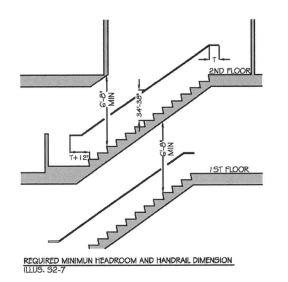

REQUIRED MINIMUM HEADROOM AND HANDRAIL DIMENSION
ILLUS. S2-7

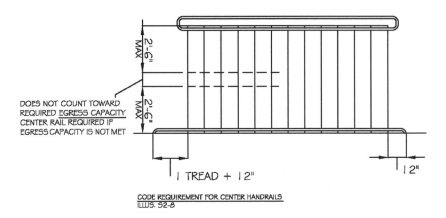

DOES NOT COUNT TOWARD REQUIRED EGRESS CAPACITY CENTER RAIL REQUIRED IF EGRESS CAPACITY IS NOT MET

CODE REQUIREMENT FOR CENTER HANDRAILS
ILLUS. S2-8

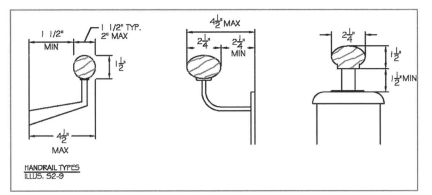

HANDRAIL TYPES
ILLUS. S2-9

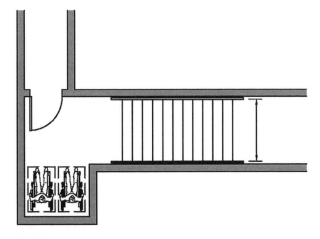

TYPICAL AREA OF REFUGE
ILLUS. S2-10

Headroom

Stairs must have headroom of at least 80 inches at any point, as shown in Illustration S2-7.

Handrails

Handrails are required on both sides of a stair. Stair rail height should be 34" to 38" above the stair nosing. They must extend 12 inches beyond the top riser, and one tread depth plus 12 inches beyond the bottom riser. When handrails don't continue to another level, they must return to the wall or the walking surface. Extensions are not required when handrails are continuous between flights, or in residential stairs, where newel posts or turnouts are acceptable. See Illustration S2-8 for these dimensional details.

Only the portions of a stairway within 30 inches of a handrail may count toward the required width for egress capacity, as calculated by the occupancy load. In practical terms, this means that stair widths required to be more than 60 inches between the handrails must have an intermediate handrail. See Illustration S2-9.

Handrails must be graspable. The minimum radius is 1¼ inches. Noncircular shapes are permitted. The overall perimeter should be between 4" and 6". Minimum distance from a wall is 1½ inches. Maximum projection from the wall is 4½". Sharp edges are not permitted and edges should have a minimum radius of ⅛ inch. See Illustration S2-9.

Stair Enclosures

Enclosed stairs are not required in residences and are not commonly found there. Stair enclosures are commonplace in nonresidential buildings, primarily to provide a safe, smoke- and fume-free exit path in case of fire and other emergencies, and to a lesser extent, to limit access for building security purposes. The enclosing walls and doors are generally required to have a one- or two-hour fire resistance rating, depending upon the building's height and type of occupancy. There are many specific code requirements related to the details of stair enclosures; those requirements are discussed and further developed in Case Study 2 on page 146.

Materials

Codes play a role in the selection of materials used in stair construction. Code issues are related to the flammability and/or fire resistiveness of material for the stair structure and/or enclosing walls, as well as the coefficient of friction of stair tread materials. The issues related to the selection of materials for stair construction and finishes are dealt with further in this section on page 134.

Lighting

Well designed electric lighting is necessary for the safe 24-hour/day use of stairs, particularly because stairs always present the potential for accidents. There is no single best or preferred approach to providing light for stairs. There is one caution: avoid shadows that obscure the leading edges of the stair's treads. Generally, lighting from above works well because it minimizes shadows. Lighting sources at landings work well for an ascending flight but will place the treads of the descending flight in shadow. Wall sconces can be effective if they are placed high enough for stair users to be out of contact with them. There are specialty lighting techniques, such as linear sources placed in the underside of handrails or individual treads. Code requirements include the need for emergency lighting to provide minimal (one foot candle) visibility during power failures.

Americans with Disabilities Act

There are specific Americans with Disabilities Act (ADA) standards related to stairs. In general, they do not vary from building code standards. Because people with significant physical disabilities are unable to use stairs without personal help, and conventional elevators do not operate in fire or some other panic situations, an enclosed area of refuge is required in accessible stairways for every 200 occupants on each floor level. Typically, areas of refuge are incorporated within required egress stairways, providing 30" x 48" wheelchair spaces for the number required by occupancy count. While spe-

cific floor plan conditions will vary, the plan arrangement shown in Illustration S2-10 (see page 130) is typical for most buildings.

In addition to the requirement for areas of refuge, the minimum required width of accessible stairs is 48 inches between the handrails for unsprinklered buildings.

Other Code-Related Issues

There are two additional building code requirements that are stair related and are critical to making buildings safe. While these two requirements are not directly related to the design of stairs, they are integrally related to the design process:

* A basic exiting principle is that at least two different egress paths should lead from the interior of the building to the outside at ground level. The rationale is that if one path is blocked or endangered by a hazard, then the other path will be available. There are exceptions to this rule for situations involving relatively small numbers of occupants, but the designer should always begin with the basic design concept that two ways out of all public spaces should typically be provided in case of an emergency situation. The application of this principle is dealt with in some detail in Case Study 2, Section 3, page 146.

* Travel distance to a required exit stair is limited by the building code. In exceptionally long buildings, more than two required exit stairs may be necessary, not due to the occupancy load, but rather due to an excessive travel distance. For most occupancies the allowable exit-access travel distance is 200 feet without a sprinkler system, and from 250 to 300 feet with a sprinkler system. These regulations are fairly complex and the code's tables must be accessed for specific applications. The designer should always be aware of the need to conform to travel distance requirements and consult the code when needed.

There are many stair-related code details not covered in this section. While some of these details are dealt with in the case studies, codes related to stairs are numerous and complex. For those who are uninitiated in these complexities, reviewing the code details related to occupancy loads and means of egress is recommended.

Additional information related to the general construction of stairs can be found on the companion Web site that serves as an addendum to this Stair Design Resource.

Materials for Construction

The materials available for stair treads are extremely varied. Each of the basic materials itemized below are potentially appropriate for tread surfaces, depending upon the stair's setting:

- *Wood*—including composite wood products and bamboo; the wood may be integral to the construction of the stair or applied to a substrate material. The finish applied to the wood has an important bearing on the stair's safety and maintenance characteristics.

- *Concrete*—smooth surface or with textured, non-slip aggregate finish; non-slip nosing strips are often embedded in the concrete.

- *Resilient tile or sheet goods*—characteristics vary with products, such as rubber, vinyl, and vinyl composition.

- *Ceramic tile*—unglazed and/or textured for non-slip finish.

- *Carpet*—pile height and toughness of construction and fiber content are important in determining stair safety.

- *Stone*—finishes range from polished (and slippery) to heavily textured; some can last for centuries.

- *Terrazzo*—smooth toweled or with textured non-slip finish; non-slip nosing strips can be embedded.

- *Glass*—tempered and of appropriate thickness, with non-slip finish.

- *Steel*—available in smooth, textured, stamped, and perforated finishes; most often used for exterior stairs.

- *Other products*—such as trowelled-on epoxies and metallic alloys with textured finishes.

There are three major factors involved in selecting tread materials and finishes: (1) appropriateness to the stair's setting and/or intended use, (2) safety, and (3) maintenance/sustainability. All three factors should be taken into account in the selection process, including the conflicts and compromises that are inevitable.

Appropriateness to the stair's setting or intended use

First is the issue of frequency of use; there's a huge difference if the stair is in a conventional residence or a highly trafficked public building, such as a high school or a subway entrance. Putting aside the special concerns of exterior stairs, will the treads be subject to wet conditions, as in a food service or science lab facility, or other conditions that might create significant safety hazards? Footsteps are easily heard on hard surfaces, but much reduced on carpet; when acoustic qualities are important, soft surfaces are called for. Except for utility stairs, such as required fire stairs, where appearance is not a major consideration, aesthetic qualities are typically quite important, including color, texture, and pattern. Each stair setting will present a different set of criteria for material and finish selection.

Safety

Because stairs hold the potential for serious accidents caused by slips, trips, and falls, it is very important that safety factors are a major consideration in selecting tread and landing materials. All three of the major testing/regulatory agencies (ANSI, ASTM, and ADA) have standards or recommendations for slip resistance for stair and flooring surfaces. Typically referred to as the "coefficient of friction," a value greater than 0.5 is generally accepted for most floor surfaces. Higher ratings of 0.6 to 0.8 are even safer for stair use. All tread surfaces are less safe when wet, but rubber tile or sheet material has a much wider differential between dry (rated "very good") and wet (rated "very poor"). The many varieties of applied wood finishes can have a major effect on tread slip resistance. Surprisingly, the building code does not identify a specific standard for stair tread material or finish; despite this, safety should be a primary criterion when making those selections.

Maintenance/Sustainability

Stair tread surfaces are subject to a much higher level of wear and abuse than floor surfaces, due to the manner in which feet normally make contact with treads. Selecting materials that can stand up to that abuse is of prime importance. Designers have a responsibility to select materials that are relatively easy to clean and maintain. There are materials, such as most stones, that can and have lasted for centuries; there are materials, such as wood, that can last for decades but require periodic refinishing; and there are materials, such as carpet and resilient flooring, that cannot be refinished and require replacement after a period of time. All of these factors are of major importance to building owners who must live with their buildings long after the designer is out of the picture. In addition to these concerns of day-to-day and long-term maintenance, there are the normal concerns for global sustainability that all designers are responsible for, including the construction processes employed, energy consumption, off-gassing, and the use of endangered materials.

Finally the selection of materials for risers must be made. Unlike treads, riser materials have relatively little bearing on stair safety or wear and abuse, making the selection criteria much less complex. Typically, the same material is used for both risers and treads. Occasionally, the riser surface will be used as a decorative element, with the use of color or figurative or patterned ceramic tile. There should be reasonable compatibility between the riser and tread materials, but that rarely presents a problem.

Handrails

Much of the basic information, written and graphic, related to handrails is in Sections 3 and 4, including the need for both the physical and perceived safety that they provide. Materials for handrails are of particular importance because of the immediacy of one's tactile experience with them. Most woods and plastics are comfortable to the touch, most metals are equally comfortable to the touch, but grasping a metal handrail on a very cold day can be quite uncomfortable, unless the metal is coated with a thermally nonconductive material. In general, designers should be sensitive to direct tactile contact experience with handrails, including avoidance of obstructions for the hand sometimes caused by the use of inappropriately selected hardware that supports the handrail.

Design solutions for supporting handrails vary greatly, from the simplest of solid partition extensions with wood cap trim, to extremely complex customized fabrications. A few basic solutions are illustrated in the drawings of this section, as well as additional drawings in Sections 3 and 4. Several of the publications noted in the Recommended Reading List at the end of this book have many photographs of railing design solutions, some of which are accompanied by detailed drawings of their construction techniques.

Stair Configurations

The 14 stair configurations shown here represent the most basic plan arrangements to be considered during the first stage of the stair design process (Illustrations S2-11 and S2-12). There are innumerable variations to these basic planning ideas, including some quite complex approaches which may be best for a specific design condition. These basic stair configurations are presented in the spirit of depicting possible starting points for stair design solutions.

Ramps

Ramps are often a viable alternative to stairs. They are required by code for all changes in levels in public buildings for people with physical disabilities when elevators are not present.

Most people use ramps quite often, whether it is a hilly urban sidewalk (take San Francisco as a case in point), or the sloped walk to a building on a hilly site. Ramps, both interior and exterior, have been in much wider use since the advent of Americans with Disabilities legislation in the early 1990s. Generally, they are safer than stairs (interior or exterior) for all users, except when there is ice or snow on an exterior ramp. Exterior ramps are much more commonplace than interior ramps because there is usually more exterior space available for the additional expanse required for ramps, as opposed to the amount of space required for an interior stair of reasonable (or even generous) riser/tread dimensions.

Code requirements for ramps are relatively simple and easy to apply. The critical issues are as follows:

• Maximum ramp slope is 1 inch rise for every 1 foot of ramp length.

• Ramp width minimum is 3 feet 8 inches.

• Maximum uninterrupted ramp length is 35 feet; for ramps requiring greater length, a 3-foot, 8-inch minimum level landing must be provided.

• Handrails are required on both sides; rail height should equal 34 to 38 inches.

ILLUS. S2-11

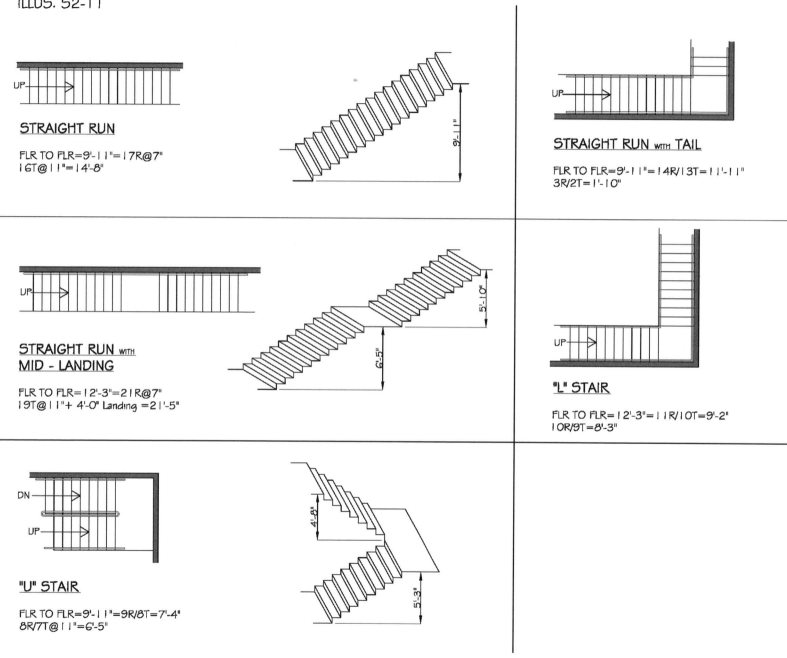

STRAIGHT RUN

FLR TO FLR=9'-11"=17R@7"
16T@11"=14'-8"

STRAIGHT RUN with **TAIL**

FLR TO FLR=9'-11"=14R/13T=11'-11"
3R/2T=1'-10"

STRAIGHT RUN with **MID - LANDING**

FLR TO FLR=12'-3"=21R@7"
19T@11"+ 4'-0" Landing =21'-5"

"L" STAIR

FLR TO FLR=12'-3"=11R/10T=9'-2"
10R/9T=8'-3"

"U" STAIR

FLR TO FLR=9'-11"=9R/8T=7'-4"
8R/7T@11"=6'-5"

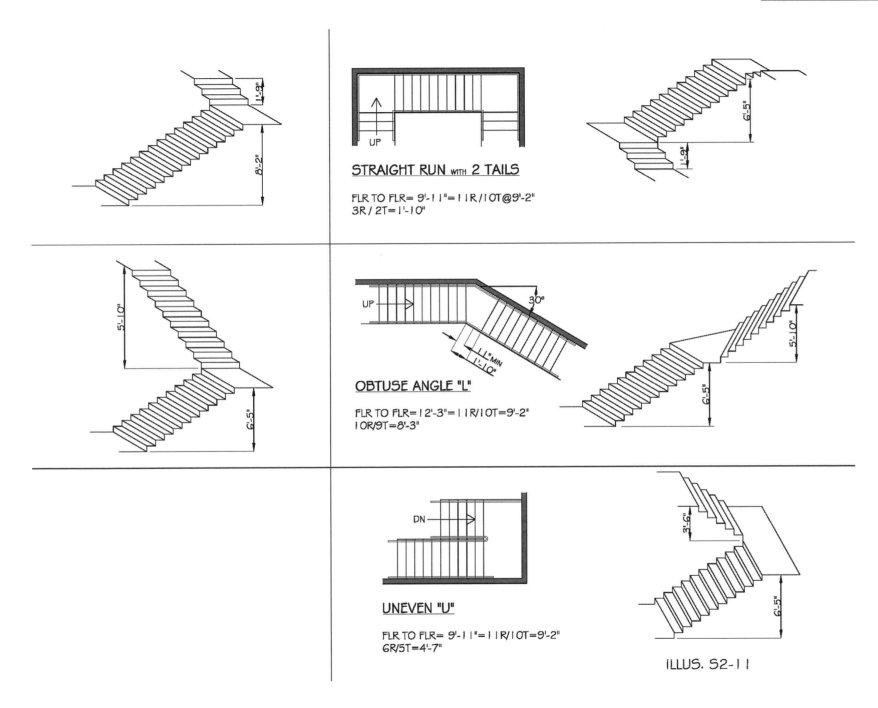

STRAIGHT RUN WITH **2 TAILS**

FLR TO FLR= 9'-11"=11R/10T@9'-2"
3R / 2T=1'-10"

OBTUSE ANGLE "L"

FLR TO FLR= 12'-3"=11R/10T=9'-2"
10R/9T=8'-3"

UNEVEN "U"

FLR TO FLR= 9'-11"=11R/10T=9'-2"
6R/5T=4'-7"

ILLUS. S2-11

ILLUS. S2–12

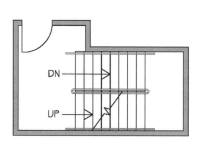

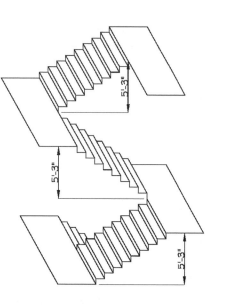

EXTENDED "U" (2 MID-LANDING)

FLR TO FLR= 15'-9"=9R/8T=7'-4"

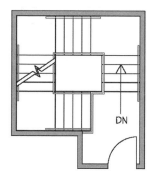

SQUARE

FLR TO FLR= 11'-8"=20R@7"
4x4T@11"=3'-8" + 4 Landings

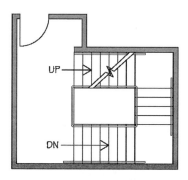

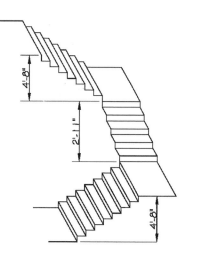

WIDE "U" STAIR

FLR TO FLR= 12'-3"=21R@7
18T@11"+2 Landings

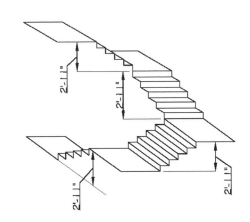

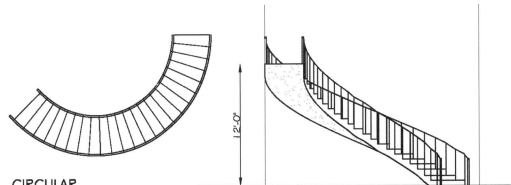

CIRCULAR

FLR TO FLR= 12'-0"=24R@6"
23T @ 10" Inner Dia., 12"@ 8'-0" Rad., 14.75"@ Outer Dia.

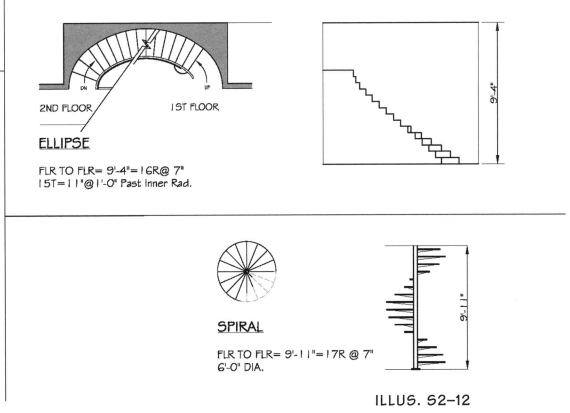

2ND FLOOR   1ST FLOOR

ELLIPSE

FLR TO FLR= 9'-4"=16R@ 7"
15T=11"@1'-0" Past Inner Rad.

SPIRAL

FLR TO FLR= 9'-11"=17R @ 7"
6'-0" DIA.

ILLUS. S2-12

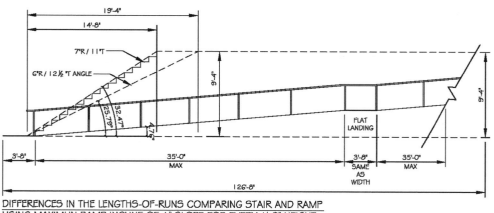

DIFFERENCES IN THE LENGTHS-OF-RUNS COMPARING STAIR AND RAMP
USING MAXIMUN RAMP INCLINE OF 1" SLOPE FOR EVERY 1'-0" HEIGHT
SCALE: 1/8" = 1'-0"
ILLUS. S2-13

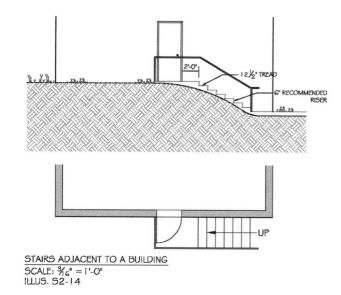

STAIRS ADJACENT TO A BUILDING
SCALE: 3/16" = 1'-0"
ILLUS. S2-14

Illustration S2-13 shows the basic dimensional requirements, plus a graphic comparison between the length of a ramp compared to a stair between two floor levels 9 feet, 4 inches apart. This clearly demonstrates why ramps are not in general interior use.

Materials for interior ramp surfaces should be slip resistant. Unlike stairs, where carpeted treads are frequently and appropriately used, most carpet products, except those with very low and dense pile, make travel by wheelchair difficult. Despite this, there is a great variety of appropriate, slip-resistant surface materials for ramps, from relatively soft surfaces, such as resilient floor products, to mid-level hardness, such as wood, to quite hard surfaces, such as concrete and unpolished stone.

Surface materials for exterior ramps have the added concern of water, snow, and ice during inclement weather, as well as the maintenance concerns of weathering. Again, there is a wide variety of appropriate materials, from exterior carpet products (typically with very low and dense pile), to natural and composite woods, to concrete and unpolished stone.

While the primary criteria in selecting a surface material for ramps must be on human safety, one should not overlook the issues of sustainability and users' tactile sense. The designer should consider all aspects of touch while keeping in mind that users' feet may be bare in some cases, or wearing soft and thin-soled shoes, or shod in heavy boots: How does it feel? Is the experience pleasant or difficult?

Exterior Stairs

The code requirements for stairs apply to both interior and exterior stairs. There are no special code requirements related to exterior stairs. Despite that, several factors related to exterior stairs strongly suggest that special attention be given to their design and dimensional characteristics. The first is weather. Water, snow, and ice on stair treads make them much more susceptible to causing trips and falls. Even in warm climates, wet treads are more dangerous to users. Second, peoples' gait when walking outside is generally longer than when walking inside. Transitioning from walking to using a stair makes a deeper tread much more comfortable for an exterior stair, whether ascending or descending, and the deeper tread requires a lower riser. Despite the fact that the code does not make a distinction, risers for exterior stairs should not be greater than 6 inches, accompanied by 12.5-inch treads. And even lower risers of 5.5 inches (14.75-inch treads) or 5-inch risers (16-inch treads) are safer and more comfortable. Risers of less than 5 inches create a step-ramp condition, a unique combination of stair and ramp that is described below.

There are three generalized categories of exterior stairs:

1. Stairs that are directly connected to a building (Illustration S2-14).

2. Garden stairs that are set in the landscape and are generally remote from buildings (Illustration S2-15).

3. Step-ramps, a hybrid combination of stairs and ramps. They are described and dimensioned in Illustration S2-16.

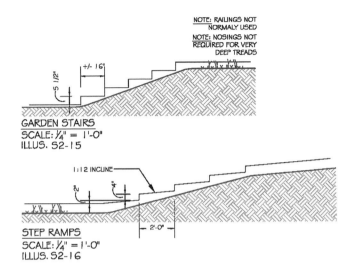

NOTE: RAILINGS NOT NORMALLY USED

NOTE: NOSINGS NOT REQUIRED FOR VERY DEEP TREADS

+/- 16"

5 1/2"

GARDEN STAIRS
SCALE: ¼" = 1'-0"
ILLUS. S2-15

1:12 INCLINE

2-0"

STEP RAMPS
SCALE: ¼" = 1'-0"
ILLUS. S2-16

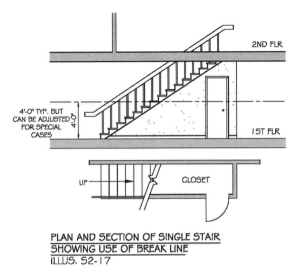

2ND FLR

4'-0" TYP. BUT CAN BE ADJUSTED FOR SPECIAL CASES

1ST FLR

UP   CLOSET

PLAN AND SECTION OF SINGLE STAIR
SHOWING USE OF BREAK LINE
ILLUS. S2-17

Selecting materials for exterior stair treads presents the same issues when selecting materials for exterior ramps, and the same wide range of materials and products are equally appropriate. Focus should be kept on human safety and comfort, with attention also to tactile quality underfoot.

For exterior stairs adjacent to buildings, such as the one shown in Illustration S2-14, railings are required, and with the same dimensional standards that apply to interior stairs. The one exception is for exterior stairs in which the adjacent grade follows the slope of the stair, making it impossible for a serious accident to occur if a small child were to fall through railing support openings; the requirement to limit railing support openings to the passage of a 4-inch sphere can be ignored. Tactile qualities for interior handrail materials are discussed later in this section and in Section 4. For exterior handrails in temperate climates, it is wise to avoid the use of metals, so that the less-than-pleasant sensation of grabbing a very cold handrail on a wintry day is eliminated.

Handrails are often not required for other exterior stairs because they usually have short runs; and particularly if they have very low risers, they are not as necessary for safety. In addition, they do not fall within building code jurisdiction. Despite this, it is never a mistake to provide them, and they are particularly welcomed by elderly users.

Beyond the basic ramp and exterior stair conditions presented here, there are many less conventional and/or adventurous design concepts and configurations that should be explored when facing similar design challenges. There are a multitude of creative solutions from the past, such as the famous Spanish Steps in Rome, to Frank Lloyd Wright's Guggenheim Museum in New York City.

Stair Drawing Basics

It is important to remember that designers' work products, i.e., their drawings, are usually small-scale simulations of a three-dimensional element or space to be constructed by others. Those drawings are the primary communication tool between designer and builder. The conventions of that tool, or language, must be clearly understood for the finished product to duplicate the designer's intent. Simply said, the conventions for drawing stairs are well established and designers must know and use them correctly for their stair designs to be understood and correctly executed.

Floor plans are commonly understood by designers and builders. Most of the elements in plan drawings are on the floor plane or are raised plane elements, such as tables, or counters, or desks. But stairs ascend and/or descend, and if the correct drawing conventions are not carefully adhered to, the design may not be understood and therefore not correctly built. Because of the ascending and descending nature of stairs, it is necessary to employ the use of break lines. To explain their use, the following illustrations demonstrate the primary uses of break lines as they relate to drawing stairs.

Illustration S2-17 shows a fairly typical residential setting in which a straight-run stair connects the first and second floors of the house, and a closet is under the stair to utilize that otherwise unused space. The section drawing shows the stair with its railing and the door to the closet. A dashed line is shown 4 feet, 0 inches above the first floor, (not usually shown on construction drawings, but shown here for instructional purposes) indicating that the plan can only show the plan elements that are below that line. (The 4-foot, 0-inch height of the plan section line is the standard drawing convention, but designers may raise or lower that line if it will help to better understand the plan drawing, and if the change from that standard is clearly noted on the drawings.) Because a major portion of the stair is above the 4-foot, 0-inch line, that portion of the stair will not be seen in the plan drawing. A break line is employed to visually cut off the portion of the stair above 4 feet, 0 inches. In floor plan drawings, break lines are typically shown at an angle rather than parallel or perpendicular to the normally orthogonal building, so as not to be confused with the typically orthogonal lines of the actual plan elements. Beyond the break line, the plan drawing shows the partition below the stair, including the closet door. Note that a double break line is used in order to indicate the transition from what lies above and below the plan section line. Also note that the line of the wall on the far side of the stair is not broken, because it is continuous and remains the same both above and below the plan section line.

Illustration S2-18 shows another fairly typical residential situation, in which there are two straight-run stairs, one directly above the other. One stair connects the first floor to the second floor, and the other stair connects the first floor with the basement. The section drawing shows both stairs with their railings, as well as the additional railings required to prevent someone from falling into the open stair well. A dashed plan section line is drawn 4 feet, 0 inches above the first floor, indicating that which can be seen below that line. A double break line is used to separate the ascending and descending stairs, including their railings, but the line of the wall on the far side of the stairs as well as the horizontal safety or guard rail on the first floor, are not broken because it is continuous and remains the same both above and below the plan section line.

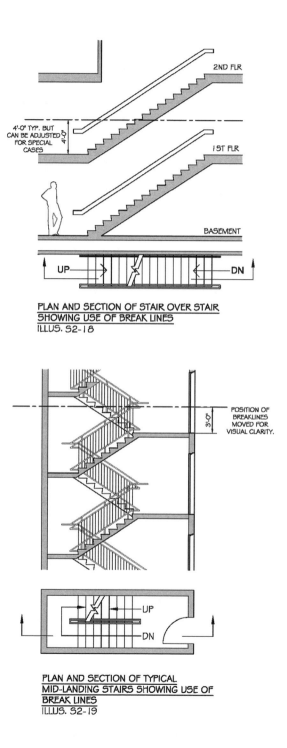

PLAN AND SECTION OF STAIR OVER STAIR SHOWING USE OF BREAK LINES
ILLUS. S2-18

PLAN AND SECTION OF TYPICAL MID-LANDING STAIRS SHOWING USE OF BREAK LINES
ILLUS. S2-19

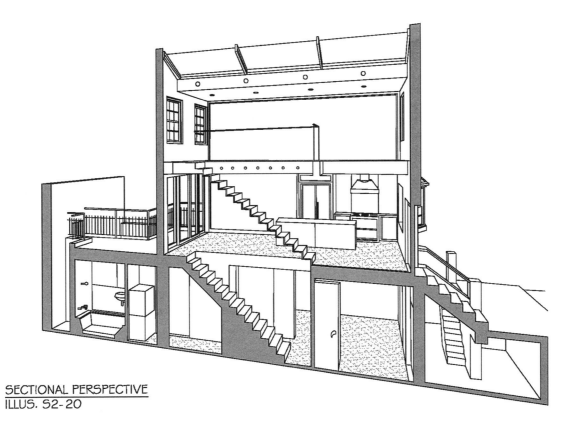

SECTIONAL PERSPECTIVE
ILLUS. S2-20

Illustration S2-19 shows a typical concrete fire stair with mid-floor landings between all floors of a hi-rise office building. Except for the first and top floors, the floor plans are identical to one another. The section drawing shows the stairs between two typical upper floors. As occupants enter the stair on the fifteenth floor from the building's main corridor, they can go up the stair to the sixteenth floor, or down the other side of the stair to the fourteenth floor below. The dashed plan section line is shown 4 feet, 0 inches above the fifteenth floor line, permitting the first several treads of the ascending flight to be shown before it is interrupted by a break line. The plan drawing of the top half of the descending flight can be seen in full, as well as the mid-floor landing; from that point the bottom half of the descending flight can be seen until it is interrupted by the break line of the ascending flight above, where a second break line is used to differentiate the ascending and descending flights. Make note that the break lines engage the handrails, but do not engage the surrounding masonry wall.

Illustration S2-20 is a sectional perspective, a drawing type that can be very effective in describing the three-dimensional qualities of a stair (or stairs) in a larger context. This drawing approach takes a section through a stair and the remainder of the surrounding building and then looks into the building beyond the vertical plane of the section. The descriptiveness of this drawing approachis useful for one's own visualization purposes, as well as an excellent presentation tool for others to better understand the three dimensional implications of the stair design.

There are unique stair designs in which the basic drawing conventions cannot be strictly applied. The designer is best advised to use the drawing conventions as far as they are applicable and then improvise upon the conventions in as sensible a manner as possible, remembering that the drawing must speak for itself when the designer is not present to explain the stair's unique characteristics.

A BRIEF REVIEW OF BASIC FACTORS INVOLVED IN MAKING STAIR DESIGN DECISIONS

SITE FACTORS

- In new buildings: the building type and its proposed occupancy type and users (general public and/or special populations)

- In existing buildings: building history and context (its age and purpose) and the intended new use and users (general public and/or special populations)

- Design expectations (utilitarian, monumental, or somewhere in between)

- Existing structural system and its degree of flexibility

FLOOR-TO-FLOOR HEIGHTS

- Is a simple straight-run stair possible?

- Does the stair require one or more mid-landings?

- Are more than two floor levels involved?

FLOOR PLAN CONDITIONS

- Is floor space limited, requiring tight planning, or may the stair be planned more generously?

- Is floor plan fixed, or may plan adjustments be made?

- Is direction of pedestrian flow or circulation/egress a stair-planning consideration?

- Stair configuration possibilities

RISER/TREAD RELATIONSHIP

- Code considerations

- Safety/comfort considerations

- Length-of-run implications and floor space limitations

CODE CONSIDERATIONS

- Stair placement in terms of egress

- Stair width requirements

- Need for enclosure (type, how much, hourly rating)

SAFETY

- Precautions against trips, falls, etc.

- Headroom clearance

THE ONE OVERRIDING FACTOR: THE HUMAN FACTOR

- Does the stair serve its users well and appropriately? Is it well integrated with the site and its purposes, permitting users to feel comfortable with its presence?

SECTION 3

STAIR DESIGN CASE STUDIES—PHASE I

The following case studies have been developed to take the reader through an interactive process that will lead to successful stair design solutions. The preceding sections examined the many factors that must be considered in the design process. This section organizes and prioritizes those factors into a useful format and employs the case studies as demonstrations of the process. The case studies are sequentially presented, starting with a very simple example and increasing in complexity with each succeeding example.

In this section, the case studies are primarily concerned with stair planning and configuration, and do not explore the necessary and more detailed aspects of stair construction, railings, materials, and architectural detailing. The case studies of this section are used again in Section 4, in order to further explore and explain those necessary and more detailed aspects of good stair design.

| CASE STUDY

The setting is a basic contemporary townhouse, still in the design stage. It is one of many identical townhouses that are part of a developer's large-scale "planned unit development." It is 22 feet, 0 inches wide from centerline to centerline of its party walls, and 43 feet, 4 inches long (plus second-floor balcony overhangs at both ends), and it is two stories tall plus an unplanned/unfinished basement, as seen in the floor plans and sections in Illustration S3-1. The floor-to-floor heights have been established at 9 feet, 1½ inches, based on a 1 foot, 1 inch floor construction thickness, resulting in an 8 foot, ½ inch finished ceiling height to accommodate the use of uncut (standard) 8 foot, 0 inch high drywall panels, for the sake of construction economy.

The most typical stair design solution in townhouses is the use of a straight-run stair that is adjacent to one of the party walls. A floor plan of this kind is shown in the Case Study Illustrations. With a floor-to-floor height of 9 feet, 1½", there are five reasonably appropriate riser/tread combinations that are permitted by the building code:

- **15 risers** at 7.30 inches with 10¾-inch treads (14 x 10¾" = 12' 6½" length-of-run)

- **16 risers** at 6.84 inches with 11½-inch treads (15 x 11½"= 14' 4½" length-of-run)

- **17 risers** at 6.44 inches with 12½-inch treads (16 x 12½" = 16'8" length-of-run)

- **18 risers** at 6.08 inches with 13½-inch treads (17 x 13½" = 19'1" length-of-run)

- **19 risers** at 5.76 inches with 14-inch treads (18 x 14" = 21' 0" length-of-run)

Take note that with only 1½-inch difference from the highest (7.30 inches) to lowest (5.76 inches) riser heights, there is a variation of 6 feet, 7 inches in length-of-run. Also note that with a code minimum requirement of 6 feet, 8 inches headroom, and a ceiling height of 8 feet, 0½" inches, not more than two risers (or one tread) can be covered by the ceiling above, regardless of the riser height selected. See the sectional sketch in Illustration S3-1 to better understand the headroom requirement.

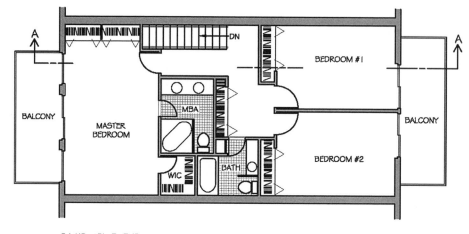

2ND FLOOR

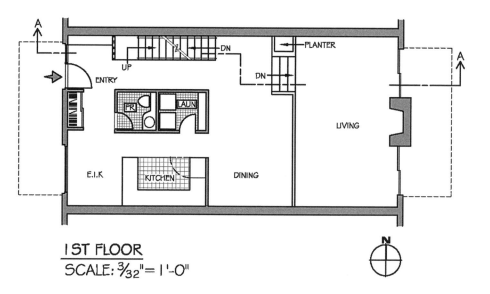

1ST FLOOR
SCALE: ³⁄₃₂"= 1'-0"

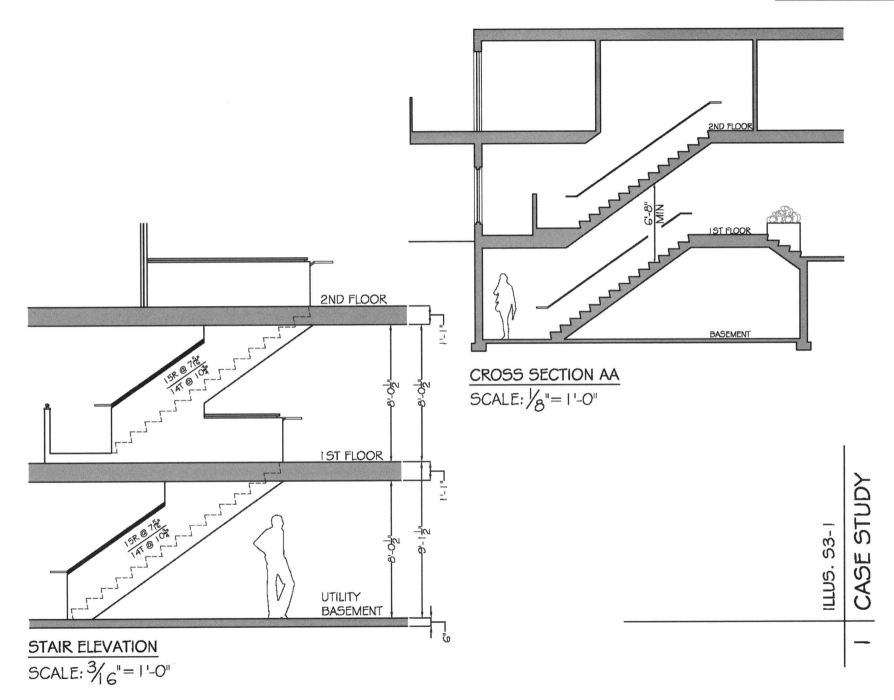

2ND FLOOR

15R @ 7⅝"
14T @ 10¾"

1ST FLOOR

8'-0½"

1'-1"

15R @ 7⅝"
14T @ 10¾"

8'-0½"

9'-1½"

UTILITY
BASEMENT

6"

STAIR ELEVATION
SCALE: 3/16" = 1'-0"

2ND FLOOR

6'-8" MIN

1ST FLOOR

BASEMENT

CROSS SECTION AA
SCALE: 1/8" = 1'-0"

ILLUS. S3-1 | CASE STUDY

Stair width is the remaining important dimensional issue not yet addressed. The building code requires a minimum width of 3 feet, 0 inches, which is commonplace and generally acceptable in a contemporary townhouse. While making the stair a few inches wider in order to make it feel a bit more generous would be possible, say to 3 feet, 4 inches, the tentative design decision here is to keep the stair width at 3 feet, 0 inches. We can re-examine the width after the stair has been designed to see if widening it can be accomplished without having a negative effect on other aspects of space planning, particularly on the second floor where bed and bathroom dimensions are critical and a few inches can make a significant difference.

Similarly, because modest-sized townhouses are limited in square footage, a riser/tread selection must be geared to the size of the house. A low riser/deep tread selection will have a negative impact on overall space planning due to its excessive length-of-run. For the purposes of a first-try solution, a 7.3" riser/10.75" tread combination is an appropriate tentative selection, producing a 15 riser/14 tread stair with a 12 foot, 6½ inch length-of-run. A plan and section solution for this riser/tread combination is shown in Illustration S3-1. Note that the master bedroom configuration cannot be purely rectangular due to the need for headroom as one starts up the stair.

Also note that a design decision has been made to keep the stair to the basement open, divided from the dining area with only a railing, rather than enclosing it with a wall and door.

A design decision was made to lower the living room floor approximately 2 feet, 0 inches in order to give it a higher ceiling, providing a more open spatial quality without visually separating it from the dining area. The short run of steps from the dining area to the lowered living room floor has different riser/tread dimensions than the stairs to the second floor or the basement. If the 7.3-inch riser height of the two main stairs had been used, three risers would have resulted in a 21.9-inch level change, and a four-riser run would create a 29.2-inch level change. Because the short run of steps to the living room is substantially separated from the two main stairs, the change in riser/tread dimensions can be used without creating discomfort or potential trips and falls for those in the house. The four 6-inch risers, with 13½-inch treads create a 2-foot, 0-inch level change and provide a more comfortable and gracious transition to the living room.

For an additional case study of a wood residential stair, see this guidebook's Companion Web site—Case Study 1A (Illustration CW-4).

2 | CASE STUDY

In all cases, required egress stairs must meet building code and ADA requirements. The code issues described in some detail in Section 2 are reiterated here in outline form as case study #2 focuses here on enclosed exit stairs:

Riser/Tread Relationship	Stair Width
Headroom	Handrails
Stair Enclosures	ADA Requirements
Two Means of Egress	Areas of Refuge

Floor-to-floor heights in multi-story buildings vary greatly, from as little as 8 feet, 8 inches (as in apartment or hotel buildings with pre-cast concrete plank floors and no ceiling plenum) to as much as 12 feet, 0 inches to 13 feet, 0 inches (as in hi-rise speculative office buildings with large structural bays and deep ceiling plenums).

Most multi-story buildings, except for houses and very small apartment buildings, have building code–required enclosed exit stairs or "fire stairs." In most cases, particularly in buildings with more than three stories, elevators serve the great bulk of vertical travel, and the required fire stairs are used almost exclusively for emergency exit purposes. These stairways are typically utilitarian in quality, designed to meet minimum building code requirements, and are usually devoid of aesthetic intent. Despite this, there are some fire stairs that are also meant to be used for day-to-day personal travel from floor to floor; these stairs often receive much more design attention in order to provide a more pleasant daily experience for its users, as specifically shown in Case Study 2A, which can be seen in this guidebook's Companion Web site Illustration CW-5.

The building type selected is a typical six-story suburban speculative office building with 10-foot, 4-inch floor-to-floor heights and strictly utilitarian fire/exit stairs. Because the building has a large branch bank on the first floor, as well as some small retail tenants, the first-to-second floor-to-floor dimension is 13 feet, 9 inches. A typical floor plan and through-section are shown in Illustration S3-2.1.

In the great majority of fire/exit stairs, the code maximum riser height is used; in this case the riser height will be 6.89 inches (10'-4" or 124" ÷ 18 = 6.89), with an 11-inch tread. The code minimum stair and landing width of 3 feet, 8 inches produces a typical fire/exit stair configuration as shown in the plan and section drawings of Illustration S3-2.1.

This conventional "U" shaped fire/exit stair is very commonplace because it is particularly compact and economical in its use of space. In addition, it conveniently repeats floor after floor, resulting in an ease and simplicity of planning with the stair entry door always in the same location on each floor. Note that the door is in a recessed position; this is not required by code, but it provides a safer and more comfortable condition. There is less chance that someone coming down the stair will be hit by the door being opened by someone else; this is of particular concern when there is an emergency condition and occupants are rushing to get out of the building. Code compliance permits the door to swing into the landing as long as the required width of the stair is not reduced by more than one half, or 1 foot, 10 inches, as shown in Illustration S3-2.1. Despite this, and particularly in cases where the fire/exit stair is used for daily travel (and not just for emergency use), a recessed door provides a better design solution.

ILLUS. S3-2.1

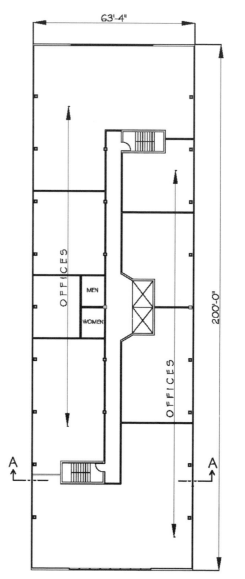

KEY PLAN
SCALE: 1/32" = 1'-0"

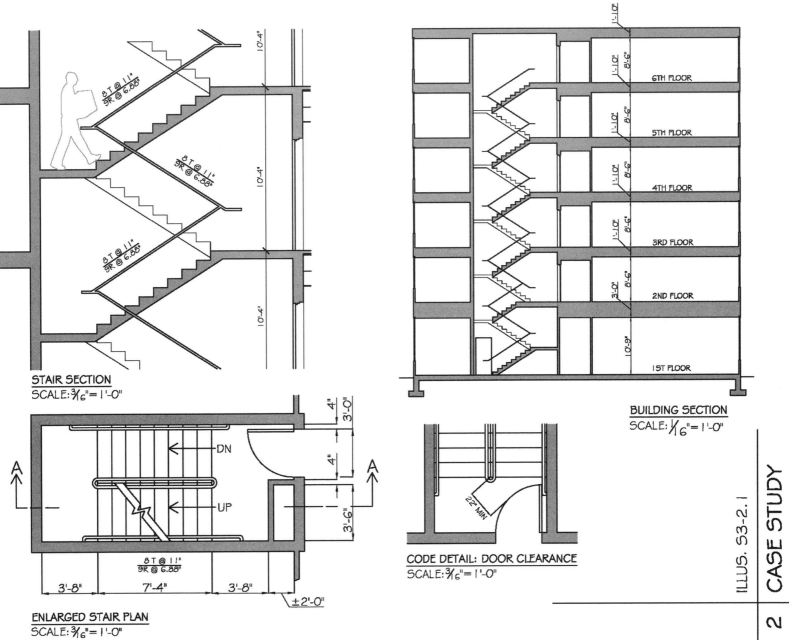

STAIR SECTION
SCALE: 3/16" = 1'-0"

ENLARGED STAIR PLAN
SCALE: 3/16" = 1'-0"

CODE DETAIL: DOOR CLEARANCE
SCALE: 3/16" = 1'-0"

BUILDING SECTION
SCALE: 1/16" = 1'-0"

ILLUS. S3-2.1

2 | CASE STUDY

TECHNIQUES FOR GETTING REQUIRED EGRESS STAIRS EXITING DIRECTLY TO THE ENTRANCE

ILLUS. S3-2.2

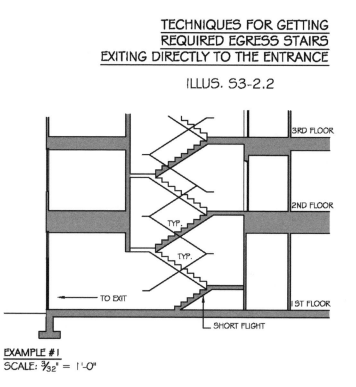

EXAMPLE #1
SCALE: ³⁄₃₂" = 1'-0"

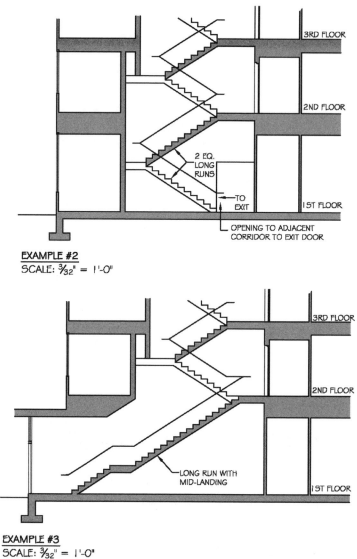

EXAMPLE #2
SCALE: ³⁄₃₂" = 1'-0"

EXAMPLE #3
SCALE: ³⁄₃₂" = 1'-0"

Before leaving the area of required fire/egress stairs, it is necessary to explain and describe a not-too-infrequent, and sometimes problematic, stair design condition. The building code, with its primary concern for human safety, requires that exit stairs discharge the building's occupants directly to the exterior. More specifically, the stair may not discharge occupants to another part of the building, such as a first-floor corridor. Access to fire/exit stairs is typically from an internal corridor in a floor-to-floor pattern, as seen in the through-section drawings of Case Study 2 (Illustration S3-2.1). At the first, or ground floor level, if floor space is available, a very simple solution is to provide an adjacent corridor directly to the exterior. If additional space is not available, a three-flight/two mid-landing stair can be created. A straight-run stair with a mid-landing is still another viable solution. All three of these solutions will comply with code requirements and are shown in Illustration S3-2.2.

The six-story office building used as the setting for these three examples presents an uncomplicated case in point. Many building conditions are not as free of complexities, particularly with difficult urban sites and/or buildings, and methods for getting occupants to the exterior can become quite complex. Despite any possible complexities, it is the concept of safe egress that must be remembered.

For an additional case study of a code-required egress stair that is designed for day-to-day use, and therefore given more careful design attention, see Case Study 2A in this guidebook's Companion Web site, which also includes photographs of some well designed, everyday-use, code-compliant egress stairs (Illustration CW-5).

3 | CASE STUDY

The setting for Case Study 3 is a two-story boutique hotel lobby, with an overlooking second-floor space that serves as a bar and lounge, as shown in the schematic plan and section of Illustration S3-3.1.

Despite its relatively small size, the design intent is to create a special space that is gracious and modestly dramatic, with the stair to the second floor as a central sculptural element. The floor-to-floor height is 12 feet, 0 inches. Because a gracious ambiance is desired, an ergonomically comfortable 6-inch riser is selected, resulting in a stair with 24 risers (24 risers x 6" = 144" or 12'0"). A dramatic curving stair to the second floor provides the desired spatial effect. For a curved stair that is part of this building's egress system, the building code requires:

• Minimum stair width of 3 feet, 8 inches

• The smaller radius must be at least twice the stair width (7 feet, 4 inches)

• Tread depth must be at least 10 inches at its narrow end, and at least 11 inches when measured 12 inches from the narrow end of the tread

To provide a somewhat more generously dimensioned stair, a width of 4 feet, 0 inches is selected, producing a minimum outer radius of 12 feet, 0 inches. As shown in the larger-scale sketch of Illustration S3-3.1, a 10-inch tread depth at the inner (8 foot, 0 inch) radius produces a tread depth of 11.25 inches when measured 12 inches from the narrow end of the tread, and a 15-inch tread depth when measured at the wide end of the tread.

The design solution selected is shown in the plan and section drawings of Illustration S3-3.1. This curved stair fits comfortably within the space and helps to visually articulate the functional elements of entrance, guest registration, concierge desk, path to elevator, and the approach to the bar and lounge above. The detailing of this sculptural element is critical to its success; that process is described in Section 4.

There are many very successful sculptural curved stairs in open lobby settings that may stimulate one's creative thoughts when faced with similar design problems.

At the entrance to many public buildings, there is often the need and/or desire for an open and impressive stair. Their purpose can vary a great deal, and they often get very little use because elevators are usually nearby and preferred by most people. They are commonplace in many old and/or historic buildings that were built before the advent or common use of elevators. This design tradition is still in common use, to a great degree because the grand gesture of these stairs often symbolizes the importance of their setting. They also provide architects and designers with the opportunity to make a strong sculptural statement at a building's point of entrance. Entrances themselves are symbolic spaces because they create the building's primary ambiance and set the stage for what will follow in the spaces beyond the entrance.

Multi-story buildings require enclosed stairwells that exit directly to the exterior. Codes do permit one flight to be unenclosed, typically from the second floor down to the entry level, with the provision that the stair terminates near the ground-level entrance to the building. The advent of sophisticated fire suppression technology over the past few decades has permitted a much greater openness of spaces in buildings, such as hotel and shopping mall atria, adventurous interior configurations of mezzanines, overhanging corridors and balconies, as well as complex level changes. Despite this, the monumental, ceremonial, or sculptural lobby stair is still an often used design tool. Case Study 3 focuses on a relatively simple, two-floor level sculptural stair, leaving the complexities of multi-level stairs for Case Study 4.

Curved, or curvilinear or helical stairs (all three terms are appropriate), have been part of our building heritage for many hundreds of years. The inherent grace and sculptural potential of the curved stair is immense, particularly in our typically rectangular and/or straight-line buildings. The geometry of curved stairs can be kept relatively simple, although more adventurous curved stairs can present some quite complex geometric configurations requiring extensive calculations. The curved stair demonstrated in Case Study 3 is not overly complex and should provide an appropriate introduction for designing these elegant stairs.

> For an additional case study of a curved stair see the elliptical stair in Case Study 3A in this guidebook's Companion Web site (Illustration CW-6).

3 | CASE STUDY

ILLUS. S3-3.1

2ND FLOOR

1ST FLOOR
SCALE: $\frac{1}{16}$" = 1'-0"

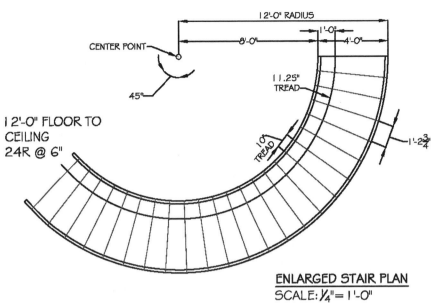

CENTER POINT

12'-0" RADIUS

8'-0"

1'-0"

4'-0"

45°

11.25"
TREAD

10"
TREAD

1'-2¾"

12'-0" FLOOR TO
CEILING
24R @ 6"

ENLARGED STAIR PLAN
SCALE: ¼" = 1'-0"

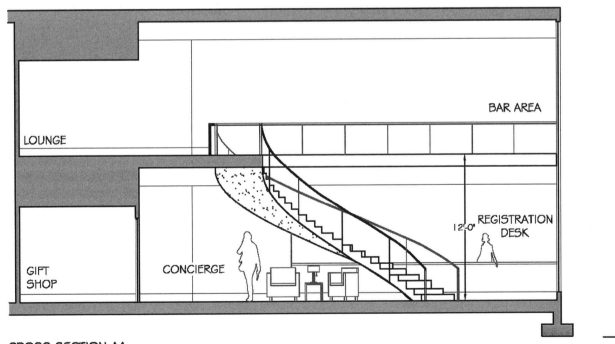

LOUNGE

BAR AREA

GIFT
SHOP

CONCIERGE

REGISTRATION
DESK

12'-0"

CROSS SECTION AA
SCALE: ⅛" = 1'-0"

ILLUS. S3-3.1

3 | CASE STUDY

In a desire to create more open and flowing spaces geared to today's lifestyles, the renovation proposal calls for the removal of all of the original second floor and portions of the original first and third floors, as well as all of the original stairs. The result is a six-level house with high-ceilinged living and entertaining spaces opening out to a rear garden, as seen in the revised floor plans and section of Illustration S3-4. New floor levels have been designated, starting with the original basement (level B) for the family room, the original first floor (level 1F) for the entry and library, the newly created floor levels 1R (living room) and 2F (master bedroom), the original third floor (level 2R) for a guest room, and the original fourth floor (level 3) for guest/maid rooms and a studio with abundant light. The new central stair should have risers at a comfortable height, consistent with the relative luxury of the house, and the risers must maintain a consistent height throughout.

The two unchanged floor-to-floor dimensions are from the entry (level 1F) to the basement (level B) of 8', 1", or 97", and from the rear guest room (level 2R) to the studio (level 3) of 9 feet, 1" or 109". The entry level to the basement can be accomplished with 15 risers at 6.466 inches (87 inches divided by 15), and the rear guest level (2R) to the studio (level 3) can be accomplished with 17 risers at 6.441 inches (109.5 inches divided by 17). Connecting the entry (level 1F) to the rear guest room (level 2R), a vertical

distance of 19 feet, 5 inches or 233 inches can be accomplished with 36 risers at 6.472 inches (233 inches divided by 36); with levels 1R and 2F established by the desired number of risers between levels. Level 1R is set 11 risers above level 1F (approximately 5 feet, 11 inches); level 2F is set 14 risers above level 1R (approximately 7 feet, 6 inches); and level 2R is set 11 risers above level 2F (approximately 5 feet, 11 inches). With all risers virtually the same height (between 6.441 and 6.472 inches), a tread depth of 12 inches has been selected, and a new stair width of 3 feet, 6 inches used throughout all levels of the contiguous dog-leg stair. With this proposed renovation, a very different kind of residence, with a more dynamic spatial quality, has been created.

The arithmetic manipulations required to create new floor levels can be complex and tedious, but the rewards of potentially interesting spaces connected by stairs that contribute to the sequential flow may more than balance the tedium.

For additional case studies of stairs that serve intermediate floor levels, see Case Studies 4A and 4B in this resource guidebook's Companion Web site (Illustrations CW-7 and CW-8).

4 | CASE STUDY

The case studies to this point have dealt primarily with stairs between two full-height floors. While most stairs are designed for settings of this kind, it is not at all uncommon for stairs to serve intermediate floor levels. The "split level" houses of the 1950s were based on creating intermediate levels for different living functions. Sloping terrain will often generate a design solution with staggered floor levels. On occasion, in the renovation of older buildings, particularly those with low or constraining ceiling heights, floor levels will be adjusted to open up spaces. And there is the occasional need to join two adjacent buildings with unaligned floor levels.

Buildings with intermediate floor levels have the potential for creating visually exciting spaces and vistas. They also tend to present complex and difficult to resolve stair design problems. Because interior conditions with intermediate floor levels are not the norm, it is not possible to present a typical condition or conditions; they tend to be special cases directly related to specific conditions or settings. The case study presented here illustrates one of the several possible intermediate floor level circumstances that designers may encounter.

This case study involves an early twentieth-century townhouse in Chicago's affluent "Gold Coast" residential area. Those townhouses are typically large and grand, but rarely satisfy contemporary lifestyles without significant renovation. As was typical of many of the large urban houses of this type, it went through significant renovations, including conversion to six small apartments in the 1940s. While the original exterior condition is essentially intact, most of its original interior architectural detail has been lost.

ILLUS. S3-4

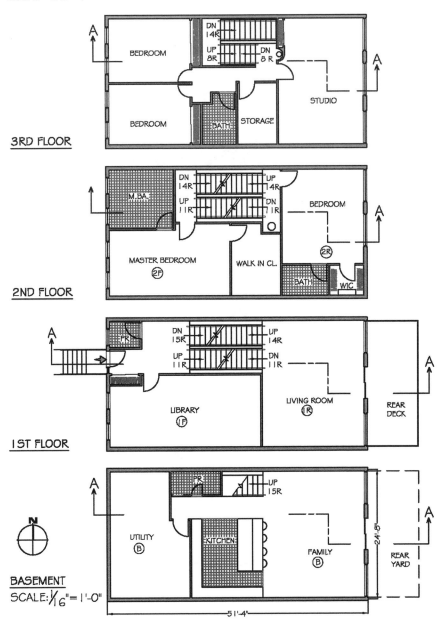

3RD FLOOR

2ND FLOOR

1ST FLOOR

BASEMENT

SCALE: 1/16" = 1'-0"

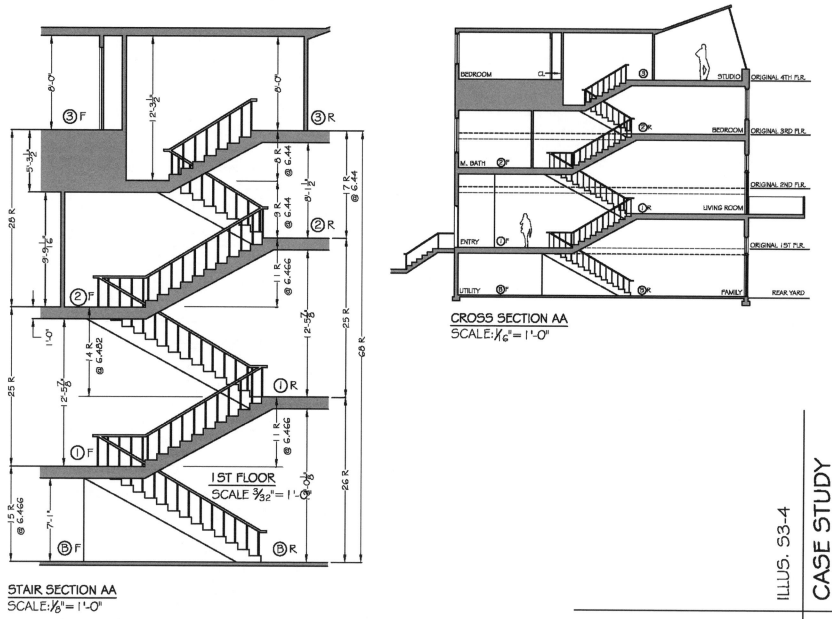

STAIR SECTION AA
SCALE: 1/8" = 1'-0"

1ST FLOOR
SCALE 3/32" = 1'-0"

CROSS SECTION AA
SCALE: 1/16" = 1'-0"

ILLUS. S3-4

4 | CASE STUDY

SECTION 4

STAIR DESIGN CASE STUDIES—PHASE II

The case studies in Section 3 focused exclusively on stair planning, without concern for stair construction or architectural details. While detailed stair elements, such as handrails and tread nosings, are shown in the small-scale plan and section drawings of the Section 3 case studies, the more detailed issues relating to dimensions, configurations, and materials were not addressed. The case studies in this section will focus on the basics of those details, providing studies based on wood, steel, and concrete construction. The possible variations in stair detailing are unlimited. There are several publications with photographs; some of them with detailed drawings of highly customized stair design solutions (see the recommended reading list on page 219). A note of caution: Many of the photographed stairs do not comply with the requirements of the International Building Code; in some cases because they pre-date the code, or because the code requirements did not apply or were ignored. The stair details in this section are essentially conventional in nature and are meant to serve as an introduction for each reader's development of less conventional future design solutions.

For the sake of continuity, Case Study 5 is specifically related to the residential wood stair shown in Case Study 1 presented in Section 3; Case Study 6 is specifically related to the enclosed steel fire stair shown in Case Study 2; and Case Study 7 is specifically related to the circular concrete stair shown in Case Study 3. In addition to publications in the recommended reading list at the end of this text, there is a great deal of useful information about stair materials and detailing (particularly for handrail systems) available in manufacturers' product literature and Web sites.

To provide appropriate context for this section's case studies, the diagrammatic sketches of Illustrations S4-1A through S4-1G provide an overview of the basic construction configurations typically employed to support stairs. Again, there are innumerable variations that can be devised.

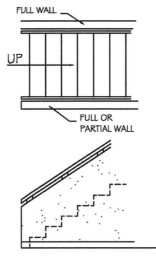

Walls or solid railings on both sides of the stair

As illustrated, there is a full wall on one side and a wall on the other side that goes up to handrail height and down to the floor below, enclosing a storage closet below the stair. If the closet is not needed or desired, that enclosing wall can be limited to a solid railing with the underside of the stair exposed or finished with panel material, such as gypsum wall board or MDF plywood. Open risers are also a possible design solution.

A **WALLS ON BOTH SIDES**
SCALE: NTS
ILLUS. S4-1

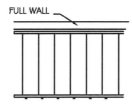
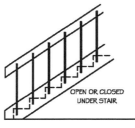

Wall on one side, exposed stringer on the other

As illustrated, there is a full wall on one side and an exposed stringer supporting a stock steel rod railing with a wood cap handrail on the other side. The exposed stringer can be placed on top of a partition that goes to the floor below, or it can be left freestanding with the underside of the stair exposed. Many other railing design solutions are possible with an exposed stringer, as well as the use of open risers.

B **EXPOSED STRINGER, HIDDEN TREADS**
SCALE: NTS
ILLUS. S4-1

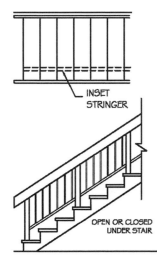

INSET
STRINGER

OPEN OR CLOSED
UNDER STAIR

Wall on one side, cut or notched stringer on the other

As illustrated, there is a full wall on one side, and a cut or notched stringer on the other side, exposing and expressing the ends of the individual treads. The stringer can be minimally inset from the ends of the treads (less than 1 inch), or inset several inches from the ends of the treads for a visually more effective result. In this case, the railing is shown with steel balusters supported between wood posts placed every fourth tread.

© **NOTCHED & EXPOSED STRINGER**
SCALE: NTS
ILLUS. S4-1

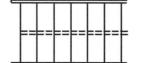

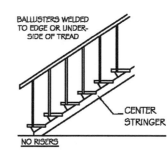

BALLUSTERS WELDED
TO EDGE OR UNDER-
SIDE OF TREAD

CENTER
STRINGER

NO RISERS

Freestanding stair supported by a central stringer

The central stringer, supported by the floor construction at both ends, can be a diagonal beam of laminated wood, steel, or pre-cast concrete. The treads must be very securely attached to the stringer to avoid tipping in the event that a very heavy person places all of their weight on one end of the tread. These attachments can be bolted or welded. As shown in Illustration S4-1F, the treads are fabricated of formed steel plate and welded to the fabricated steel stringer. The railing is supported by steel balusters that are welded to the underside of the steel plate treads, with the handrail supported by individual steel brackets welded to the balusters.

Ⓓ **SINGLE CENTER STRINGER**
SCALE: NTS
ILLUS. S4-1

Further Discussion

The stair types shown in sketches S4-1A, B, C, &- E indicate a full wall on one side of the stair and an open opposite side. All of these stair types can become freestanding stairs by making both sides open, using the same railing type shown on the open side.

All of the stair types illustrated here may be used residentially, as well as in public buildings. Several of the railings in these illustrations do not comply with IBC standards for public buildings because their openings are too large; they could be revised to comply by adding additional horizontal members. Materials for stair structures must be appropriate to the buildings of which they are a part. In typical residential construction, it would be inappropriate to incorporate a concrete stair. In most steel structures, a fabricated steel stair would be most appropriate. Decisions related to the materials used to build a stair should be made very early in the stair design process.

Materials for the fabrication of railings and handrails must be appropriate for the stair of which they are a part. A mix of materials can often be entirely appropriate; a wood stair need not have a railing and handrail made of wood, and the same is true of steel and concrete stairs. But the size, proportion, and design characteristics of the railing and handrail must be consistent with the design characteristics of the stair. There are no hard and fast rules to be followed in these design decisions; this is where the designer's aesthetic judgments are involved.

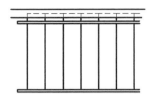

Wall on one side, individual treads cantilevered from wall

As illustrated, the full wall on one side supports the cantilevered treads, requiring a wall structure capable of supporting the treads. This is typically accomplished with the tread embedded and counterbalanced in a massive masonry wall, or with steel treads welded to a steel structure within the wall. The illustrated railing is supported by steel balusters that are individually welded to the supporting steel underside of the cast stone treads. The handrail is supported on steel brackets that are welded to the balusters.

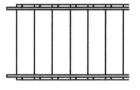

PLASTIC HANDRAIL
1/2" GLASS PANEL
GLASS BOLTED TO ENDS OF TREADS
STEEL TREADS WELDED TO STEEL STRUCTURE IN WALL & CANTILEVERED FROM WALL
CAST STONE TREAD WITH STEEL PLATE ANCHORED IN WALL

E CANTILEVERED TREADS
SCALE: NTS
ILLUS. S4-1

Freestanding concrete stairs

Concrete, both cast-in-place and pre-cast, has the potential for creating very sculptural stairs. The two stair profiles shown in the accompanying sketches are typical profiles for concrete stairs. Railing fabrications can be welded or bolted to embedded steel plates or machined nuts, resulting in the use of steel balusters, or bolted plate glass railings with plastic or wood handrails applied (Illustration S4-1G). Because of the completely plastic quality of concrete, the possibilities are endless.

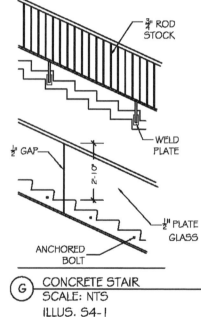

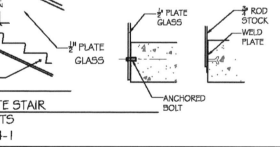

G CONCRETE STAIR
SCALE: NTS
ILLUS. S4-1

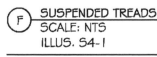
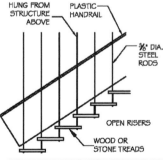

Wall on one side, treads individually suspended on the other

As illustrated, there is a full, tread-supporting wall on one side, and the treads on the other side are individually suspended by steel suspension rods from above, resulting in a stair without a supporting stringer. This kind of suspended stair obviously requires a floor structure or beam above capable of supporting the stair. Typically, suspended stairs require a solid connection to the floor below in order to prevent excessive swaying movement. The treads could be one of many appropriate materials such as wood, steel, or reinforced cast stone. The handrail is attached to the suspension rods by welded handrail brackets, similar to those used for attaching a handrail to a wall surface, eliminating the need for a linear supporting element.

F SUSPENDED TREADS
SCALE: NTS
ILLUS. S4-1

5 | CASE STUDY

ILLUS. S4-2

The stairs developed in Case Study 1 (Section 3) ended at the planning phase, its details left undefined. The detailed drawings of Illustration S4-2 complete the design process. As shown here, the contained stringers and traditional riser and tread profile are typical of the shop-fabricated wood stair that is shipped to the construction site and attached to the floor construction at the bottom and top of each run. Even the rectangular landing at the bottom of the run from the first to the second floors would most likely be part of the shop fabrication. The solid railing on the open side of the stairs avoids the potential complications of fabricating and attaching baluster members. The railing is constructed as a typical stud (wood or steel) and drywall partition and capped with a trimmed down 1-by-6. The wood handrail is a typical millwork shape (sold by lumber suppliers), cut to length and attached with the use of custom cut lengths of support pieces, each about 5" to 6" long and 1½" high, of 5/4-inch (1⅛-inch finished) trim stock. They are nailed to and through the wood cap, leaving enough space (1¼ inches minimum) for the grasping hand to get under the handrail. The handrail is then finish-nailed and countersunk to the 5/4-inch support pieces, each about 5" to 6" long and 1½" high. The finish for the wood treads and risers is typically a durable polyurethane coating, or a prime coat of polyurethane with a dense and durable underlayment. The carpet is then installed over the wood. The finish for the exposed wood stringers, cap, and handrail can be a durable "natural" finish to expose the wood grain, or a durable semi-gloss or gloss paint. Lighting is accomplished through the use of recessed down lights; two in the second floor ceiling, one directly over the oversized tread at the first floor; and two in the soffit above the stair to the basement.

For an additional example of details for a residential stair, see Case Study 5A in this guidebook's companion Web site (Illustration CW-9).

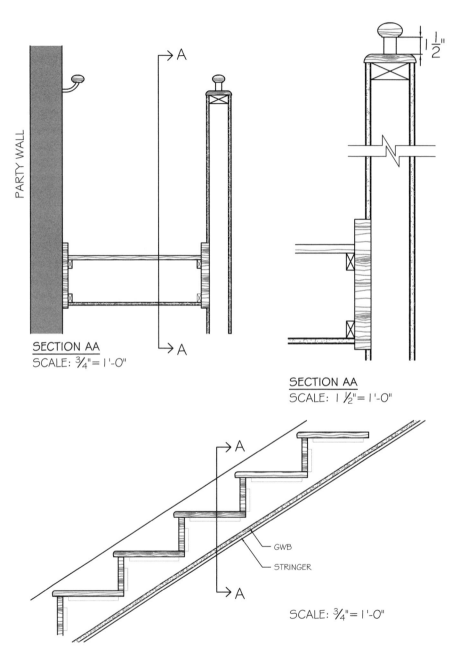

PARTY WALL

SECTION AA
SCALE: ¾" = 1'-0"

SECTION AA
SCALE: 1½" = 1'-0"

GWB

STRINGER

SCALE: ¾" = 1'-0"

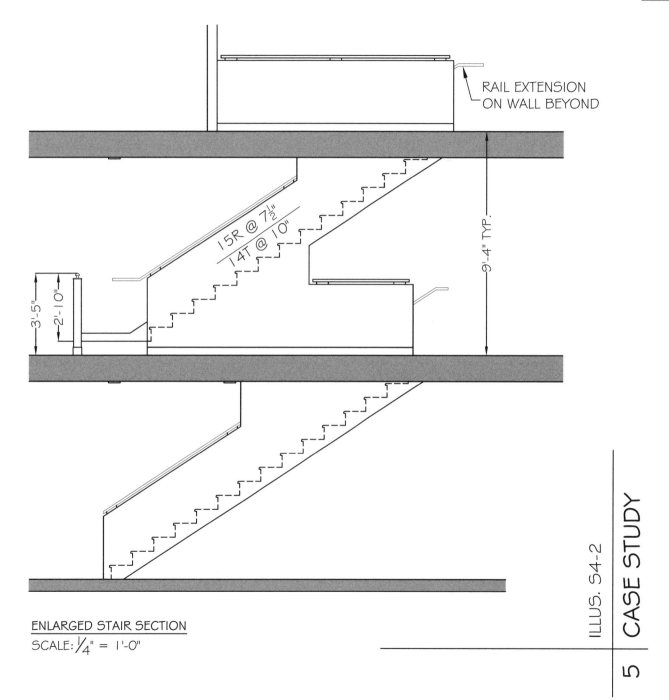

RAIL EXTENSION
ON WALL BEYOND

15R @ 7½"
14T @ 10"

9'-4" TYP.

3'-5"

2'-10"

ENLARGED STAIR SECTION
SCALE: ¼" = 1'-0"

ILLUS. S4-2

5 | CASE STUDY

6 | CASE STUDY

ILLUS. S4-3

The stair developed for Case Study 2 in Section 3 is the basis for this case study. The detailed drawings of Illustration S4-3 complete the design process. The details for this stair are extremely rudimentary, reflecting the "emergency exit" nature of the stair's expected use. The steel channel stringers directly support the vertical members of the aluminum pipe rail system, employing a bolted sleeve connection. Framed aluminum mesh panels are suspended between the vertical pipe members, employing aluminum rod connectors that run through the vertical pipe, conforming to code requirements of openings not greater than 4 inches. The treads are concrete steel pans with a 3-inch-wide abrasive safety strip anchored in the concrete. There are countless variations of these details for basic railing systems; a look through the catalogs of the many manufacturers of railing systems will illustrate the great variety of standard components that are available. The wall surfaces are exposed and painted masonry. Lighting is provided by a 48-inch-long, wall-mounted and lensed fluorescent fixture, with a 6-foot, 8-inch AFF mounting height above each mid-landing and main floor level; the result is a safe lighting condition.

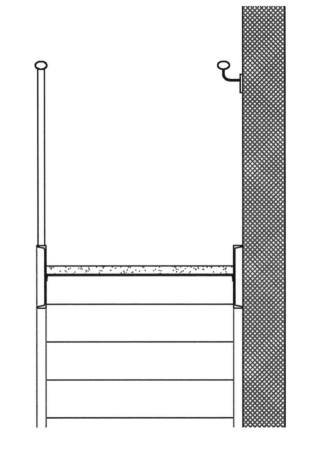

STAIR SECTION
SCALE: 1"= 1'-0"

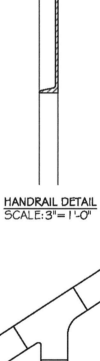

HANDRAIL DETAIL
SCALE: 3"= 1'-0"

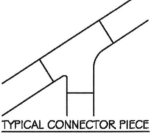

TYPICAL CONNECTOR PIECE

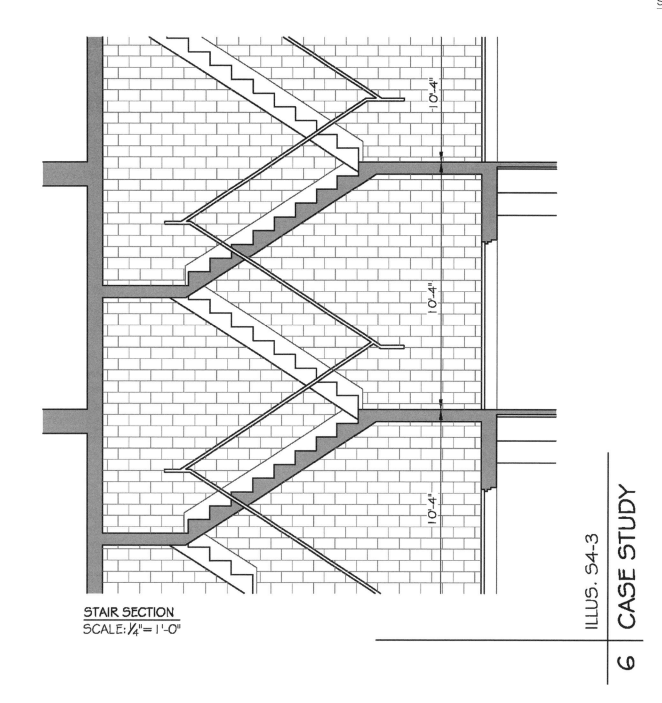

STAIR SECTION
SCALE: $\frac{1}{4}$" = 1'-0"

ILLUS. S4-3

6 | CASE STUDY

7 | CASE STUDY

ILLUS. S4-4

The stair developed for Case Study 3 is further developed here for this case study and is shown in Illustration S4-4. The stair is a one-piece, freestanding concrete structure that could be poured on site or pre-cast in a shop and delivered to the site and set in place by crane and bolted or welded to pre-set connections. Because of concrete's plasticity, the material is appropriate for the stair's curvilinear form. The stair treads receive a fine abrasive aggregate coating before the concrete sets, creating a slip-resistant surface. Bolt sleeves are set in the concrete form to receive the bolts that secure the ½-inch-thick glass railing to the concrete. The glass is obviously custom formed to perfectly match the curve of the stair. Cushioned grommets are used to ensure a perfect fit of the glass to the concrete. The handrail is a stock extruded and anodized aluminum shape that is shop fabricated to match the stair's curve; the shape is grooved to receive a cushioned sleeve that in turn attaches to the glass railing panels. The color of the concrete, the glass, and the aluminum railing must be selected to coordinate with the hotel lobby's overall design. Lighting for the stair is integral to the overall space and is not separated from the overall lighting design solution.

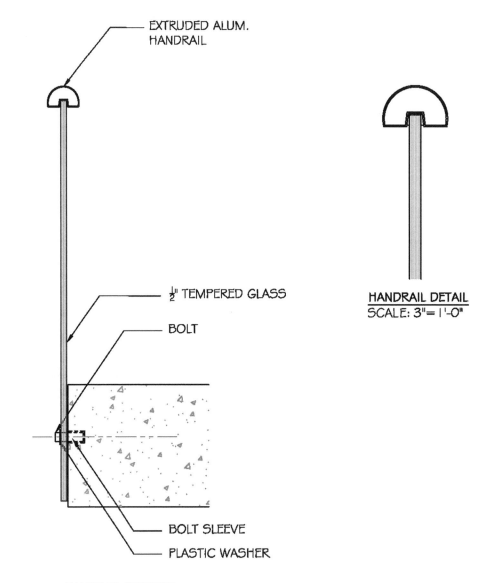

EXTRUDED ALUM. HANDRAIL

½" TEMPERED GLASS

BOLT

BOLT SLEEVE

PLASTIC WASHER

HANDRAIL SECTION

HANDRAIL DETAIL
SCALE: 3"= 1'-0"

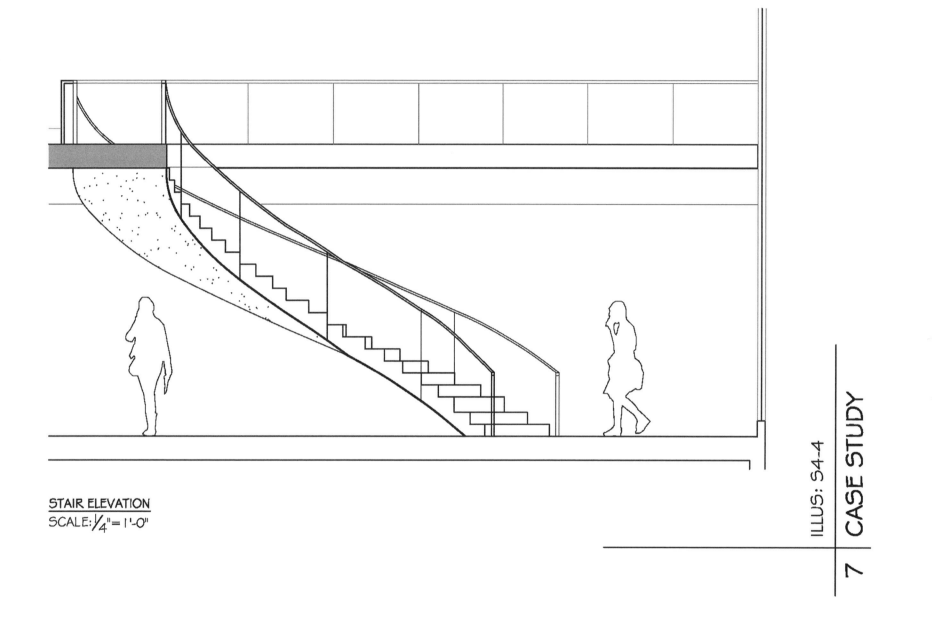

STAIR ELEVATION
SCALE: 1/4" = 1'-0"

7 | CASE STUDY

Appendix

DESIGN PROGRAMS
and BUILDING SHELLS

DESIGN PROGRAMS

1A, 1B, 1C: 1,500 square feet

2A, 2B, 2C, 2S: 2,500 square feet

3A, 3B, 3C: 4,000 square feet

- Design Programs 1A, 1B and 1C are specifically meant to be used with the 1,500-square-foot Building Shells 1A, 1B, and 1C; they can be used interchangeably, providing nine separate space planning exercises of that size.

- Design Programs 2A, 2B, 2C and 2S are specifically meant to be used with the 2,500-square-foot Building Shells 2A, 2B, 2C, and 2S; they can be used interchangeably, providing 16 separate space planning exercises of that size. The "S" designation connotes "sample," in which program 2S and shell 2S are the demonstration sample used throughout the text.

- Design Programs 3A, 3B, and 3C are specifically meant to be used with the 4,000-square-foot Building Shells 3A, 3B, and 3C; they can be used interchangeably, providing nine separate space planning exercises of that size.

DESIGN PROGRAM 1A
Suite for Dual Pediatric Practice

A partnership of two pediatricians requires a new office facility. Their practice is neighborhood-oriented, dealing with a complete range of pediatric care. Although the atmosphere should be professional and businesslike, the primary concern in terms of ambience is to create a relaxed atmosphere throughout to minimize the typical anxiety that most people, parents and children, feel when entering a doctor's office. The practice employs a receptionist/secretary, a medical technician, and a part-time bookkeeper for billing and other business functions. A medical equipment manufacturer has been selected; its representative has prescribed the size and shape of the typical exam room and the nurse's station.

SPECIAL REQUIREMENTS

1. The receptionist controls the movement of patients; consequently, that station must be centrally and uniquely situated to perform that function.
2. The exam rooms and the consulting offices must have acoustic privacy.
3. The business office and workroom functions may be combined into one space, assuming that all the detailed requirements are met; if not combined, they should be adjacent to one another.
4. Where the building configuration permits, the partners would like an "escape hatch" exit, so that they can leave without walking through the reception/waiting area.
5. Exterior view and natural light are desirable but not at a premium—first priority is for the waiting/reception area, and second priority is for the consulting offices.
6. All patient areas shall be barrier-free in concept and dimension.

PROGRAM REQUIREMENTS

A. Reception/Business Office
1. The reception station is the hub of activity, with all patients checking in there upon arrival and making or arranging for payment before leaving.
2. Primary work surface of at least 12 sq. ft., secondary surface of at least 8 sq. ft., transaction counter for patients 4' to 6' long, a box/file drawer pedestal, flat screen monitor, pull-out keyboard tray, and a small desktop printer.

3. 60 lin. ft. of lateral files within easy reach of receptionist.
4. Part-time bookkeeper's station with 10 to 12 sq. ft. desk surface, plus a small return for a flat screen and printer identical to the receptionist's, and a box/file drawer pedestal.
5. Two task chairs.
6. Easy eye contact between the two workstations is desirable.

B. Workroom
1. Desktop copier (26" w × 20" d × 14" h) on base 30" w × 24" d.
2. Storage closet or cabinet, min. 18 lin. ft. of 12" d shelves and min. 18 lin. ft. of 18" d shelves.
3. Coat closet, 3 lin. ft. hanging rod.
4. Worktable, 10 to 12 sq. ft.

C. Waiting Area
1. Seating for five adults and three children.
2. Magazine rack or display.
3. Set aside approx. 60 sq. ft. for a children's play area.
4. This area presents the greatest challenge in creating psychological comfort for patients, particularly considering the children's age range, from infancy through puberty.

D. Nurse's Station
1. Regularly shaped space of 70 to 80 sq. ft., with a min. dimension of 7'-0".
2. Station shall present a transaction counter to entering patients that shall be directly in the line of vision when entering from the waiting area, and the station must also conveniently serve the three exam rooms.
3. Station shall contain a laboratory sink on one of its long walls; its placement is not restricted by distance to plumbing lines or chases.

E. Exam Rooms (three)
1. Regularly shaped spaces of 85 to 95 sq. ft. with a min. dimension of 8'-0".
2. A regular or irregular placement of rooms is acceptable; comfortable access for patients and staff is the first priority.
3. Plumbing tie-in requirements are not restricted by distance to the plumbing lines or chases, despite the installation of a lavatory in each room.

F. Consulting Offices (two)

1. Comfortable spaces for talking to patients and parents, as well as private desk work; atmosphere should be informal, even residential in ambience.
2. Desk with 12 to 15 sq. ft. surface, plus credenza or return with 5 to 8 sq. ft. secondary surface, and two box/file drawer pedestals. Include a flat screen monitor, a keyboard tray, and a small desktop printer.
3. Swivel-tilt desk chair and three guest chairs.
4. 36 lin. ft. of book/artifact shelves, 12" d.

G. Powder Rooms (two)

1. Lavatory and toilet (only one room shall be barrier-free), for patients and staff.

H. Storage Closet

1. Approx. 50 sq. ft., placed for easy access to both workroom and nurse's station.

DESIGN PROGRAM 1B
Township Youth Organization

A suburban township has decided to establish and support a youth organization for its sizable and growing population. To a great degree, the organization's purpose will be to provide a meeting place for several established small organizations and programs. In addition, it will coordinate programs with the township's schools and fill gaps where programmatic voids exist. The organization will generally serve an age range of 8 to 16, with primary hours of activity during the afternoon and evening on weekdays and daylight hours on the weekend; a complete seven-day-a-week schedule will be maintained during the summer vacation period. The range of activities is immense, including a chess club, a hiking/camping club, intramural-level sports competitions, a debating club, dance competitions, a community newsletter, theatrical productions, martial arts instruction, and even some supervised overnight activities. Flexibility of space and equipment is essential, informality of atmosphere is a given, and a critical eye to easy maintenance will make the day-to-day operations run more smoothly.

SPECIAL REQUIREMENTS

1. The director's office must be strategically placed so that it is near the entrance door and so that a glass vision panel will permit supervision of the multipurpose room. When the door is closed, acoustic privacy must be accomplished.
2. Except for the kitchen, the entire facility shall be barrier-free in concept and dimension.
3. Storage of tables, chairs, and equipment is an important aspect of planning the center. Access to and removal and replacement of stored items must be accomplished with ease and efficiency; the storage location(s) may not be remote, and the maneuvering of stored items must be kept to a minimum.

PROGRAM REQUIREMENTS

A. Multipurpose Room
  1. A room of maximum flexibility and diversity of use, capable of seating at least 30 in a classroom arrangement, at least 24 at a few or several modular tables (for games, dining, or small group use), or at least 20 at a central table in a conference arrangement.
  2. A pull-out or fold-down reception desk (24" × 48") near the entrance door for those occasions when entrance must be monitored or ticketed.
  3. Two locker alcoves (boys and girls), each with 20 half lockers, 12" w × 12" d × 36" h.

B. Toilet Rooms
  1. Boys: two lavatories, one urinal, and one toilet stall.
  2. Girls: two lavatories and two toilet stalls.

C. Kitchen
  1. Essentially residential in design, to serve a broad range of functions, from afternoon snack service to prepared dinners.
  2. Min. 14 sq. ft. countertop with full complement of base and wall cabinets.
  3. 30" w double-bowl sink, 30" w range/oven, 32" w refrigerator, 24" w under-counter dishwasher.

D. Director's Office
  1. 12 to 15 sq. ft. desk surface, 5 to 8 sq. ft. return or credenza surface, two box/file drawer pedestals.
  2. Flat screen monitor, a keyboard tray, and a small desktop printer.
  3. Swivel-tilt desk chair and two guest chairs.
  4. 30 lin. ft. of book/artifact shelves, 12" d.
  5. Closet, 5' w × 2' d; half for hanging rod and half for shelves.
  6. Private barrier-free bathroom, compact but comfortable, with lavatory, toilet, and stall shower.

E. Storage
In closets or cabinets, the following items should be stored out of sight but easily accessible for use.
  1. 24" sq. rolling dolly capable of holding 30 stacking chairs.
  2. Folding-leg tables to accommodate 20 people (table size based on multipurpose room plan).
  3. 12 sleeping bags in bins 18" w × 18" h × 24" d.
  4. A/V equipment on 12 lin. ft. of 18" d shelves (one shelf 18" h and the other two shelves 12" h).
  5. Games and equipment on 12 lin. ft. of 12" d shelves, 12" h, and 8 lin. ft. of 18" d shelves, 15" h.
  6. Supplies on 8 lin. ft. of 12" d shelves, 12" h, and 12 lin. ft. of 18" d shelves, 15" h.

DESIGN PROGRAM 1C
A Small Accounting Firm Suite

A small, well-established accounting firm must relocate its offices. Their practice is fairly conventional, with most of their client involvement in the business and small corporate areas. The two partners operate with a two-person staff: a secretary/receptionist and a per diem accountant. Their desired ambience is one of comfortable formality, reflecting their success but without a hint of pretentiousness. Although visitors are frequent, it is unusual for more than two or three to be there at one time, except for occasional conferences or meetings of five or six people.

SPECIAL REQUIREMENTS

1. The issues of privacy and confidentiality are of major concern. The partners' offices and the conference room must have visual and acoustic privacy.
2. The four permanent workspaces should ideally have exterior view and natural light.
3. The per diem accountant's work area should have some degree of privacy, not only for confidentiality, but also because the work function often demands long, uninterrupted hours of concentrated work.
4. One of the partners is wheelchair-bound. The entire suite must be barrier-free in both concept and dimensional reality.
5. If possible, the partners would like to have a secondary "escape hatch" exit, where they can leave without passing through the reception area.

PROGRAM REQUIREMENTS

A. Receptionist/Secretary
1. Minimum 15 sq. ft. primary work surface, with minimum 10 sq. ft. return, two box/file drawer pedestals, telephone, a flat screen monitor, keyboard tray, and a small desktop printer. A transaction surface is needed to provide privacy of paperwork and to screen desk clutter.
2. Task chair.
3. Minimum 24 lin. ft. of lateral files.

B. Waiting Area
1. Seating for four visitors.
2. Coat storage for six, in closet or cabinet.

3. Convenience surface(s), i.e., an end table for magazines and visitors' articles.

C. Partners' Offices (two)
1. Minimum 18 sq. ft. working surface, plus kneehole credenza or return surface for a flat screen monitor, keyboard tray, and a small desktop printer; minimum two box/file drawer pedestals.
2. Executive swivel-tilt chair and two guest pull-up chairs.
3. Minimum 12 lin. ft. of lateral files.
4. Minimum of 40 lin. ft. of book/artifact shelving, 12" d.
5. Partner A prefers an informal, conversational conference area, with lounge seating for four.
6. Partner B prefers small conference table or round conference extension of main desk surface, capable of seating four people.
7. Each office requires a small personal clothes closet.

D. Per Diem Accountant
1. Work area or station with minimum 15 sq. ft. of primary work surface, plus a secondary work surface of at least 10 sq. ft., a flat screen monitor, keyboard tray, and a small desktop printer, at least two box/file drawer pedestals, and a minimum of 12 lin. ft. of wall-hung shelves above the work surfaces.
2. Operational task chair and one guest chair.
3. Minimum of 12 lin. ft. of lateral files.

E. Conference/Library
1. Conference table and chairs to comfortably accommodate six people.
2. Credenza for beverage service and paper/pencil storage.
3. Legal-book shelves lining most wall surfaces; minimum 75 lin. ft. of shelving, 12" d, 12" h.

F. Copy/Storage/Workroom
1. Freestanding copier (42" w × 25" d × 38" h) that requires a 55" w space.
2. Collating work surfaces (min. 10 sq. ft.) with storage below.
3. Minimum of 30 lin. ft. of lateral files.
4. Lockable storage (cabinets and/or closet) with min. of 18 lin. ft. of 12" d shelving and a minimum of 18 lin. ft. of 18" d shelving.
5. Prefab "executive kitchen" unit for beverage service and refrigeration (42" w × 25" d × 36" h). Sink must be tied into plumbing lines as a conventional plumbing fixture.

G. Restroom
1. Lavatory.
2. Toilet.

DESIGN PROGRAM 2A
Regional Management Office

A national financial services firm must relocate a regional management office. This regional facility serves three functions: (1) the management of executive activities for the region, (2) a marketing center for potential clients, and (3) a home base for account executives who spend most of their time on the road. Because of the executive and marketing activities, a reasonably impressive atmosphere is desired, so that the success of the firm is clearly conveyed and visiting clients are made to feel comfortable. Visitor traffic is normally limited to the reception area, the three private offices, and the conference room, with the remainder of the facility being primarily for in-house use. The office manager, in addition to being responsible for the day-to-day in-house functions, is also the interface between the public/executive functions and in-house functions. Ideally, all personnel areas should have easy access to exterior view and natural light, except for the account executives' area, where those people will typically spend only a few hours a week in their shared workstations. The accounting staff requires a degree of separateness from other functions, while the support staff are the most accessible personnel and are directly supervised by the office manager. Restroom facilities must be strategically located to serve employees and visitors. The beverage center must serve the daily needs of employees as well as guests in the conference room.

SPECIAL REQUIREMENTS

1. Acoustic privacy is required for the three private offices, the conference room, and the office manager.
2. All facilities shall be barrier-free in concept and dimension.

PROGRAM REQUIREMENTS

A. Reception/Waiting Area
1. Receptionist shall greet visitors, control visitor traffic, and handle a part-time secretarial workload.
2. Desk shall have a primary work surface of 12 to 18 sq. ft. and a return of 7 to 10 sq. ft., plus two box/file drawer pedestals.
3. Flat screen monitor, keyboard tray, and a small desktop printer.
4. 12 lin. ft. of lateral files within easy reach.
5. Secretarial task chair.
6. Visitor seating for five, plus convenience surfaces.
7. Coat closet or cabinet for visitors, 4 lin. ft.
8. At least one major, unbroken exhibit wall for display of the company's services, 5 lin. ft. min.

B. Regional Manager's Office
1. Desk with 18 to 20 sq. ft. surface and two drawer pedestals.
2. Credenza with kneehole, 10 to 12 sq. ft. surface and maximum filing and storage capacity above and below the work surface.
3. Flat screen monitor, keyboard tray, and a small desktop printer.
4. Executive task chair and two pull-up guest chairs.
5. Lounge seating for four and convenience surfaces to create an informal conference area.
6. Personal clothes closet, with at least 3 lin. ft. of hanging rod.

C. Private Offices (two)
The office needs of the marketing manager and the accounts administrator are the same:
1. Desk with primary work surface of 20 to 24 sq. ft., containing a round conference extension to accommodate three visitors, plus a return or credenza with 8 to 12 sq. ft., and one box/file drawer pedestal.
2. Open or closed book/manual shelving of at least 8 lin. ft., placed above and/or adjacent to the credenza or return surface.
3. Flat screen monitor, keyboard tray, and a small desktop printer.
4. Management task chair and three pull-up guest chairs.
5. 12 lin. ft. of lateral files.

D. Conference Room
1. Central table to seat ten people.
2. Credenza for beverage service, pencil and paper storage, and the control panel for the video system. (A ceiling-mounted digital projector, directed toward the projection screen, is the only AV system to be considered.)
3. A motorized, ceiling-recessed projection screen, 4'-6" w.
4. A marker-board wall, at least 8' long, placed to not conflict with the projection screen.

E. Office Manager
1. Desk with 12 to 15 sq. ft. work surface, return with 7 to 10 sq. ft. surface, two box/file drawer pedestals, 8 lin. ft. of book/manual shelv-

ing, 12 lin. ft. of lateral files, and a flat screen monitor, keyboard tray, and a small desktop printer.

2. Management task chair and two pull-up guest chairs.

3. Glass vision panel for supervision of support staff.

F. Support Staff (three)

These four people work together as a team; their workstations should be arranged to facilitate that relationship. It is assumed that systems furniture will be employed, with partition panels not exceeding 60" in height.

1. Typical workstations: 45 to 60 sq. ft., containing at least 16 sq. ft. of work surface, a box/file drawer pedestal, 6 lin. ft. of lateral files, 4 lin. ft. of overhead binder bin, and a flat screen monitor, keyboard tray, and a small desktop printer.

2. Operational task chair.

G. Accounting Staff (two)

1. Two identical stations arranged as a working group with a common bank of files consisting of 36 lin. ft. of lateral files.

2. Typical station: 65 to 80 sq. ft. containing at least 18 sq. ft. of work surface, a box/file drawer pedestal, 6 lin. ft. of lateral files, 8 lin. ft. of overhead binder bin, and a flat screen monitor, keyboard tray, and a small desktop printer. Management task chair and a guest chair.

H. Account Executives (three)

1. Three stations for part-time use by six on-the-road account execs; their periods of time in the office will not often coincide.

2. Typical station: 40 to 50 sq. ft. containing at least 14 sq. ft. of work surface, two box/file drawer pedestals, 4 lin. ft. of binder bin, and a flat screen monitor, keyboard tray, and a small desktop printer. Operational task chair.

3. This area shall also contain a "huddle" space: a small, open conference space to seat four at a table, for informal and/or impromptu conferences. The huddle space is available to all personnel.

I. Workroom

Centrally located for easy access by all personnel.

1. Freestanding copier (46" w × 26" d × 35" h); requires a 54" w space for maintenance purposes.

2. Closed shelving for supplies, at least 18 lin. ft. of 12" d shelves and at least 18 lin. ft. of 18" d shelves.

3. Worktable (60" w × 24" d × 36" h), for collating, sorting, etc.

4. Employee coat closet with 5' long hanging rod.

5. 45 lin. ft. of lateral files.

J. Beverage Center

1. Min. of 8 sq. ft. of clear work counter, with full complement of base and wall cabinets.

2. Single-bowl sink, 17" w; small range/oven, 20" w; stand-up refrigerator, 24" w; cabinet-hung coffeemaker.

K. Restrooms—Unisex

1. One lavatory, one toilet stall.

L. Janitors Closet—25 sq. ft.

M. Storage Closet—40 sq. ft.

DESIGN PROGRAM 2B
Popular Culture Institute

A large urban university in a suburban-like setting at the edge of the city limits plans to house a new Popular Culture Institute. With an established reputation in the social sciences and several esteemed faculty involved in popular culture and futurism, the university expects to become part of an international network of similar institutions participating in the exchange of traveling exhibits and programs. In addition to regularly changing exhibits, the institute will initiate many conference and seminar programs. Because the exhibits will include many formats and media, it is necessary for the exhibit space to provide maximum flexibility.

The general atmosphere generated by the interior planning and design should be one of energy and currency, avoiding any suggestion of institutional quality or museum stodginess. Most traffic will flow from the entry/reception space to the main exhibit area and the meeting room, with secondary traffic to the curator's and assistant's offices. Exhibit deliveries are infrequent enough so as to not require a separate service entrance, but if the potential for a separate service entry exists, direct access from that point to the workroom is desirable.

SPECIAL REQUIREMENTS

1. The meeting room and the curator's office require acoustic privacy.
2. The curator and the administrative assistant work closely together, and their offices should be arranged to accommodate that relationship.
3. The administrative assistant will supervise shipping and receiving, as well as the part-time employees involved in exhibit construction in the workroom.
4. Natural light and view are desirable for all of the spaces and functions, but window placement in the main exhibit space must be carefully planned so as not to limit exhibit design and planning potential; all windows shall be provided with shading treatments.
5. The building code requires that rooms or spaces seating more than 30 people shall have two remote means of egress.
6. The entire facility shall be barrier-free in concept and dimension.

PROGRAM REQUIREMENTS

A. Entry/Reception
1. A reception desk, at least 4'-6" w, serviced by work-study student help, as an entry point information desk; desk shall contain pedestal drawers for the storage of handout literature.
2. Bench or benches to seat three to four people should not encourage lengthy occupancy.
3. Wall-mounted literature rack with face size of about 15 to 20 sq. ft. (4" d).
4. Bulletin board for coming events and announcements, about 20 to 24 sq. ft.

B. Meeting Room
1. Flexible lecture/seminar room to seat 24 auditorium style, or 14 at a centrally placed conference table.
2. The room should be divisible by a folding partition of high acoustic value to accommodate small conferences of six people in each part.
3. Credenza for beverage service and storage of pencils and paper; the credenza should be available when the room is used as one large space or as two smaller spaces.
4. Ceiling-recessed projection screen, 6' w, placed for classroom viewing when the room is set up to seat 24 people, and a ceiling-mounted digital projector.
5. A marker-board wall, at least 32 sq. ft. in size, shall be placed for classroom viewing, and not obscured by the projection screen.

C. Main Exhibit Area — 650 sq. ft.
1. An open, flexible space for a variety of exhibit formats. The ceiling grid shall be designed to accept the verticals of a modular exhibit system. Track lighting is the primary illumination system.
2. In special circumstances, the space will be used for lectures or presentations, seating up to 45 people.
3. Ceiling-recessed projection screen, 8' w, located for lecture/presentation viewing, and a ceiling-mounted digital projector.

D. Curator's Office
1. Primary desk surface of at least 18 sq. ft. with secondary surface of at least 10 sq. ft., a flat screen monitor, keyboard tray, and a small desktop printer, at least one box/file drawer pedestal.
2. Lateral files, 18 lin. ft.
3. Bookshelves, 30 lin. ft., 12" d.

4. Managerial task chair and three guest chairs.

5. A casual seating/conference arrangement is preferred (the curator does not have to sit behind a desk).

E. Administrative Assistant

1. A functional workstation with 20 to 25 sq. ft. of work surface, a flat screen monitor, keyboard tray, and a small desktop printer, and two box/file drawer pedestals.

2. Lateral files, 24 lin. ft.

3. Book/manual shelves, 12 lin. ft., 12" d.

4. Operational task chair and one guest chair.

F. Workroom

1. Workbench (72" w × 36" d × 36" h) with 12 lin. ft. of 8" d shelves above.

2. Modular steel shelving, two units that are 36" w × 12" d × 78" h and two units that are 36" w × 18" d × 78" h.

3. Storage area for modular exhibit system parts (56" w × 28" d × full height); this area shall be separated from other workroom areas by a partition or permanent panel.

4. Storage area for two-stack chair dollies 24" sq. and six folding tables with 72" × 36" top surface.

5. Central worktable (78" w × 42" d × 36" h).

6. Four workbench stools.

7. Lumber/crate storage, two divided spaces, each 48" w × 30" d × full height; areas to be separated from other areas by a partition or permanent panel.

8. Two portable coatracks (60" w × 18" d × 58" h).

G. Serving Kitchen

1. Min. of 12 sq. ft. counter, with full complement of base and wall cabinets.

2. Single-bowl sink, 25" w; two-burner commercial coffee urn; cabinet-hung microwave; under-counter warming oven, 30" w; stand-up refrigerator, 32" w.

H. Restrooms

1. Men: two lavatories, one urinal, one toilet stall.

2. Women: two lavatories, two toilet stalls.

DESIGN PROGRAM 2C
Meeting/Marketing Facility

A successful publishing firm wishes to create its own small meeting and marketing facility. The new facility is expected to serve a variety of functions, from in-house training sessions to sales and marketing presentations to potential buyers. While maintaining a strongly professional image, this facility is expected to reflect the firm's success and impress visitors through its design quality.

From a functional viewpoint, the most important planning and design issue is the creation of optimal presentation, classroom, and conference spaces. The only regular staff housed at the center is the reception personnel, both of whom are trained to operate the AV equipment. Presenters, workshop leaders, conveners, etc., will come from their own offices to use the conference center. Special attention should be given to corridor and aisle spaces, since relatively large numbers of people will be entering or leaving a space at one time, as well as moving from one space to another as a group.

SPECIAL REQUIREMENTS

1. Acoustic control is of primary importance; each meeting or conference space must provide acoustic privacy.
2. The entire center shall be barrier-free in concept and dimension.
3. All AV equipment is video-based. Each presentation, classroom, or conference space shall have a ceiling-mounted projection unit directed toward a projection screen.
4. Although not required, preference has been expressed for the large and small conference rooms to be placed adjacent to one another, with their common wall being a folding partition of high acoustic performance, making it possible to have a combined conference area capable of seating 18 at a central table.

PROGRAM REQUIREMENTS

A. Reception Station
1. Critically located for maximum control of visitor traffic; ideally, the station should be visible upon entry to the center. Reception personnel should always be easily available for information purposes.
2. A two-person reception desk, with 10 to 12 sq. ft. of clear work surface and a box/file drawer pedestal for each person and a flat screen monitor, keyboard tray, and a small desktop printer.
3. Transaction surface for visitors in front of each desk area.
4. Immediately adjacent storage wall, 8' to 10' long by 6'-6" to 7'-0" h by 1'-8" d, containing 12 lin. ft. of lateral files and closed cabinets for the storage of supplies and handout literature.

B. Waiting Area
1. A comfortable lounge atmosphere in visual contact with the reception station.
2. Seating for seven (min.) to eight visitors.
3. Coat storage for 70 winter coats.
4. Table(s)/convenience surface(s) for magazines, mugs, etc.
5. Wall-mounted display rack for company literature, 3' w $\times$ 4' h $\times$ 4" d.

C. Equipment Room
1. Central control and equipment storage for all of the presentation, classroom, and conference spaces, located immediately adjacent to (or at least very near) the reception station.
2. Provide a 90 to 100 sq. ft. room with lockable door (and desirably without windows), minimum dimensions of 7'-6", for a permanent control panel, equipment shelving, tape storage, and space for four 22" by 34" equipment carts that will be used in the presentation, classroom, and conference areas.

D. Presentation Room
1. A conventional lecture/presentation space with comfortable fixed seating for 24 people.
2. A speaker's lectern or a panelists' table and chairs (for four) at the front of the room.
3. A motorized, ceiling-recessed projection screen, 6' w, at the front of the room, and a ceiling-mounted digital projector.
4. A marker-board surface across the entire front of the room.
5. A closet for four stacking chairs and the panelists' folding table.

E. Training Room
1. Seating for 16 people at eight training tables, 72" w $\times$ 24' d.
2. Each table shall contain a flat screen monitor, keyboard tray, and a small desktop printer.
3. A speaker's lectern at the front of the room.
4. A motorized, ceiling-recessed projection screen, 5' w, at the front of the room, and a ceiling-mounted digital projector.
5. A marker-board surface across the entire front of the room.

F. Large Conference Room

1. A central, modular conference table for 12 people. (The modular table design will accommodate the adding of the small conference table, if space planning permits.)
2. A credenza, at least 8' long, for beverage service and pencil and paper storage.
3. A motorized, ceiling-recessed projection screen, 5' w, at the front of the room, and a ceiling-mounted digital projector.
4. A marker board, at least 10' long, for one side of the room.

G. Small Conference Room

1. A central, modular conference table for six people.
2. A credenza, at least 5' long, for beverage service and pencil and paper storage.
3. A motorized, ceiling-recessed projection screen, 4' w, placed for easy viewing, and a ceiling-mounted digital projector.
4. A marker board, at least 8' w, for a side of the room other than the projection screen side.

H. Coffee/Break Area

1. A centrally located break space for intermission periods of presentation, class, or conference programs.

2. A primarily open space for standing or seating, with stool, bench, or leaning surfaces for 12 to 18 people; comfortable seating is specifically not desired.
3. Buffet or counter surface(s) (one or two totaling 8 to 10 lin. ft.) for beverage and snack/hors d'oeuvres service.
4. Adequate wall surface for diverting graphics or other visual material. A view to the exterior is also important for this space.
5. Ideally, this space should be adjacent to (and flow into) the waiting area, so that the combined spaces can serve for larger social/reception functions.

I. Kitchen

1. A serving kitchen only (no food preparation), centrally located to serve the presentation room and conference rooms, as well as the coffee/break area.
2. At least 12 sq. ft. of counter space, with a complete complement of base and wall cabinets.
3. Single-bowl sink (25" w), two-burner commercial coffee urn (10" w × 21" d), small four-burner range/oven (20" to 24" w), and a 28" w stand-up refrigerator.
4. Enclose space to contain noise and odors.

J. Restrooms

1. Men: two lavatories, one urinal, one toilet stall.
2. Women: two lavatories, two toilet stalls, makeup bar.

DESIGN PROGRAM 2S
University Career Counseling Center

The University Career Counseling Center will become an integral part of this medium-size, state-supported university and will provide curriculum and career counseling for all levels of students. Seminar-type instruction will be provided for college and high school educators, who are themselves counselors. In addition, the director and the director's staff are considered the university's primary resource for career information and employment opportunities for graduates and have a major role to play with each of the institution's departments of professional education. The center serves not only the adjacent campus but also three other branch campuses located in other parts of the state. This statewide activity often brings overnight guests to the center, creating a need for a guest apartment, which would generally be used for one- or two-night stays.

The bulk of the center's traffic is generated by a fairly constant flow of students and recent graduates, most of whom come with a specific appointment time. Several times each week, groups ranging in size from 6 to 30 come for conferences, seminars, lectures, and group counseling. The director and assistant director will each see several visitors on a typical day, usually coming alone or in pairs.

SPECIAL REQUIREMENTS

1. The general atmosphere of the center should essentially reflect its connections to the business and corporate world, rather than its institutional and educational connections. Each visitor's experience, from reception through interview or program, should emulate a real-world or professional experience. Jeans and T-shirts are discouraged attire for visitors.
2. Wherever possible, full advantage should be taken of exterior view and natural light in areas where staff or visitors spend a considerable amount of time.
3. Except for the kitchen and bathroom in the guest apartment, all spaces and functions shall be accessible to wheelchair-bound users.
4. The director's office, the seminar room, and the guest apartment require acoustic privacy.

5. The guest apartment is expected to have an appropriate residential environment, avoiding the typical "hotel plastic" character. The entrance to the apartment should avoid a public or prominent location.
6. The director, assistant director, and secretary tend to work as an administrative team and should have their work spaces clustered together. The receptionist is the greeter and "traffic cop" for the center. The interviewers' locations need only be convenient for visitors; their other internal working relationships are not frequent or critical.

PROGRAM REQUIREMENTS

A. Reception Area
1. The reception station shall include an uninterrupted work surface of at least 12 sq. ft.; a transaction surface for visitors, 40" AFF; a flat screen monitor, keyboard tray, and a small desktop printer; two box/file drawer pedestals; a small console telephone; and a task chair.
2. Immediately adjacent to the station, 12 lin. ft. of lateral files, and a fax machine (18" w × 16" d × 9" h) must be accommodated.
3. Guest seating for five to six visitors.
4. Coat storage for 30 people.
5. Wall-hung literature rack (40" w × 60" h × 5" d), easily accessible by visitors.

B. Interview Stations (four)
1. Stations shall be created through the use of systems furniture work surfaces, acoustic partition panels, and storage elements; panel height shall not exceed 65".
2. Primary work surface and return shall provide a combined surface of 18 to 20 sq. ft. per station.
3. Provide two box/file drawer pedestals; a minimum of 4 lin. ft. of overhead storage bin; and a a flat screen monitor, keyboard tray, and a small desktop printer per station.
4. One operational task chair and one guest chair per station.
5. A minimum of 48 lin. ft. of lateral files shall be accessible to all four stations.
6. Without creating "offices," each station should, through the use of acoustic partition panels, create a sense of separateness from the other stations.

C. Director

1. A comfortable, no-frills, executive office consistent with institutional standards.
2. A double-pedestal, recessed-front executive desk with matching kneehole credenza for placement of a flat screen monitor, keyboard tray, and a small desktop printer.
3. An executive swivel-tilt desk chair and two guest pull-up chairs.
4. Minimum of 20 lin. ft. of book/artifact shelving, 12" d.

D. Assistant Director

1. A management workstation created through the use of systems furniture; acoustic panels shall not exceed 65" in height.
2. 12 to 15 sq. ft. primary work surface plus credenza or desk return (at least 8 sq. ft.) and two or three box/file drawer pedestals.
3. At least 4 lin. ft. overhead bin storage.
4. A flat screen monitor, keyboard tray, and a small desktop printer.
5. A management task chair and two guest pull-up chairs.

E. Secretary

1. Primary work relationships are with the director and assistant director. This station monitors access to the director's office.
2. An operational workstation created through the use of systems furniture; this station should have a high level of visual accessibility.
3. Minimum 12 sq. ft. primary work surface min; 6 sq. ft. return; two box/file drawer pedestals; min. 4 lin. ft. overhead shelf or bin; a flat screen monitor, keyboard tray, and a small desktop printer.
4. Operational task chair and one guest chair.
5. Min. 6 lin. ft. of lateral files.

F. Work Area

1. Freestanding copier (44" w × 27" d × 38" h), requiring 54" w space.
2. Storage cabinet, 36" w × 18" d × 78" h.
3. Min. 6 lin. ft. of lateral files.

G. Seminar Room

1. Multipurpose presentation, conference, and encounter activities, with flexible arrangement potential. Provide classroom seating for 20, conference or seminar seating for 12 at one central table, or (through the use of a folding partition) two small conference rooms, each to seat at least 6 at a central table.
2. Beverage serving surface, plus paper and pencil storage below it; this should be available when room is set up as one large space or as two small spaces.
3. Storage for tables and chairs that are not in use.
4. 6'-0" w ceiling-mounted projection screen (electric operation), and a ceiling-mounted projector.
5. 48" w × 48" h × 5" d visuals board (96" w when open) placed for use when room is set up as one large space, and not obscured by the projection screen.
6. Tackable wall surface, min. 8 lin. ft. placed for use when room is set up as one large space.

H. Public Restrooms

1. Men: two lavatories, one urinal, one toilet stall.
2. Women: two lavatories, two toilet stalls.

I. Coffee Station

For daily staff use and for support of seminar room activities.

1. Minimum of 8 sq. ft. of work counter (not including sink) plus base and overhead cabinets.
2. Double-burner commercial coffee urn, sink, under-cabinet microwave, 24" w stand-up refrigerator.

J. Guest Apartment

1. Living area: comfortable lounge seating for four or five, coffee table for informal serving, and entertainment center (TV, VCR, music) with book/artifacts shelving.
2. Dining area: minimal in size; can be part of living area or kitchen; table surface to double as desk/work surface.
3. Kitchen: small but serviceable for occasional food preparation, with sink, small four-burner range/oven (20" to 24" w), and adequate countertop space and cabinets.
4. Sleeping area can be an alcove rather than a separate room; shall contain double bed, night table and lamp, 3 to 4 lin. ft. of closet space, drawer storage, and space for a luggage rack.
5. Bathroom: basic but comfortable apartment bathroom, with lavatory, toilet, and tub or stall shower, plus small linen closet or cabinet.

DESIGN PROGRAM 3A
Market Research Group

A small and prosperous market research group is planning to relocate its offices to larger quarters because it has outgrown its current facilities. Their new design program, which was researched and written by a space-planning consultant, incorporates an estimated growth factor for the next five years. Because the firm represents a broad spectrum of services, their facility must accommodate a large number of varied tasks for a relatively small business concern. Telephone survey is the only company function not handled from this office.

Comfort and productivity for employees and visitors are the dominating planning factors here; image for its own sake is not desired. Visitors are generally limited to the reception area, group survey rooms, conference room, and the three private offices. The vice president for operations is the supervisor of day-to-day functions and must be located appropriately. The workroom should be reasonably convenient to all working functions, while the reference library gets limited use and may be placed in a relatively remote location. The beverage center must be strategically located to serve the needs of employees and visitors in the survey and conference rooms; the beverage center and the lunch/break room could be combined in one space.

SPECIAL REQUIREMENTS

1. The conference room, group survey rooms, three private offices, and the lunch/break room require acoustic privacy.
2. The group survey rooms require maximum acoustic absorption.
3. The three private offices should be arranged to permit easy interaction between those three people.
4. Access to natural light and exterior view is very desirable for all offices and workstations.
5. All facilities shall be barrier-free in concept and dimension.

PROGRAM REQUIREMENTS

A. Reception/Waiting
1. This working reception station greets visitors and controls visitors' traffic, and provides some limited secretarial services.
2. Total work surface must be at least 20 sq. ft., accommodate a flat screen monitor, keyboard tray, and a small desktop printer, and provide at least one box/file drawer pedestal.
3. A transaction counter is required for arriving visitors.
4. Lateral files, 18 lin. ft., must be within easy reach.
5. Waiting area shall include seating for 12, plus coat closet or cabinet (5 lin. ft.) and a magazine rack or display surface. Waiting periods can occasionally be lengthy; therefore, comfortable upholstered seating is desired.

B. Group Survey Rooms (two)
1. Survey Room A shall be set up as a conventional conference for 12 people. Seating should be appropriate for survey sessions of up to three hours in length.
2. Survey Room B shall be set up in a comfortable conversational circle for ten people, with one part of the circle open for reference to the marker wall or video screen.
3. Each room shall contain a marker wall (at least 8 lin. ft.), a ceiling-recessed motorized screen (6' w) to drop in front of the marker wall, and a credenza (at least 6' long) for beverage service, video controls, and supply storage. A ceiling-mounted digital projector will be ceiling-mounted and directed toward the screen.

C. Conference Room
1. Central table to seat ten.
2. Credenza for beverage service and the storage of pencils/paper.
3. A clear wall surface or a ceiling-recessed projection screen and a ceiling-mounted digital projector.
4. Marker-board wall surface, 8 to 10 lin. ft.
5. Storage closet, at least 10 sq. ft., for a video monitor cart, newsprint pad easel, and other conference paraphernalia.

D. President's Office
1. Executive desk, 18 to 22 sq. ft. credenza with kneehole space and able to accommodate a flat screen monitor, keyboard tray, and a small desktop printer, two box/file pedestals and book/artifact shelves (above), 16 to 20 lin. ft.
2. Executive task chair and two pull-up guest chairs.
3. Conversational conference area with lounge seating for four, plus appropriate space for the two pull-up chairs to become part of the conversational grouping when needed.
4. Shelving for books and artifacts, with at least 50 lin. ft.

E. Private Offices (two)

Except for the shelving requirements, the office needs of the executive vice president and the vice president of operations are the same and are as follows:

1. Desk surface of 20 to 26 sq. ft. containing a rounded conference extension to accommodate three visitors, plus a return or credenza with 7 to 10 sq. ft., a flat screen monitor, keyboard tray, and a small desktop printer, and one box/file drawer pedestal.
2. Management task chair and three pull-up guest chairs.
3. Lateral files, 12 lin. ft.
4. Shelving:
   - For exec. VP—60 lin. ft. for books and artifacts.
   - For VP for operations—16 lin. ft. for books.

F. Account Executives (two)

1. Management workstation with at least 20 sq. ft. of desk surface, a flat screen monitor, keyboard tray, and a small desktop printer, and two box/file drawer pedestals.
2. Management task chair and two pull-up guest chairs.
3. 9 lin. ft. of lateral files.

G. Administrative Assistants (four)

1. Workstation with at least 16 sq. ft. of desk surface, a flat screen monitor, keyboard tray, and a small desktop printer, and two box/file drawer pedestals.
2. Operations task chair and a guest side chair.
3. 6 lin. ft. of lateral files.

H. Workroom

1. Freestanding copier (47" w × 27" d × 38" h), requires a 56" w space for maintenance.
2. Mail sorting table, 60" w × 24" d × 36" h, with a wall-hung mail sorter above the table 48" w × 26" h × 9" d.
3. Lockable supply shelving in cabinets or closet, containing 36 lin. ft. of 12" d shelving and 36 lin. ft. of 18" d shelving.
4. Employee coat closet with 6 lin. ft. of hanging rod.
5. General storage closet, 30 sq. ft.

I. Beverage Center

1. At least 10 sq. ft. of open counter space, plus a full complement of base and wall cabinets.
2. Single-bowl sink, 19" w; small range/oven, 20" w; stand-up refrigerator, 28" w.
3. Under-counter dishwasher, two-burner coffeemaker, and a cabinet-hung microwave.

J. Lunch/Break Room

1. Flexible table arrangement for eight to ten people, accommodating groups from two to six people.
2. Service station for supplies, condiments, etc., plus trash receptacles below.

K. Rest Rooms

1. Men: two lavatories, one urinal, one toilet stall.
2. Women: two lavatories, two toilet stalls.

DESIGN PROGRAM 3B
The Cosmopolitan Club

Following the lead of other metropolitan chapters, the local chapter of a national business and professional organization has decided to initiate its own private dining club. The club's purposes are to provide a meeting place for members, a place to entertain nonmember friends and business associates, and a dining place of predictable fare and atmosphere where one is known. The design program was established after lengthy consultation with the managers of other dining clubs within the national organization and a local food service consultant.

The overall ambience should be friendly, businesslike, and more formal than informal. Lunch is the major meal of the day, although dinner will be served as well. Previous experience indicates that men and women diners will be equal in number. The bar and lounge activity is expected to be limited; again, previous experience indicates that members expect the lunch hour to be limited, without the luxury of an extended midday break. Because the membership is fairly diverse in nature, a strong theme in cuisine or decor is not desired. The general traffic patterns are obvious, but in circumstances where a separate service entrance is not possible (as in the case of a high-rise office building), service deliveries and garbage pickup must be routed with minimal passage through public spaces and strictly scheduled for non-dining hours. The manager's office should be located fairly close to the entry, and ideally it should have access to food preparation areas without having to travel through the dining area.

SPECIAL REQUIREMENTS

1. The private dining rooms and the manager's office must provide acoustic isolation.
2. The bar is primarily a service bar, and a 5' long portion of the bar length must be reserved for waiter pickup.
3. Priority for natural light and view must be given to the dining areas; the same are desirable but not necessary in the bar/lounge and the manager's office.
4. All public areas shall be barrier-free.

PROGRAM REQUIREMENTS

A. Entry
1. Seating for four to five people; the comfort level need not be very great.
2. Maître d' stand, about 3 sq. ft. in size, strategically placed to view both the bar/lounge and the main dining room.
3. Small decorative table, 6 to 10 sq. ft., for the display of club literature.
4. Self-service coatroom or alcove with at least 20 lin. ft. of hanging rod, plus umbrella stand, hatrack, and boot rack.

B. Bar/Lounge
1. A traditional bar with at least 8 lin. ft. of under-counter work area and a back bar with storage and bottle display, space for six barstools, and a waiter pickup space of 5'-0" in length.
2. Flexible table area for eight to ten people, to accommodate groups of two and four.

C. Main Dining Room
1. Seat 40 diners at tables for 2 and 4, with the flexibility for occasional arrangements for 6.
2. Service station, 6 lin. ft. of clear countertop, plus storage trays for flatware and shelves for china service, glasses, table linens, etc.; allow 50 sq. ft. for the station.

D. Private Dining Rooms (two)
1. One room to seat 6 and the other to seat 12 (at one table).
2. Each room shall have a service buffet of at least 5' and 7' long, respectively, with service storage below the buffet surface.

E. Manager's Office
1. Desk with 12 to 15 sq. ft. work surface, return with 7 to 10 sq. ft. surface, two box/file drawer pedestals, 8 lin. ft. of book/manual shelving, and a flat screen monitor, keyboard tray, and a small desktop printer.
2. Lateral files, 30 lin. ft.
3. Management task chair and two pull-up guest chairs.

F. Restrooms
1. Men: two lavatories, one urinal, one toilet stall.
2. Women: two lavatories, two toilet stalls, two-seat grooming vanity.

G. Food Service Facilities

Allow 1,000 sq. ft. for total food service area, including receiving desk, employee lockers and toilet facilities, dry and cold storage (including waste refrigeration), food preparation kitchen, dishwashing area, and waiter service line. View of kitchen should be screened from diners, and kitchen noises should be contained in the work areas. At least one major wall shall be adjacent to an existing plumbing stack.

DESIGN PROGRAM 3C
Community Counseling Consortium

The Community Counseling Consortium (CCC) has found a new space in which to house its offices and meeting facilities. The space must accommodate the administrative and counseling offices for CCC, a community seminar and conference room, and a Hot Line Center (HLC).

CCC is a nonprofit, community-funded organization that counsels both families and individuals in crisis—those facing death or a terminal illness of a family member; those dealing with drug and alcohol abuse, or physical or sexual abuse; those facing desertion or joblessness, etc. The predominant area of direct help is with individuals or families facing a terminal illness. CCC offers some health care courses, hospice programs, and group interaction seminars that address both the emotional and physical needs of the client. CCC further works as a resource center for persons facing other crisis situations through direct counseling and indirect referral to the proper specific service agency. CCC maintains a checkout library—books, CDs, and DVDs—available to individuals, families, or community service agencies. It further offers a reasonably sized seminar room for community awareness programs and group interaction sessions.

The Hot Line Center is a separate agency funded in part by CCC. The center will be housed in the new CCC facility and will offer a 24-hour telephone hot line for those persons in immediate danger or crisis. In addition to the office area, the center will include an apartment for the supervisor—a position typically held by a graduate student in social work serving a three- to six-month community internship.

SPECIAL REQUIREMENTS

1. CCC wants to maintain a personal and noninstitutional atmosphere throughout its facility. The interiors must be functional but also inviting and relaxing.

2. Particular attention must be given to the reception area and counseling offices in regard to the initial impression conveyed to those persons seeking help.
3. Window areas, and the natural light that they permit to enter, are very important features of the interior environment and must be used to full advantage.
4. As many clients are handicapped, all public spaces must be wheelchair-accessible. (The HLC, both the office and the apartment, are considered to be for private use and need not meet barrier-free codes.)
5. The HLC office and apartment must be a separate entity, with access to its spaces immediately entered from the reception area, and if possible (building configuration permitting) with its own exterior entrance door.
6. The private counseling offices should afford visual as well as acoustic privacy.
7. Though personal or residential in appearance, furniture materials and finishes must be durable and practical and meet commercial standards.

PROGRAM REQUIREMENTS

A. Reception Area
1. Reception station to accommodate a client sign-in counter, 10 sq. ft. of clear work surface, a flat screen monitor, keyboard tray, and a small desktop printer, a storage pedestal with two box drawers and one file drawer, a telephone, and a task chair.
2. 18 lin. ft. of lateral files.
3. A wall-hung literature rack for information and educational brochures. This rack must be visible from the reception area and accessible to the public.
4. Secured storage for general office supplies (24 lin. ft. of shelving, 12" d) and visual materials available for public checkout, i.e., books, CDs, DVDs, etc. (24 lin. ft. of shelving, 18" d).
5. Freestanding copier (30" w × 26" d × 38" h) accessible to the receptionist but not visible to visitors.
6. Visitor seating for four to six.
7. Coat hanging space for ten visitors.

B. Counseling Offices (three)

1. Three private offices. Each requires a work area to accommodate 12 sq. ft. of work surface, 9 lin. ft. of lateral files, and 6 lin. ft. of open shelving for books and artifacts, and a flat screen monitor, keyboard tray, and a small desktop printer. Work area should be separate, but not necessarily divided, from the actual counseling area. Each requires a managerial swivel-tilt chair.
2. Counselor A prefers a casual conference table area—a round desk-height table and four chairs.
3. Counselors B and C prefer a conversational arrangement—sofa and/or lounge chair seating for at least four.

C. CCC Director's Office

1. A private office with both a work area and a conference area.
2. Double-pedestal desk (18 sq. ft.) with full-height box/file drawer pedestals, and a flat screen monitor, keyboard tray, and a small desktop printer.
3. Credenza with a minimum of 6 lin. ft. of lateral files.
4. Swivel-tilt executive desk chair.
5. Two guest pull-up chairs.
6. 18 lin. ft. of open shelving for books and artifacts.
7. Separate conference area for four using lounge chairs around a round coffee table (15" h).

D. Community Seminar Room

1. Multipurpose room. Allow for varied and flexible seating arrangements—lecture-style layout (i.e., classroom seating) for 40, or conference setup (i.e., tables and chairs) for 20.
2. Storage for folding tables, stacking chairs, and coatracks for 40 visitors.
3. Coffee bar with under-counter refrigerator (60" w × 24" d × 36" h).
4. One tackable wall, 8 lin. ft. min.
5. One visual board (48" w × 48" h × 5" d closed, 96" w open). Includes writing surface, flip chart, and pull-down projection screen.
6. Ceiling-recessed projection screen and a ceiling-mounted digital projector.

E. Public Restrooms

1. Men: two lavatories, one urinal, one toilet.
2. Women: two lavatories, two toilets.

F. Kitchen/Lounge

Used by both clients and staff for lunches, breaks, and relaxing.

1. Tables and chairs in flexible arrangement to seat at least 16.
2. Work area: counter surface of at least 12 sq. ft., double sink, under-counter dishwasher, four-burner range/oven (30" w), microwave, standard refrigerator with icemaker (32" w), and a full complement of base and wall cabinets.

G. Hot Line Center: Office

1. Separate entry (from the exterior, if possible).
2. Two work areas, semiprivate, each to accommodate a 10 sq. ft. work surface, a telephone, a flat screen monitor, keyboard tray, and a small desktop printer, a two-file drawer pedestal, and a managerial chair.
3. 12 lin. ft. of lateral files, accessible to both workers.
4. Storage closet or cabinet (36" w × 18" d × 78" h) for forms, manuals, supplies, etc.

H. Hot Line Center: Supervisor's Apartment

1. Adjacent to the CCC office.
2. Living area: conversational seating for four, reading chair, wall unit for TV, stereo, and books, 15 lin. ft. of shelving.
3. Dining area: table and chairs for four; table will double as a writing/work surface.
4. Small kitchen: sink, refrigerator, range, microwave, counter, and cabinets; approx. 50 sq. ft. in size.
5. Sleeping area (need not be a separate room): double bed, bedside table, drawer storage, clothes closet with 4 lin. ft. of hanging rod.
6. Bathroom: lavatory, toilet, shower, linen storage.

BUILDING SHELLS

1A, 1B, 1C: 1,500 square feet

2A, 2A-RC, 2B, 2C, 2C-RC, 2S: 2,500 square feet

3A, 3B, 3C, 3C-RC: 4,000 square feet

- Building Shells 1A, 1B and 1C are 1,500 sq. ft. in size and are meant to be used interchangeably with Design Programs 1A, 1B and 1C, providing nine separate space planning exercises of that size.

- Middle: Building Shells 2A, 2B, 2C and 2S are 2,500 sq. ft. in size and are specifically meant to be used interchangeably with Design Programs 2A, 2B, 2C and 2S, providing 16 separate space planning exercises of that size. Please note that the "S" designation connotes "Sample", in which shell 2S and program 2S are the demonstration example used throughout the text.

- Building Shells 3A, 3B and 3C are 4,000 sq. ft. in size and are specifically meant to be used interchangeably with Design Programs 3A, 3B and 3C, providing nine separate space planning exercises of that size.

BUILDING DESCRIPTION

Situated on a heavily traveled street, this typical wood frame "rancher" of 1950s vintage is sited on an oversized lot with a deep and well-landscaped rear yard, making it appropriate for non-residential uses. Exterior walls are of load-bearing wood stud (16" o.c.) construction, with an insulating sheathing board and painted wood siding applied to the exterior and gypsum wallboard applied to the interior. The roof construction is of conventional clear-span wood trusses placed 24" oc., with plywood sheathing and asphalt shingles applied. Exterior doors are 7'-0" high; windows are double hung, with a 3'-0" sill (A.F.F.) and a 7'-0" head (A.F.F.).

The first floor is of wood joist construction with a plywood subfloor and t+g oak strip finish flooring. the ceiling is gypsum wallboard, 8'-0" A.F.F. The partitions surrounding the basement stair are of wood stud and gypsum wallboard construction; these partitions have a 6" high wood clamshell baseboard. The door to the stair is a 7'-0" high painted flush door. The heating system is a perimeter baseboard type, 6" high, presenting a continuous appearance on all exterior walls. Because of the existing waste line location in the basement, all of the plumbing fixtures must be placed within 10'-0" of the north and west walls of the building. All incoming utility lines and metering equipment are in the full basement.

Because this structure does not have architectural distinction or historic significance, modest revisions to its exterior may be made. The basic provisions of standard regional building codes, including those provisions related to barrier-free access and design, shall be complied with.

SITE PLAN

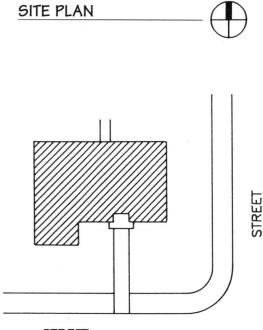

STREET

STREET

N

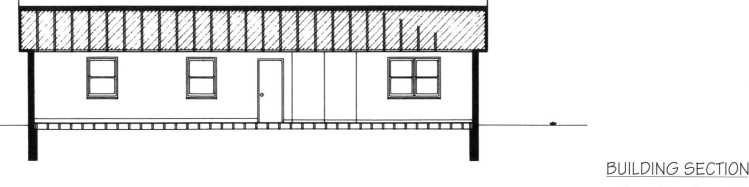

BUILDING SECTION

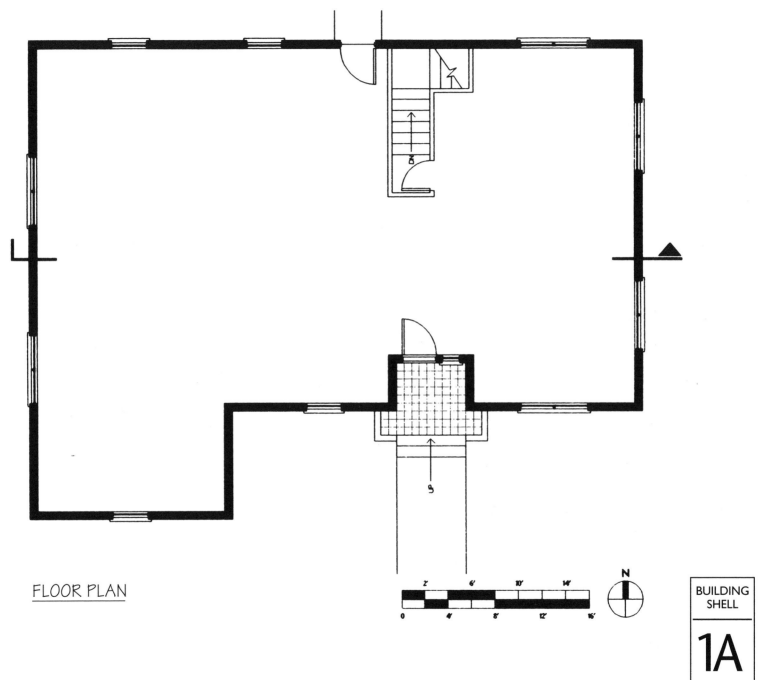

FLOOR PLAN

BUILDING
SHELL

1A

BUILDING DESCRIPTION

This turn-of-the-century firehouse has been retired from active service after many years. It is part of a small cluster of commercial buildings that are separated by load-bearing masonry fire walls in row-house-like manner. The front and rear walls are of non-bearing masonry construction. The second floor and roof structures are of typical wood joist construction. The garage door openings in the south wall have arched lintels, 12'-0" high at their mid-point. The side doors in the south wall have glass transoms above 7'-0" high doors, with arched lintels over the transoms, 9'-0" high at their midpoint. The rear service door is 7'-0" high, and the windows in the north and west walls have sills at 3'-0" A.F.F. and heads at 9'-0" A.F.F. For the purpose of this design problem, the second floor will be used for future expansion purposes only, with access to the existing stair a basic planning consideration.

The ground floor is a reinforced concrete slab on grade. The interior face of the exterior walls and the party wall are exposed brick. The free-standing interior columns are 6" diameter steel lally columns. The first floor ceiling is plaster, on wood lath attached to the underside of the second-floor joists and is at 14'-0" A.F.F. A new HVAC system is planned for rooftop installation, with supply and return ducts to be fed down adjacent to the east party wall; new interior construction on the first floor may expose new ductwork, or construct a new suspended ceiling to conceal the new ductwork. All plumbing fixtures must be placed within 10'-0" of the east and west walls in order to connect with the main drain lines along those walls in trenches below the finished floor.

Because of its clear period character, the south wall of the building may not be altered. But the infill windows within the garage door openings may be designed to fit the needs of the new interior use. The basic provisions of standard regional building codes, including those provisions related to barrier-free access and design, shall be complied with.

SITE PLAN

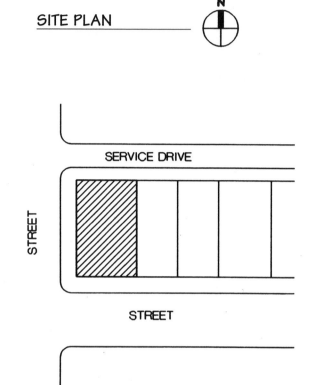

BUILDING SECTION

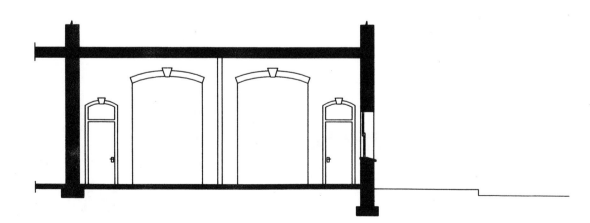

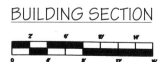

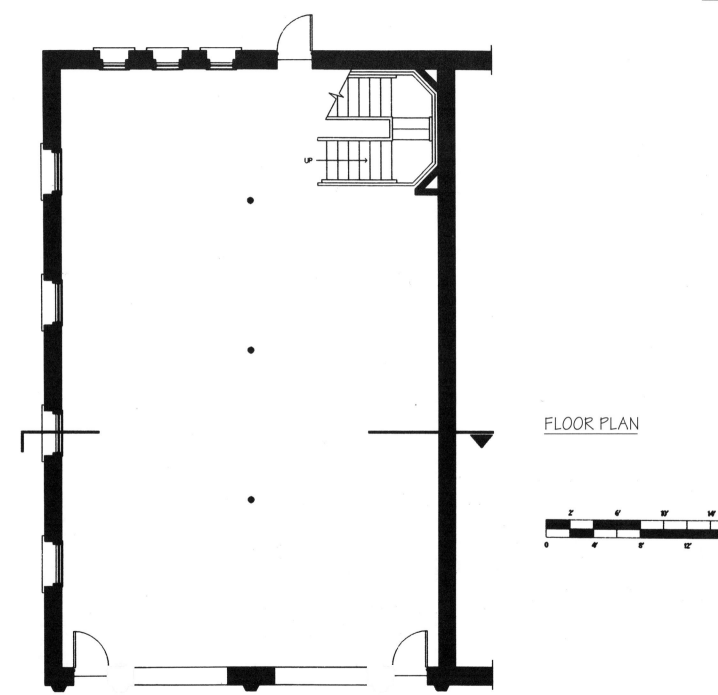

FLOOR PLAN

2'   6'   10'   14'

0   4'   8'   12'   16'

N

BUILDING
SHELL

1B

BUILDING DESCRIPTION

Built in the 1920s, this former municipal office building, designed with classical detail and situated in a parklike setting, has been made available for rent for both professional offices and community agency use. The specific space described here is at one end of the first floor of this three-story-plus-basement building. The basic structure is masonry bearing wall with reinforced concrete floors. The exterior walls are brick with a plaster interior finish;the interior bearing wall is also of brick with a plaster finish. Windows are double hung, with the sill at 3'-0" A.F.F. and the head at 8'-0" A.F.F. The window trim is 6" wide.

The exsisting floor surface is terrazzo, in smooth but unpresentable condition. Interior wall surfaces are plaster with an 8" high three-piece wood baseboard. The interior bearing wall may be penetrated with an additional opening up to 6'-0" wide, but the length of the wall at either end of the opening must be at least 3'-6" long. The entry to the space must be closed off with a door. The plaster ceiling is just below the concrete beams of the floor above and is 10'-0" A.F.F. A new central HVAC system has been installed to accommodate supply ductwork. A 1'-0" deep by 2'-0" wide (min. dimension) soffit must be placed along the exterior walls. Plumbing fixtures must be placed within 12'-0" of the designated pipe chases.

Changes to the exterior of the building are not permitted. The basic provisions of standard regional building codes, including those provisions related to barrier-free access and design shall be complied with.

KEY PLAN

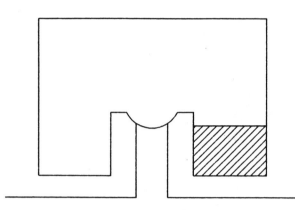

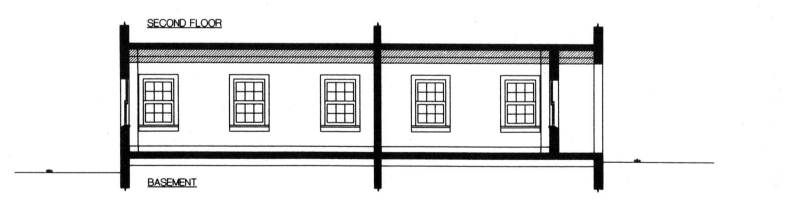

SECOND FLOOR

BASEMENT

BUILDING SECTION

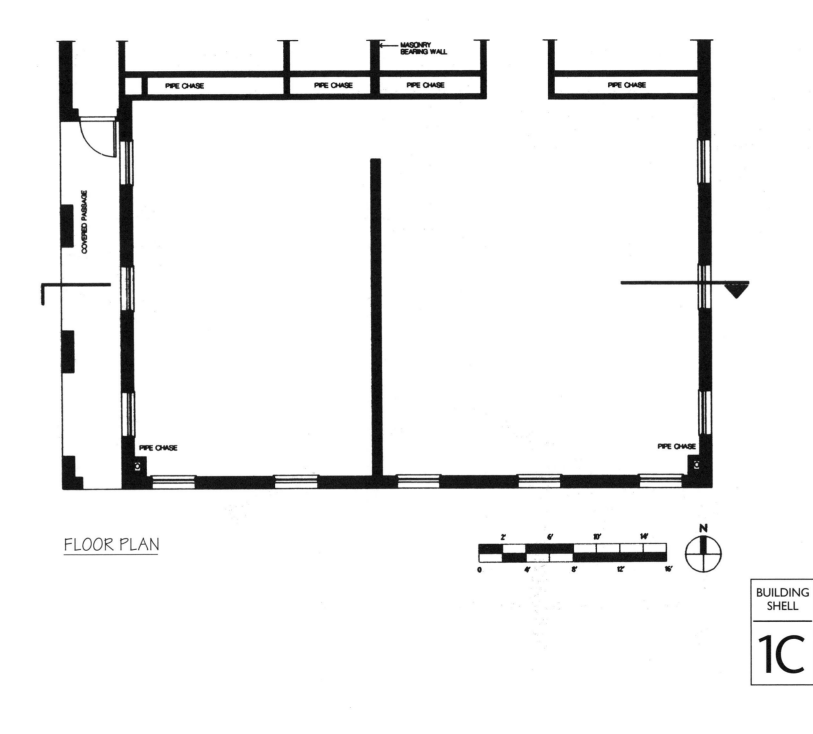

MASONRY
BEARING WALL

PIPE CHASE   PIPE CHASE   PIPE CHASE   PIPE CHASE

COVERED PASSAGE

PIPE CHASE   PIPE CHASE

FLOOR PLAN

BUILDING
SHELL

1C

BUILDING DESCRIPTION

This turn-of-the-century boathouse is sited on a river drive in a parklike setting. It is of ordinary construction. The lower level will continue to be used for rowing sports and will be entered only from the exterior on the river (east) side of the building. The combination Hip/Gable roof is shingled with slate. All windows have sills at 3'-0" A.F.F., and all doors and windows have heads at 10'-0" A,F,F, (doors and recently installed sliding glass doors have transoms over 7'-0" operating doors). All operating windows are double hung; the two projecting bay windows have fixed glass center sections.

The floor is the orginal oak parquet. The wall surfaces are plaster with a 7" high wood baseboard. The ceiling is plaster, the flat part of which is 12'-0" A.F.F.; see the reflected ceiling plan for height variations in the center bay. A new HVAC system will provide heating and cooling through forced-air duckwork above the ceiling. Plumbing waste and supply lines are contained in the designated chases and tight against the south wall of the building, just below the first-floor joists. Flush fixtures (such as toilets and urinals) must be placed within 10'-6" of a pipe chase or the south wall of the building. All other fixtures must be placed within 12'-6" of a pipe chase or the south wall of the building.

Changes to the exterior of the building are not permitted. The basic provisions of standard regional building codes, including those provisions related to barrier-free access and design, shall be complied with.

SITE PLAN

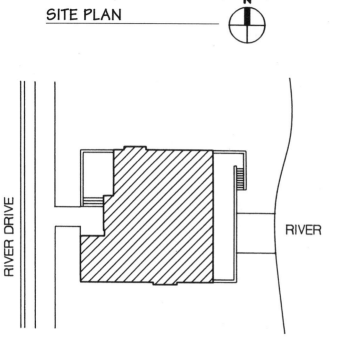

BUILDING SECTION

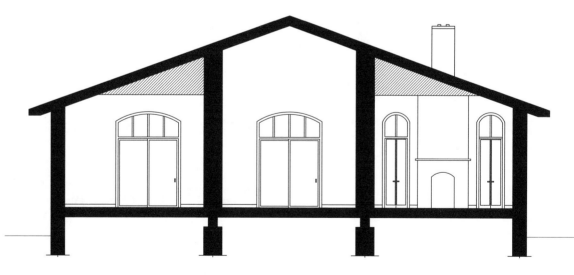

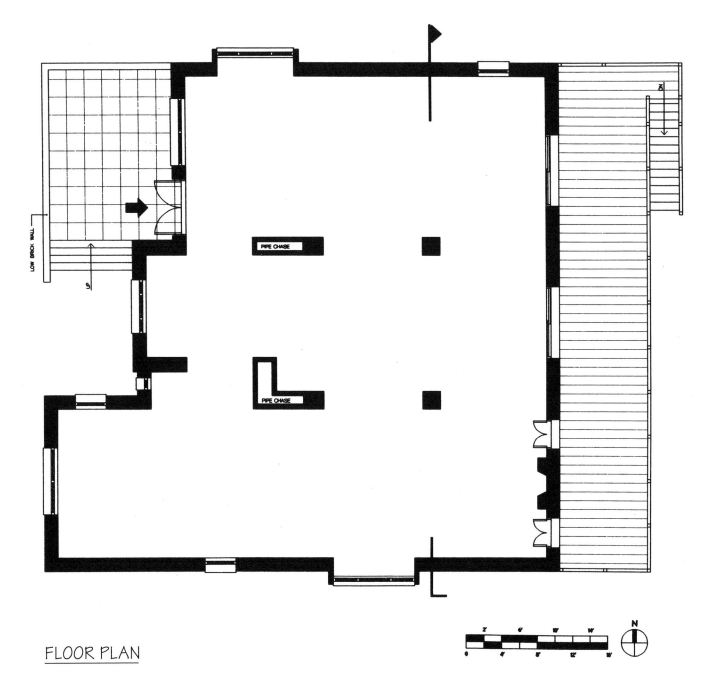

PIPE CHASE

PIPE CHASE

LOW BRICK WALL

FLOOR PLAN

BUILDING
SHELL

2A

REFLECTED CEILING PLAN

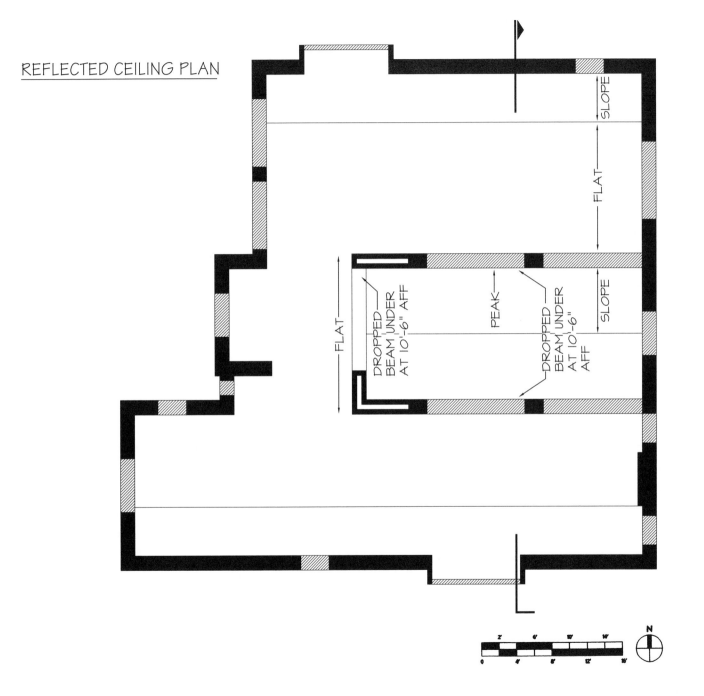

SLOPE

FLAT

FLAT

PEAK

SLOPE

DROPPED BEAM UNDER AT 10'-6" AFF

DROPPED BEAM UNDER AT 10'-6" AFF

FLAT

REFLECTED CEILING PLAN

2A
RC

BUILDING DESCRIPTION

This 1980s building is part of a suburban office park consisting of many small and medium-sized one- and two-story buildings in a green campus setting. The buildings are of load-bearing steel stud and roof truss construction, with the ground floor of slab-on-grade concrete, and the exterior walls sheathed and surfaced with brick veneer. This particular building is a one-story structure with a shingled intersecting center ridge roof, and a suspended 2' x 2' lay-in acoustic tile ceiling set at 8'-6" A.F.F. The 3'-0" wide (fixed) and the 6'-0" wide (slider) windows have sills set at 2'-6" A.F.F.; the sliding glass door (6'-0" wide), hinged doors, and all windows have heads at 8'-0" A.F.F.

Interior wall surfaces are painted gypsum wall board with 4" high straight vinyl base. HVAC equipment and duckwork are concealed above the ceiling. Plumbing supply and waste lines are contained in the two identified pipe chases and in the two exposed pipe clusters in the western portion of the building (these clusters must be enclosed in a chase or incorporated into partition work). Plumbing fixtures must be placed with 12'-0" of existing soil stacks.

In consultation with the developer's architect, very modest exterior changes, such as door and window locations, may be made. The basic provsions of standard regional building codes, including those provisions related to barrier-free access and design, shall be complied with.

SITE PLAN

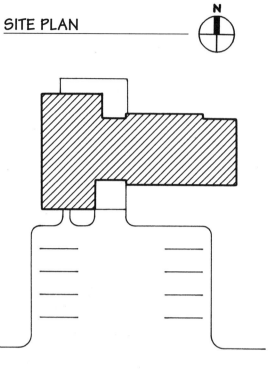

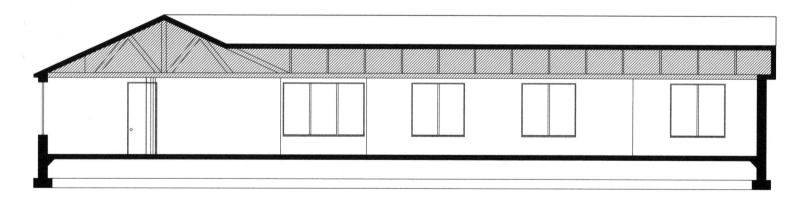

BUILDING SECTION

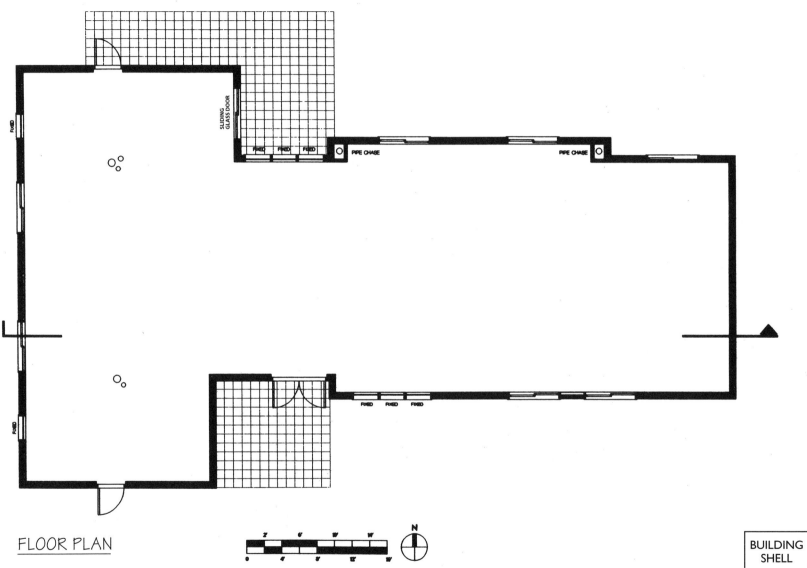

FLOOR PLAN

BUILDING
SHELL

2B

BUILDING DESCRIPTION

This space is at the end of one wing of a typical floor of a large, urban core office building constructed during the first decade of the century in the grand manner of the Beaux Arts tradition. As was typical of the period, it is of steel frame construction and reinforced concrete floors, with unusually heavy limestone clad masonry walls. All of the windows are double-hung, with sills at 2'-6" A.F.F. and heads at 9'-6" A.F.F.

The existing floors are bare concrete. The interior walls are plaster with a 9" high wood base-board. The original ceiling has been removed, and a new suspended lay-in type acoustic tile ceiling will be installed at 10'-0" A.F.F. The ductwork of a recent-vintage, central HVAC system will be concealed above the suspended ceiling, except for one major duct trunk line, shown on the reflected ceiling plan, which will require a ceiling height of not more than 8'-9" A.F.F.; partitions and ceiling configuration must accommodate the lower-than-normal duct. All plumbing fixtures must be placed within 12'-0" of the two pipe chases adjacent to the freestanding columns, the three large pipe chases between the east demising wall and the building's fire stair, or the north exterior wall. The unpochéd partition shown at the east edge of the space indicates where the acquired space ends; a demising partition must be placed there, with an entrance door to the space placed as desired within that partition.

Changes to the exterior of the building are not permitted. The basic provisions of standard regional building codes, including those provisions related to barrier-free access and design, shall be complied with.

See reflected ceiling plan for additional information.

KEY PLAN

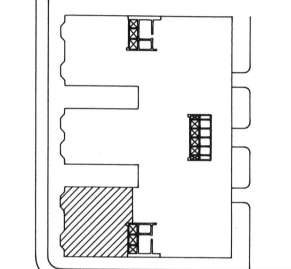

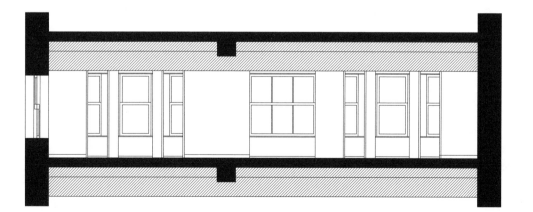

BUILDING SECTION

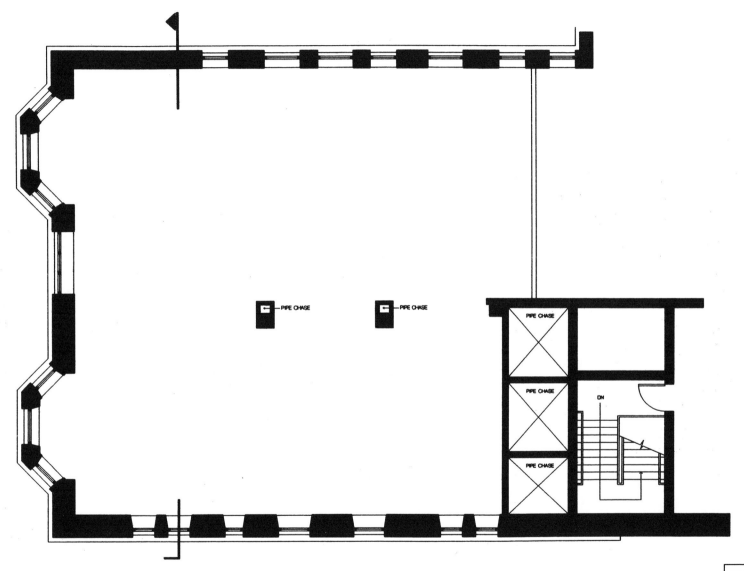

FLOOR PLAN

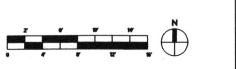

BUILDING
SHELL

2C

REFLECTED CEILING PLAN

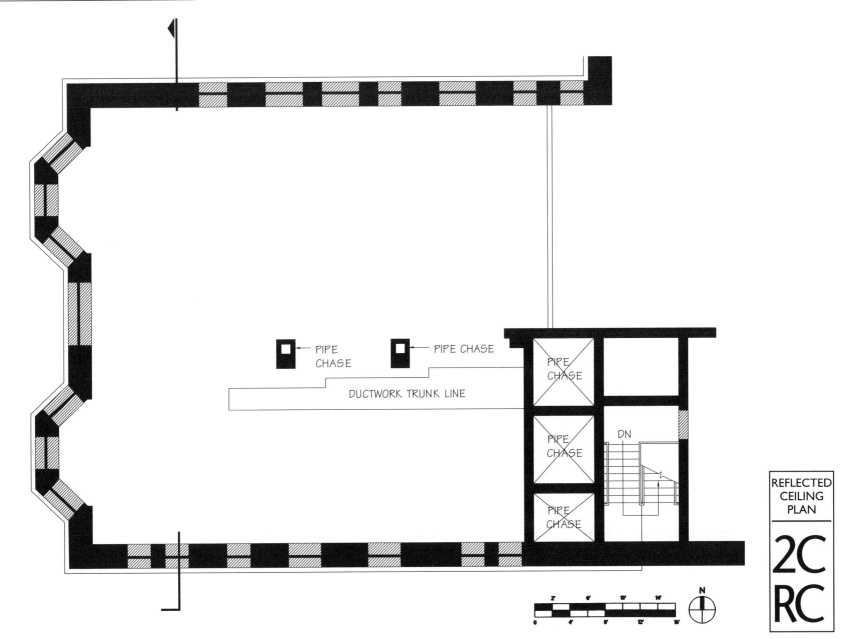

PIPE CHASE

PIPE CHASE

PIPE CHASE

DUCTWORK TRUNK LINE

PIPE CHASE

PIPE CHASE

DN

PIPE CHASE

N

REFLECTED
CEILING
PLAN

2C
RC

BUILDING DESCRIPTION

This former branch bank facility is of light steel frame construction, with load-bearing steel frame construction, with load-bearing steel stud exterior walls faced with 4" (nominal) brick veneer, which projects above the essentially flat roof, creating a capped parapet wall. Decorative square column covers occur at 10'-0" intervals where the glazing is continuous. This recently constructed building is contextually appropriate in its commercial setting and is architecturally pleasing but has no architectural significance. The bank's vault and other interior partitions have been removed with the exception of the mechanical room, which is to remain. The drive-in-teller's window on the north wall has been replaced by a bay window, similar in appearance to the other commercial aluminum windows. Windowsills are 2'-6" A.F.F., and heads are at 8'-6" A.F.F.

The floor is an exposed concrete slab on grade. The interior wall and column surfaces are painted gypsum wallboard, with 4" high straight vinyl base. The original acoustic tile ceiling has been removed and shall be replaced by a suspended system with acoustic tile and/or gypsum wallboard; tile size and style are at the designer's discretion. The maximum ceiling height is 9'-0" A.F.F. All HVAC ductwork shall be concealed above the ceiling. All plumbing fixtures must be placed within 12'-0" of the north wall of the building, or within 12'-0" of either or both of the free-standing internal columns; the vent stacks adjacent to the columns must be enclosed. The existing entrance vestibule shall remain intact.

Changes to the exterior of the building are not permitted. The basic provisions of standard regional building codes, including the provisions related to barrier-free and design, shall be complied with.

SITE PLAN

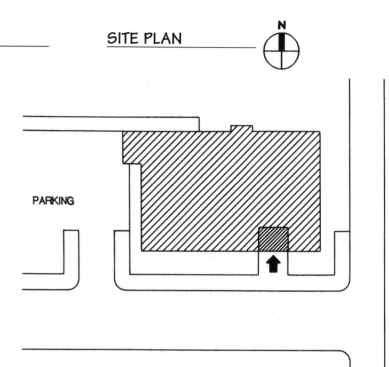

PARKING

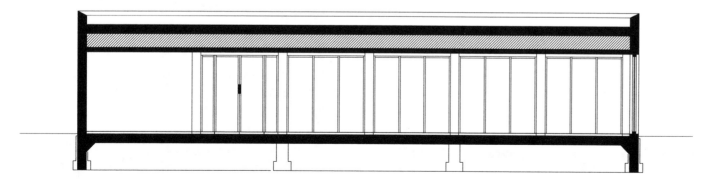

BUILDING SECTION

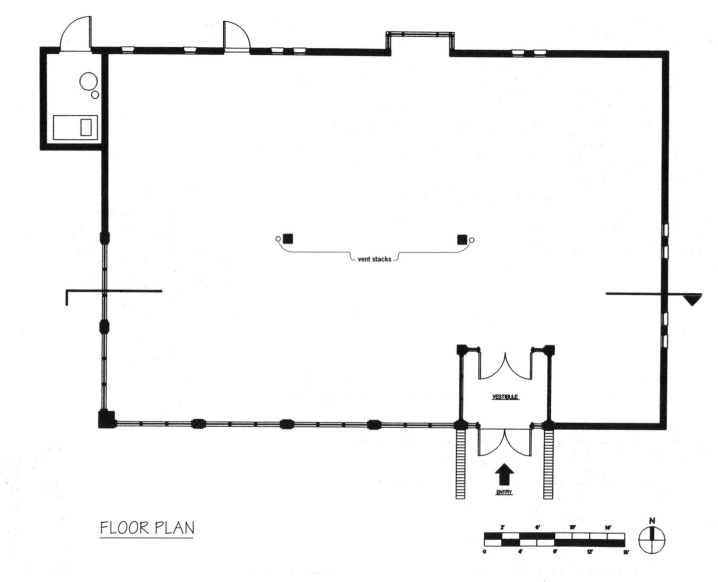

FLOOR PLAN

vent stacks

VESTIBULE

ENTRY

BUILDING DESCRIPTION

This one-story Savings Bank building of contemporary design in an urban residential setting is of 1960s vintage. Its exterior bearing walls are of brick-veneered steel studs, and the clear span roof is framed with light steel trusses; the floor construction is slab on grade. The building section indicates the general character of the sloped hip roof which covers the building. The sidelight windows adjacent to the main entrance door and the windows on the west wall of the patio, have sills at 6" A.F.F. All other windowsills are 2'-8" A.F.F., and all windows heads and door heads are at 8'-0" A.F.F.

The interior wall surfaces are painted gypsum wallboard with 4" high straight vinyl base. It is expected that a new suspended acoustic tile ceiling will be installed at 9'-6" A.F.F. (maximum height); the specific size and type of ceiling material have not yet been selected.

HVAC equipment is housed in the small mechanical room, which is accessed from the exterior on the north wall; all duckwork shall be concealed above the suspended ceiling. Plumbing supply and waste lines are contained in the three exposed pipe clusters in the center of the building (these clusters must be enclosed in a chase or incorporated into partition work). Plumbing fixtures must be placed within 15'-0" of existing soil stacks. The existing entrance vestibule must remain intact.

Changes to the building's exterior may be made only to the north wall of the building, although the location of the secondary exit door and the mechanical room may not be changed. The basic provisions of standard regional building codes, including those provisions related to barrier-free access and design, shall be complied with.

SITE PLAN

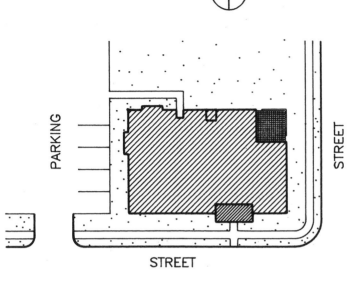

BUILDING SECTION

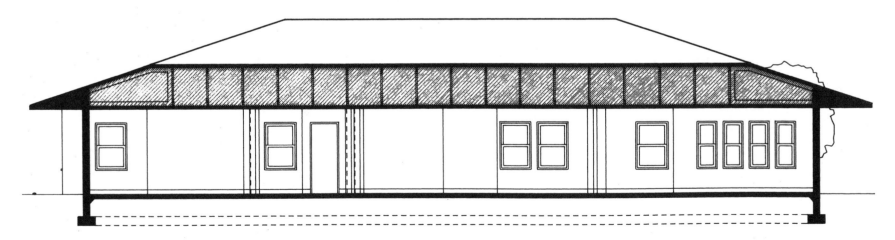

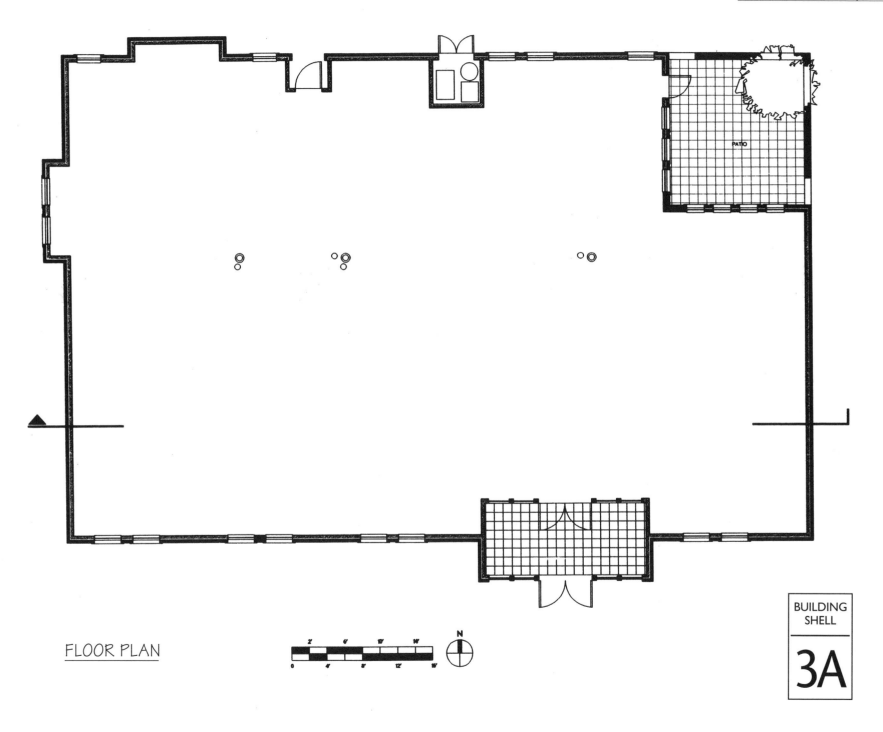

PATIO

FLOOR PLAN

N

BUILDING DESCRIPTION

This barn structure of unknown vintage is in a once rural but now suburban setting, facing a heavily traveled commerical street. The remaining original stone portion faces the street, and the back portion, reconstructed with wood frame, faces a wooded rear yard with a stream at the far end. The fieldstone walls have never been finished on the interior, and the frame walls at the rear of the building have a board-and-batten exterior with recently insulated in-fill and hardboard finish on the interior. The roof structure, interior columns, and floor/loft structures are all of heavy timber contstuction, none of which has been closed-in. The original roof, a traditional gable-end ridge roof, is intact and covers the entire structure. The lower level can be entered only from the exterior (on the north wall) and will be used exclusively for storage and utility purposes only. The upper loft level will be reserved for future expansion purposes. Windows in the original structure are wood double hung, with a 3'-0" sill A.F.F. and a 9'-0" head A.F.F. in the south wall and a 5'-0" sill A.F.F. and an 8'-0" head A.F.F. in the east and west walls.

Windows of appropriate size, style, and placement shall be installed in the wood frame walls of the addition. Existing door openings shall be retained as such, or converted to window openings. The two existing rough openings in the existing masonry walls in the building's entranceway shall become window openings, with sill and head heights to be determined by interior use.

The existing floor is rough wood plank. There are no finished ceilings; the height to the underside of the loft beams above is 12'-0" A.F.F. For this first phase of reconstruction, all HVAC equipment and duckwork will be contained in the basement. All plumbing fixtures must be placed within 12'-0" of the main east and west walls.

Except as noted above, concerning new window openings, changes to the exterior of the building are not permitted. The basic provisions of standard regional building codes, including those provisions related to barrier-free access and design, shall be complied with.

SITE PLAN

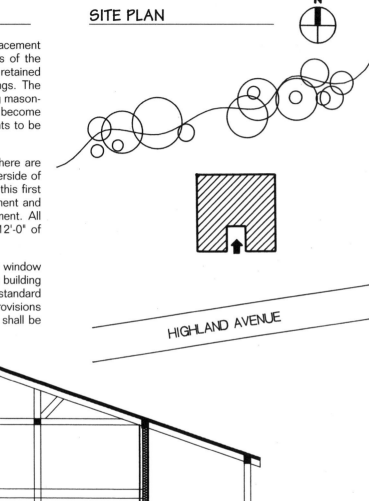

HIGHLAND AVENUE

BUILDING SECTION

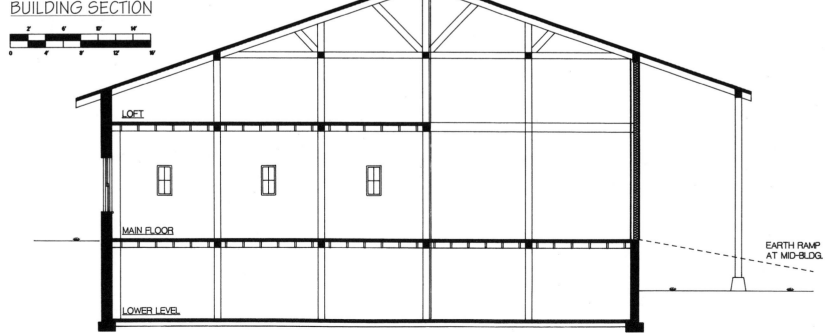

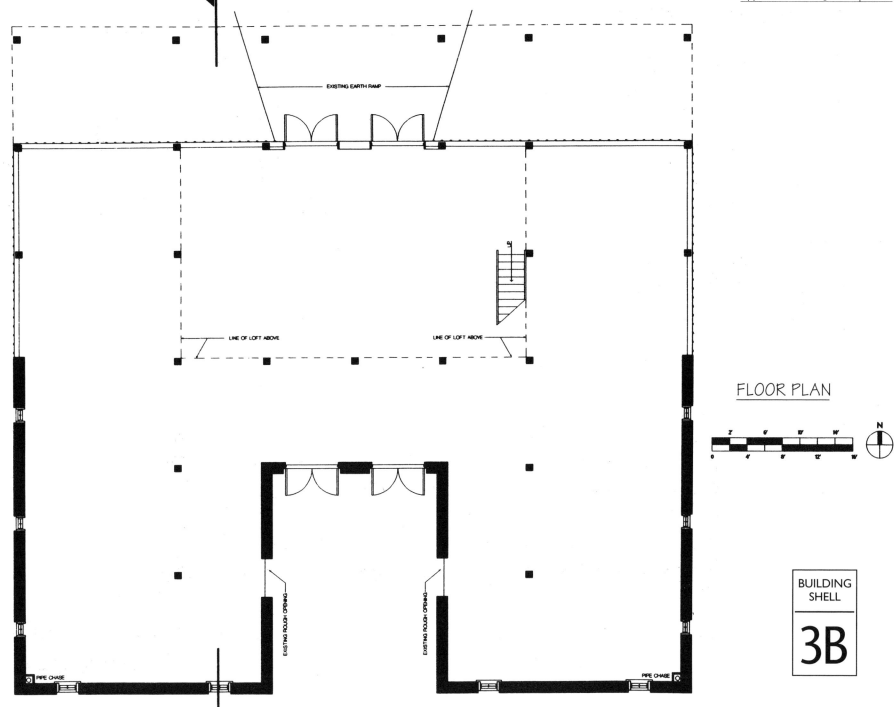

EXISTING EARTH RAMP

LINE OF LOFT ABOVE

LINE OF LOFT ABOVE

FLOOR PLAN

EXISTING ROUGH OPENING

EXISTING ROUGH OPENING

PIPE CHASE

PIPE CHASE

N

BUILDING
SHELL

3B

BUILDING DESCRIPTION

This space is on a typical floor of a recently built, suburban high-rise office building. It is of steel frame construction, with a central service core and an exterior wall of brick spandrels and non-operating aluminum ribbon windows that are broken by brick panels at the building's corners. The window sill is at 2'-6" A.F.F. and the head is at 8'-0" A.F.F.

The existing floor is concrete. The interior wall surfaces are painted gypsum wallboard, with 4" high straight vinyl base. The existing suspended acoustic tile ceiling, including the lay-in fluorescent lighting fixtures, may be reconfigured to accommo-date the revised floor plan; the ceiling is set at 8'-6" A.F.F. All HVAC equipment and duck-work is concealed above the ceiling. All plumbing fixtures must be placed within 15'-0" of the free-standing wet columns or any of four large pipe chases adjacent to the east demising wall.

Changes to the exterior of the building are not permitted. The basic provisions of standard regional building codes, including those provisions related to barrier-free access and design shall be complied with.

See reflected ceiling plan for additional information.

SITE PLAN

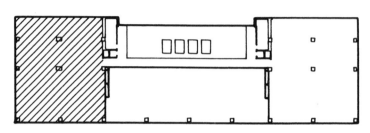

BUILDING SECTION

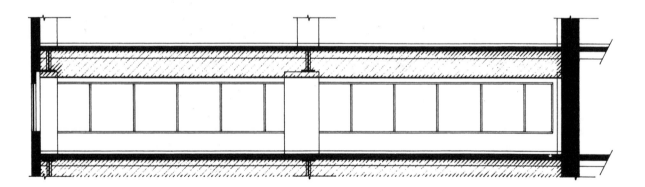

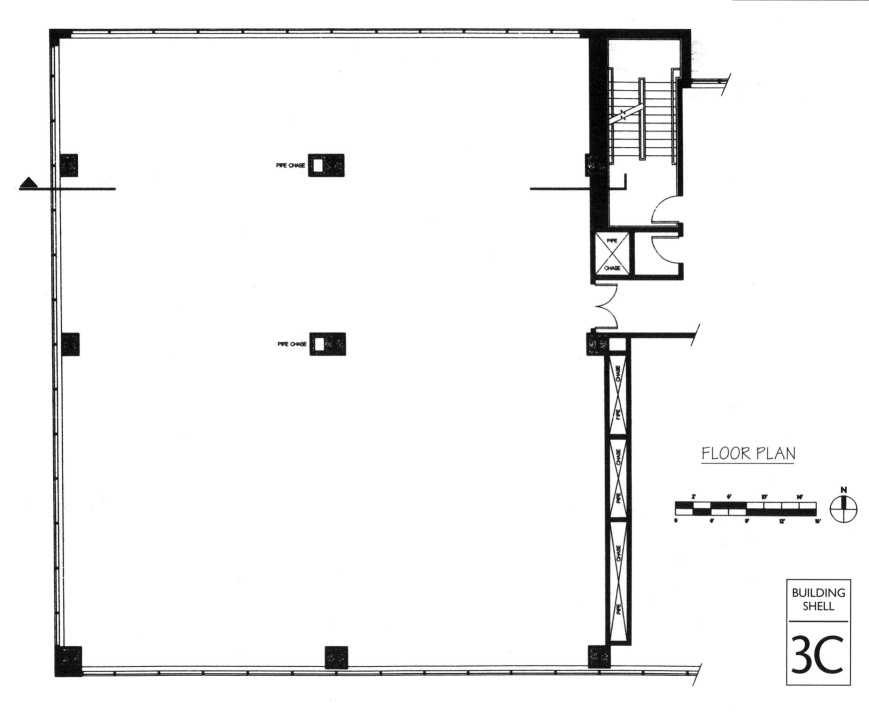

PIPE CHASE

PIPE CHASE

PIPE

CHASE

CHASE

PIPE

CHASE

PIPE

CHASE

PIPE

FLOOR PLAN

N

BUILDING
SHELL

3C

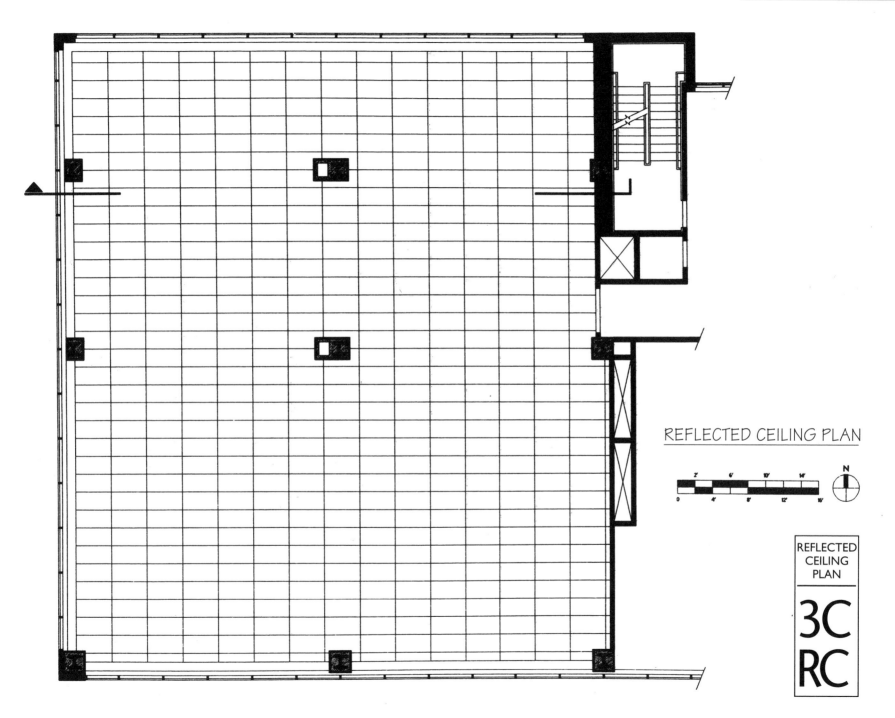

REFLECTED CEILING PLAN

REFLECTED
CEILING
PLAN

3C
RC

GLOSSARY

There are many words and phrases directly related to describing stairs, parts of stairs, and elements adjacent to or related to stairs. The terminology used by architects, designers, and builders, although generally consistent, is not universal, with several words and terms that may be synonymous or on conflict with one another. The glossary of terms that follows has been kept concise, and its purpose is to help the reader to understand the use of stair terminology that is used in this *Stair Design Resource.*

Abbreviations: ADA—Americans with Disabilities Act
ANSI—American National Standards Institute
ASTM—American Society for Testing Materials
IBC—International Building Code

Baluster: One of a series of vertical members supporting a handrail.

Balustrade: A handrail supported by a series of balusters running along the open edge of a level floor, protecting people from falling to the floor level below. A balustrade is sometimes referred to as a guardrail.

Banister: A handrail that follows the incline or decline of a flight of stairs along its open edge (or edges), supported by balusters or other vertical supports.

Circular Stair: A curvilinear stair, typically in one of two forms: (1) a compact spiral stair in which all treads are pie-shaped winders, or (2) a larger circular form in which the smaller radius is at least two times the width of the stair (as per IBC standards).

Dogleg Stair: See *"U" Stair,* below.

Flight: A series of steps uninterrupted by landings.

Guardrail: A protective railing designed to prevent people and large objects from falling into an open well, stairwell, or other similar spaces (sometimes referred to as a balustrade).

Handrail: A railing of a convenient height to be grasped for support when ascending or descending a stairway, attached to an adjacent wall or supported by balusters.

"L" Stair: A stair consisting of two parts connected by a mid-landing, forming an "L" shaped stair.

Landing: A platform between flights of steps that allows the climber to rest, or makes it possible for a stairway to change direction.

Length-of-Run: The horizontal distance between the bottom riser and the top riser.

Newel: The central supporting column of a spiral stairway.

Newel Post: A post that terminates the handrail at the foot or at the head of a staircase, or at a landing.

Nosing: The front or leading edge of the tread, projecting beyond the base of the riser.

Pitch: The degree of incline of the stair; a pitch of 45 degrees is not easy to climb, and one under 27 degrees is tedious and slow.

Railing: See *Handrail*, above.

Ramp: An inclined plane for passage between unaligned levels.

Run: See *Length-of-Run*, above.

Riser: The vertical member of a step.

Spiral Stair: See *Circular Stair*, above.

Stair: A series of steps, with or without landings, giving access from level to level.

Staircase: The entire structure housing a flight or flights of steps, including the supporting framework, landings, balusters, railings, etc. (It is synonymous with stairway.)

Stair Foot: The level space in front of the lowest step of a stairway.

Stair Head: The level space at the top of a stairway.

Stairway: See *Staircase*, above.

Stairwell: The vertical volume of space occupied by a staircase.

Step: One unit of a stair, consisting of a riser and tread.

Stringer: A sloping board at each end of the tread that carries the risers and treads of the stair. A "closed stringer" covers the ends of the treads and risers; an "open stringer" shows the ends of the treads.

Tread: The horizontal surface of a step.

"U" Stair: A stair consisting of two parallel flights of steps connected by a mid-landing, forming a "U" shaped stair.

Winder: A non-rectangular tread; usually pie-shaped in spiral stairs; triangular or wedge-shaped when used to turn corners.

BIBLIOGRAPHY

This bibliography is a compilation of the recommended reading lists accompanying each chapter. It is separated into *reference* sources (denoted by an asterisk*) and *reading materials*. The reference sources provide in-depth information related to basic and recurring planning and design issues and questions. The reading materials are intended to develop knowledge and skills in general planning and design areas and in some peripheral to space planning. One's personal selections in the reading areas will depend heavily upon previous background and experience.

A concerted effort has been made to keep this list to essential books only. It is suggested that the student prioritize his or her planned reading efforts while using this book. More specifically, concentrate on the space planning issues and let the less critical "influencing factors" such as plumbing, acoustics, and interior construction wait until later.

Many other worthwhile texts deal with space planning and related information and skills. An excellent source for locating additional reading related to space planning is the Interior Design Educators Council's (IDEC)

Comprehensive Bibliography for Interior Design, available in many libraries; it can also be purchased directly from IDEC by contacting that organization online at www.idec.org or by writing to:

9202 North Meridian Street, Suite 200
Indianapolis, IN 46260-1810

1. Allen, Edward. *How Buildings Work: The Natural Order of Architecture,* 2nd edition. New York: Oxford University Press, 1995.
*2. American National Standards Institute. *Specifications for Making Buildings and Facilities Accessible to and Usable by Physically Handicapped People.* New York: American National Standards Institute, 1980. (Available from ANSI, 25 West 43rd St., New York, NY 10036.)
3. Binggeli, Corky. *Building Systems for Interior Designers.* Hoboken: John Wiley & Sons, 2003.
*4. Ching, Francis D. K. *Building Codes Illustrated: A Guide to Understanding the International Building Code.* Hoboken: John Wiley & Sons, 2003.

*5. ———. *Architectural Graphics,* 4th edition. Hoboken: John Wiley & Sons, 2002.

*6. ———. *Interior Design Illustrated,* 2nd edition. Hoboken: John Wiley & Sons, 1987.

*7. Ching, Francis D. K., and Cassandra Adams. *Building Construction Illustrated,* 3rd edition. Hoboken: John Wiley & Sons, 2000.

8. Deasy, C. M., and Thomas Laswell. *Designing Places for People.* New York: Whitney Library of Design, 1990.

*9. DiChiara, Joseph, and John H. Callender, eds. *Time-Savers Standards for Building Types,* 4th edition. New York: McGraw Hill, 2001.

8. Egan, M. David. *Architectural Acoustics.* New York: McGraw-Hill, 1988.

10. ———. *Concepts in Architectural Lighting.* New York: McGraw-Hill, 1983.

*11. Groom, James N., and Sarah Harkness. *Building Without Barriers for the Disabled.* New York: Watson-Guptill Publications, 1976.

12. Hall, Edward I. *Hidden Dimension.* New York: Anchor, 1990.

13. Harmon, Sharon Koomen, and Katherine E. Kennon. *The Codes Guidebook for Interiors.* Hoboken: John Wiley & Sons, 2001.

*14. Illuminating Engineering Society. *IES Lighting Handbook: Student Volume.* New York: Illuminating Engineering Society, 1987.

15. Kilmer, Rosemary, and W. Otie Kilmer. *Designing Interiors.* Fort Worth: Harcourt Brace Jovanovich College, 1992.

16. Kira, Alexander. *The Bathroom.* New York: Viking, 1976.

17. Kirkpatrick, James M. *The AutoCAD Book.* Upper Saddle River: Prentice Hall, 2000.

18. Laseau, Paul. *Graphic Thinking for Architects and Designers.* New York: Van Nostrand Reinhold, 1988.

19. Lockard, William K. *Design Drawing.* New York: W. W. Norton, 2000.

20. McGowan, *Interior Graphics Standards.* Hoboken: John Wiley & Sons, 2003.

*21. Panero, Julius, and Martin Zelnik. *Human Dimension and Interior Space.* New York: Watson-Guptill, 1989.

22. Pena, William. *Problem Seeking.* Hoboken: John Wiley & Sons, 2001.

23. Pile, John F. *Interior Design.* New York: Harry N. Abrams, 2002.

*24. Ramsey, Charles G., and Harold R Sleeper. *Architectural Graphic Standards.* Hoboken: John Wiley & Sons, 2000.

*25. Reznikoff, S. C. *Specifications for Commercial Interiors.* New York: Whitney Library of Design, 1989.

*26. ———. *Interior Graphics and Design Standards.* New York: Whitney Library of Design, 1989.

27. Sommer, Robert. *Personal Space: The Behavioral Basis of Design.* New York: Prentice Hall, 1969.

28. White, Edward. *Space Adjacency Analysis.* Tucson: Architectural Media Ltd., 1995.

29. ———. *Introduction to Architectural Programming.* Tucson: Architectural Media Ltd., 1972.

30. Ziesel, Jon. *Inquiry by Design: Tools for Environment-Behavior Research.* Cambridge University Press, 1999.

*31. Major and Regional Building Codes:

- International Building Code 2000. International Conference of Building Officials. February, 2000.
- BOCA—Building Officials and Code Administrators International
- ICBO—International Conference of Building Officials
- Life Safety Code of the National Fire Protection Association
- National Building Code of Canada
- National Fire Code of Canada
- NBD—Basic/National Building Code
- SBC—Standard Building Code
- SBCCI—Southern Building Code Congress International
- UBC—Uniform Building Code

RECOMMENDED READING

Baldon, Cleo. *Steps and Stairways,* New York, Rizzoli, 1989. An excellent, wide-ranging collection of color photographs of stairs around the world, with greater focus on twentieth-century buildings.

Blanc, Alan and Blanc, Sylvia. *Stairs, 2nd edition,* Oxford, Architectural Press, 2001. Its primary value is in several small, detailed drawings of stair construction (including handrails), accompanied by photographs.

Chueca, Pilar. *The Art of Staircases,* Barcelona, International Key Services, 2006. An excellent collection of color photographs of contemporary stairs, accompanied by several diagrammatic drawings.

Falkenberg, Haike. *Staircases,* Te Neues Pub Group, 2002 [ISBN 3823855727]. An excellent collection of color photographs of contemporary stairs.

Haberman, Karl J. *Staircases: Design and construction,* Basel, Birkhauser, 2003 [ISBN 3764364912]. An excellent series of staircase studies in photographs and detailed construction drawings.

Mannes, Willibald. *Designing Staircases,* New York, Van Nostrand Reinhold, 1982. Many drawings of wood stair construction and details.

Slessor, Catherine. *Contemporary Staircases,* London, Mitchell Beazley, 2000. A good, short history of stairs and many good color photos of contemporary stairs.

Spens, Michael. *Staircases,* London, Academy Editions, 1995. A good, short history of stairs, some photographs, and many excellent drawings of stairs.

Staebler, Wendy. *Architectural Detailing in Contract Interiors,* New York, Watson Guptill Publications, 1988. Some stair projects shown, with photographs and construction details.

Templer, John A. *The Staircase,* Cambridge, MIT Press, 1992, in two (very thin) volumes. An excellent scholarly study of stair history and theory (Vol. 1), and analysis of stair trips and falls (Vol. 2).

INDEX